"Many believers are wondering how they can serve the Lord best where He has placed them. This book will enable every believer to discover their gifts so that they can better serve God among the body of believers where they are involved. I wholeheartedly and enthusiastically endorse the concepts of this book for every believer."

—David Younggi Cho
Seoul, Korea

"I found it fascinating. A long-overdue idea presented with skill, charm and common sense. The self-tests are particularly exciting. Every Christian should own a copy, certainly every Christian leader. In short, invaluable!"

—Marjorie Holmes

"Katie's teaching and administration gifts shine here! No one seems to have been forgotten. The teaching in this book and the tests that go with it will help you better understand yourself and others. You will find it easier to forgive and be less critical of others; and helps with interpersonal relationships will enable the Body of Christ to function better. It will be evident to the reader that the Holy Spirit has breathed a fresh touch on the Scriptures they share."

—Rita Bennett, co-founder, Christian Renewal Association; author, *You Can Be Emotionally Free*

In the New Testament, the apostle Paul teaches about three groupings of spiritual gifts. These include the motivational—or personality—gifts: perceiving, exhorting, serving, teaching, giving, administrating and having compassion. How fulfilled or frustrated you are depends on your use or neglect of your motivational gifts. Therefore, it's imperative (and enjoyable, too) to know with which gifts you have been blessed. Through charts, tests and information, Don and Katie Fortune help you recognize your gifts. In addition, *Discover Your God-Given Gifts* reveals:

- why you relate to people the way you do
- what your primary and secondary gifts are
- the character traits associated with each gift
- typical problem areas for each gift
- biblical characters who demonstrate each gift

You'll experience great joy as you *Discover Your God-Given Gifts* and learn to use them as He intended.

Revised and Expanded Edition!

Discover Your God-Given Gifts

Biblical Handbook to Help You Discover . . .
- Why You Think and Act the Way You Do
- How Gifts Affect Your Relationships
- What Career or Ministry Suits You Best
- How Using Your Gifts Will Bring You Joy

Don & Katie Fortune

Chosen
a division of Baker Publishing Group
Grand Rapids, Michigan

© 1987, 2009 by Don & Katie Fortune

Published by Chosen Books
A division of Baker Publishing Group
P.O. Box 6287, Grand Rapids, MI 49516-6287
www.chosenbooks.com

Printed in the United States of America

Library of Congress Cataloging-in-Publication Data

Fortune, Don.
    Discover your God-given gifts / Don & Katie Fortune. –Repackaged ed.
        p. cm.
    Originally published: Old Tappan, NJ : F.H. Revell Co., c1987
    Includes bibliographical references.
    ISBN 978-0-8007-9467-5 (pbk.)
    1. Gifts, Spiritual. 2. Spiritual life–Christianity. I. Fortune, Katie. II. Title.
BY767.3.F67 2009
243′.13–dc22   2009016987

In keeping with biblical principles of creation stewardship, Baker Publishing Group advocates the responsible use of our natural resources. As a member of the Green Press Initiative, our company uses recycled paper when possible. The text paper of this book is comprised of 30% post-consumer waste.

10 11 12 13 14 15   7 6 5 4 3 2

Contents

Part III: Practical Applications

Foreword

Only heaven will reveal the untold number of lives that have been affected by Don and Katie Fortune's book *Discover Your God-Given Gifts*.

Following a mandate from the Lord to help people know and understand the gifts He has given them for the furtherance of the Kingdom, Don and Katie have been teaching on the motivational gifts for more than thirty years. They have taught seminars in 37 nations and in most of the United States and Canada. Translated into many languages, this teaching has released people the world over to become all God intends them to be, and to embrace the calling on their lives through their gifts.

Katie was an integral part of the Aglow ministry in the early years of its inception. She began the first *Aglow* magazine in 1968 and served as its editor for eight years. Katie also served on the first Aglow International board as vice president of communications. She has taught seminars and spoken in Aglow conferences, retreats and groups in many nations. Her materials were used in leadership training throughout Aglow for many years, equipping and empowering women to use their gifts in leading others.

In addition to her teaching on the gifts, one of Katie's booklets, *Receive All God Has to Give*, has been used extensively throughout the Aglow ministry and has sold millions of copies and been translated into thirty languages. Written in the early 1970s, it is the only booklet from that time that continues to be reproduced and sold to this day.

Katie and Don are truly gifts to the Body of Christ, and their ministry has produced effective and lasting fruit for the Kingdom. Aglow has been blessed by its longstanding association with this couple.

As you read this new edition of *Discovering Your God-Given Gifts*, you will learn and grow in your God-given gifting. It will be a wonderful blessing in your life.

Jane Hansen Hoyt
President/CEO, Aglow International

Introduction

It was in 1974 that friends of ours, Lynn and Glenn Koontz, invited us over to their home to share with us what they had learned about motivational gifts during the advanced Basic Youth Conflicts seminar taught by Bill Gothard. We were excited as Glenn went through his notes regarding these Romans 12 gifts. We could suddenly see why we were each so different from one another. It helped us to understand things about ourselves that had eluded us before.

"Ah!" Don said to me. "Now I understand why you are always eager to organize things, including me and the kids!"

"Uh-huh," I replied, "and I see why you are always telling everyone to look for good in every situation."

I soon recognized that administration was my primary gift. For the first time in my life I understood why I always felt such zeal for whatever I was involved in. I could see that it was "all right" for me to prefer to delegate tasks instead of doing them myself. I could at last release myself from self-imposed guilt for not measuring up to the "ideal homemaker" image. I felt relieved that my interest in pioneering projects outside the home was within the range of expected and acceptable behavior for my particular gift. I also recognized some of the problem areas of my life as being characteristic of an administrator. Now I would be able to work on them with greater understanding.

Don identified his primary gift as that of exhortation. He could see why he was so eager to give advice to people . . . sometimes whether they asked for it or not. He realized that the Lord had equipped him to be an encourager, to build people up in the Body of Christ, and that he needed to persevere in doing so even when no immediate results were visible.

"I could begin to accept some of Katie's puzzling-to-me ideas and behavior," he admitted later. "Knowing that she was operating within the motivational gifts that God had given her, I could stop trying to convert her to my way of thinking and doing."

For my part, I realized I needed to release Don to be what God has made him to be. Our differences no longer needed to be a threat to either one of us. Rather, we could delight in them, knowing that God had brought us together in marriage with different gifts that could enrich both of our lives.

We began also to recognize the unique giftedness in each of our three children. Linda is a classic compassion person. David is an interesting mixture of his parents' gifts, an administrator-teacher-exhorter. Dan is a perceiver modified by compassion. How much fun it was to see their personalities grow and blossom as we allowed them to be what God created them to be. It helped us to know better how to discipline and encourage.

We also became sensitive to the gifts of family members, friends and colleagues. We could better understand why some of our actions caused a reaction rather than a response in others, and why we sometimes felt threatened by certain people. Former personality conflicts diminished—in many cases even disappeared.

Soon we were applying our new understanding to all our interpersonal relationships. We saw why our pastor's sermons typically gravitated to certain themes. Why a particular person who had been placed in a leadership position couldn't handle it. Why our older son cultivated a large group of friends while our younger son was happier with one or two close ones. Why our daughter consistently befriended the unlovable.

It all began to make sense!

Additional Research

Our perspective was further enriched when we received a set of tapes on the biblical gifts by the Rev. Don Pickerill, president of Life Bible College in California. The more we searched the Scriptures the more excited we became. The biblical characters came alive. Their ministries, motives and methods began to fall into the broader framework of the purpose and plan of God for their lives.

At the same time, the Holy Spirit began to confirm that this was a subject He wanted me to teach. (I'd identified a secondary gift of teaching.) So, taking what others had discovered and adding what we were learning from the Scriptures and from experience, I began to teach about these gifts in women's groups, Bible studies—wherever the Lord opened up doors of opportunity.

And of course, the more I taught, the more I learned. The feedback from the groups was fantastic. More insights! More indication that the teaching was indeed essential and life-changing. I collected data from each group I taught, and developed a scoring method (my administration gift in action) that enabled people to identify their gifts.

Several other women from our area began to teach on the subject and we decided to get together each month to share findings and brainstorm. I told Margaret Ann Hardwick, Judy Walker, Bobbie Elmore and Barbara Walsh that I was preparing a book on the subject and asked for their input. We had some wonderful times together, researching, revising and enlarging.

Special thanks go to those who later helped with the research compilations: Colleen McGowan, Lydia Mathre and Carol Miller. Gigantic thanks to Helen Bishop who gave endless hours of help on the computer. I also want to thank Elizabeth Sherrill for her sensitive and thorough editing.

Broad Exposure of the Teaching

During the past 35 years Don and I have taught our motivational gift seminar across the country, from Washington to Florida, and from California to New York. We have taught in churches, Bible schools, Christian schools, Bible study groups, prayer groups, conferences, retreats, pastors' groups, Aglow, FGBMFI, YWAM, U.S. Base Chapels and other groups around the world including Australia, Belgium, Canada, Czechoslovakia, Denmark, England, the Feroe Islands, France, Germany, Greece, Holland, Honduras, Hong Kong, India, Israel, Italy, Japan, Korea, New Zealand, Norway, Panama, the Philippines, Poland, Russia, Scotland, Singapore, South Africa, Spain, Swaziland, Sweden, Switzerland and most of the United States and Canada.

The testing materials have been translated into Chinese, Danish, Dutch, Finnish, French, German, Indonesian, Japanese, Korean, Norwegian, Polish, Portuguese, Romanian, Russian, Spanish, Swedish and Ukranian.

We have been privileged to work with some wonderful interpreters. In Panama, one would have thought Karen Hines (wife of evangelist Mike Hines) had been teaching the subject for years. In Germany, Waltraud Keil (a teacher with the Berlitz School of Languages) picked up our very gestures and inflections. In Japan a young pastor named Kai interacted with us in a way that could only have been the work of the Spirit.

In Korea, theologian Archer Torrey, grandson of theologian-writer R. A. Torrey, was our interpreter at the Jesus Abbey. When we asked why his interpretations were often longer than the original, he explained that he was getting such clear insights from the Holy Spirit that he added those, too.

We've also had some funny things happen, like the time in Japan when Don was saying, "A perceiver will often fast and pray." Our missionary friend, Ron Sisco, jumped in with a quick correction when the interpreter said, "A perceiver will often pray fast."

We have found that the teaching appeals to and applies to not only people in every nation and culture, but also to people from every type of church, denomination and parachurch organization. We get enthusiastic responses from teenagers, college groups, adults and senior citizens. All tell us basically: "This seminar has changed my life!"

Good Tidings of Great Joy

There is a simple acrostic often used in Christian circles:

J ESUS
O THERS
Y OU

It is because *Jesus*, our Lord, has tugged on our hearts to do so that we have written this book.

It is because *others*, in fact hundreds of you, have asked us to commit this teaching to writing that we have written this book.

It is because we have seen so many lives changed and enriched by this understanding that we know it will enrich *you*.

We know without a doubt that the end-product of the adventure you are starting today will release *joy* in your life in a new and exciting dimension!

Joy is the byproduct of operating in the sphere of *your* God-given gifts!

Part I
Perspective

1
Three Categories of Gifts

If you have a basket of apples, oranges and bananas—what do you have? A basket of apples? No. You have a basket of fruit. So it is with the three categories of gifts enumerated in the New Testament. All three groups are composed of gifts but, like the fruit in the basket, each group is unique and distinct from the others.

One of these groups of God-given gifts holds the key to understanding many things about yourself—why you think and act the way you do, how you relate to other people and the circumstances around you, and what makes you the special individual you are. This group of gifts will be the focus of this book, and are primarily spoken of in 1 Peter:

> As each of you has received a gift (a particular spiritual talent, a gracious divine endowment), employ it for one another as [befits] good trustees of God's many-sided grace [faithful stewards of the extremely diverse powers and gifts granted to Christians by unmerited favor].
>
> 1 Peter 4:10

Here, unmistakably, is a statement that every believer has been given a gift. Here, also, is a command to employ it for the benefit of others. We can be confident that God would not command us to use something we do not possess—but how do we get it?

The Greek word for "gift" in this verse is *charisma,* defined in my Greek dictionary as "a divine gratuity . . . a spiritual endowment . . . a free gift." So this is not something we can earn; in fact, the command is not to try to deserve it, but to *use* it. This kind of gift is a possession, something already given to each one of us by God at our creation.

As I mentioned, this is true of only one of the three groups of gifts found in the New Testament. Let's look briefly at each listing to see which one falls into this category of special gifts that reveal so much about the way God made us.

The Manifestation Gifts

The first group of gifts is found in 1 Corinthians 12:

> But to each one is given the manifestation of the [Holy] Spirit [the evidence, the spiritual illumination of the Spirit] for good and profit. To one is given in and through the [Holy] Spirit [the power to speak] a message of wisdom, and to another [the power to express] a word of knowledge and understanding according to the same [Holy] Spirit; to another [wonder-working] faith by the same [Holy] Spirit, to another the extraordinary powers of healing by the one Spirit; to another the working of miracles, to another prophetic insight (the gift of interpreting the divine will and purpose); to another the ability to discern and distinguish between [the utterance of true] spirits [and false ones], to another various kinds of [unknown] tongues, to another the ability to interpret [such] tongues.
>
> verses 7–10

There are nine gifts listed here:

1. *The word of wisdom,* a revelation of wisdom beyond natural human wisdom that enables a person to know what to do or say.
2. *The word of knowledge,* a revelation of information for a person, group or situation that could not have been known by any natural means.
3. *Faith,* the kind of wonder-working faith that moves mountains and waits expectantly for results.
4. *Gifts of healings,* the many different ways and varieties of degrees in which God manifests healing.
5. *Working of miracles,* the demonstration of the power and action of God that goes beyond natural laws.
6. *Prophecy,* an anointed proclamation of God through an individual to encourage, exhort or comfort.
7. *Discerning of spirits,* a person's ability to perceive what type of spirit is in operation in a given situation.
8. *Various kinds of tongues,* the languages, directed to God, given to the believer by the Holy Spirit but not learned or understood by the speaker.
9. *Interpretation of tongues,* the supernatural ability to express the content of what has been spoken in tongues.

Some call these the "manifestation gifts" because Paul used the Greek word *phanerosis*, meaning "an exhibition, expression or manifestation."

The concept is like a water pipe through which water flows from a source, through the pipe and to a person who takes a drink. The pipe is not the recipient of the water, but only its conduit. The person who drinks the water is the recipient. In other words, Paul defined these as supernatural manifestations of the Holy Spirit at work through a believer.

This listing of gifts does not match our 1 Peter 4:10 reference, since these gifts flow through the believer but do not become the possession of the person. Also, no one can dictate when the gift is to be operated; the Holy Spirit is the Source and the One in charge of the gift, working through an available and expectant vessel.

The Ministry Gifts

The second listing of gifts is found in Ephesians 4. In this instance, the word for "gift" in verse 8—"He ascended up on high . . . and gave gifts [*doma*] unto men" (KJV)—means literally "a present." Looking at this verse in context we see that after Jesus ascended to the Father He presented gifts of *people* who were called and gifted to lead and train the rest of the Body of Christ.

While many versions do not repeat the implied word "gift" in verse 11, the Amplified Bible does:

> And His gifts were [varied; He Himself appointed and gave men to us] some to be apostles (special messengers), some prophets (inspired preachers and expounders), some evangelists (preachers of the Gospel, traveling missionaries), some pastors (shepherds of His flock) and teachers.
>
> Ephesians 4:11

It is important to note that in this verse the words "men" (AMP) or "some" (NASB) are used in the sense of "mankind"—men and women. Therefore, both can be *domas* to minister to the Body of Christ.

There are five ministry gifts listed in this passage:

1. The *apostle*, one who establishes and strengthens churches.
2. The *prophet*, one who speaks forth the message of God.
3. The *evangelist*, one who is called to preach the Gospel.
4. The *pastor*, one who feeds and shepherds the believers.
5. The *teacher*, one who instructs believers in the Word of God.

We purposely list these gifts in lower-case type to emphasize the fact that these are not titles, but functions. A person does not become a prophet by being given the name. Rather, he becomes a prophet as he develops his God-given ability to function in prophet-like ways, responding to God's specific call with a willing heart.

The purpose of these ministry gifts is clear.

> And He gave some as apostles, and some as prophets, and some as evangelists, and some as pastors and teachers, for the equipping of the saints for the work of service, to the building up of the body of Christ; until we all attain to the unity of the faith, and of the knowledge of the Son of God.
>
> Ephesians 4:11–13, NASB

These five ministry gifts might equally well be called "equipping" gifts, enabling the saints (believers) to do the work of the ministry so that Christ's Body on earth (the Church) can function as His true representative.

Therefore, these gifts are not the possessions—the things that belong to us—spoken of in 1 Peter 4:10. Rather they are *people* who are gifted to be equippers of the rest of the Body of Christ.

The Motivational Gifts

Now turn to the third listing of gifts in the New Testament, found in the book of Romans.

> Having gifts (faculties, talents, qualities) that differ according to the grace given us, let us use them: [He whose gift is] prophecy, [let him prophesy] according to the proportion of his faith; [he whose gift is] practical service, let him give himself to serving; he who teaches, to his teaching; he who exhorts (encourages), to his exhortation; he who contributes, let him do it in simplicity and liberality; he who gives aid and superintends, with zeal and singleness of mind; he who does acts of mercy, with genuine cheerfulness and joyful eagerness.
>
> Romans 12:6–8

Charisma is the Greek word here, the same word used in 1 Peter 4:10. We believe this list is the category of gifts that Peter was referring to when he said we were to employ them to benefit one another. Notice the Romans passage urges us to use them. This verse is like a repetition, an echo of Peter's statement.

This list of gifts is the focus of this book. These are the gifts we *possess*. These are the gifts that God has built into us and made part of us to be used for the benefit of others and for His glory. Like all the others, they are grace gifts. We do not deserve them. But because God loves us He gives them to us. Since they provide the motivating force for our lives, they have been called motivational gifts. They are the gifts that *shape our personalities*.

Because God has created us with free will, we can choose to use our motivational gifts appropriately, or we can choose to neglect them or even to abuse them. To be able to choose to use these gifts according to the will of God, it is important to have some understanding of what they are and how they function. That will be our goal in the following pages.

Right now we will just touch on the seven gifts briefly by presenting the seven key words we have chosen to identify the various recipients.

1. *Perceiver,* one who clearly perceives the will of God. We have purposely chosen this word rather than the word "prophet" to avoid confusion, since the same root word is also used in the two other categories of gifts. Also, in today's culture the word "prophet" has rather ominous connotations.
2. *Server,* one who loves to serve others. Another appropriate word is "doer."
3. *Teacher,* one who loves to research and communicate truth. We almost selected the word "researcher," since that motivation is so strong.
4. *Exhorter,* one who loves to encourage others to live a victorious life. These are extremely positive people who can equally well be called "encouragers."
5. *Giver,* one who loves to give time, talent, energy and means to benefit others and advance the Gospel. Another word could be "contributor."
6. *Administrator,* one who loves to organize, lead or direct. Other words could be "facilitator" and "leader."
7. *Compassion person,* one who shows compassion, love and care to those in need. We say "compassion" instead of "mercy" since this word is more comprehensive in today's usage.

The Gifts in Context

It is always important to look at any verses you plan to study in the context of the entire passage. In this case, we will focus briefly on the first five verses of Romans 12, the verses preceding the list of motivational gifts.

I appeal to you therefore, brethren, and beg of you in view of [all] the mercies of God, to make a decisive dedication of your bodies [presenting all your members and faculties] as a living sacrifice, holy (devoted, consecrated) and well pleasing to God, which is your reasonable (rational, intelligent) service and spiritual worship.

Do not be conformed to this world (this age), [fashioned after and adapted to its external, superficial customs], but be transformed (changed) by the [entire] renewal of your mind [by its new ideals and its new attitude] so that you may prove [for yourselves] what is the good and acceptable and perfect will of God, even the thing which is good and acceptable and perfect [in His sight for you].

For by the grace (unmerited favor of God) given to me I warn everyone among you not to estimate and think of himself more highly than he ought [not to have an exaggerated opinion of his own importance], but to rate his ability with sober judgment, each according to the degree of faith apportioned by God to him.

For as in one physical body we have many parts (organs, members) and all of these parts do not have the same function or use,

So we, numerous as we are, are one body in Christ (the Messiah) and individually we are parts one of another [mutually dependent on one another].

Romans 12:1–5

In the first verse Paul, writing the Christians in Rome, states that all believers are to present themselves to God as living sacrifices. It is only by this wholehearted dedication that our motivational gifts can be used as they were intended.

In the second verse we learn that we need to have our minds renewed. How do we do this? By the Word of God. As we prayerfully read and study the Bible, it becomes a living, personalized revelation of God and our minds are cleansed and renewed. The key word "transformation" is the Greek word *metamorphosis*, which we also use to describe the process of a caterpillar becoming a butterfly. Such is the power of God's Word.

In the third verse we learn that we are to have a right attitude about ourselves—gratefulness and humility rather than conceit, and an objective sense of value rather than self-abasement. And we also learn that each of us has been given a degree of faith that will allow us to operate effectively in our motivational gifts: The *perceiver* has faith that God will answer petitions; the *server* has faith that enables him to complete whatever task is started; the *teacher* has faith that she can ferret out the facts of any matter; the *exhorter* has faith that there is a solution to every problem; the *giver* has faith that God will supply all needs; the *administrator* has faith that any project can be accomplished if the right people are brought together to do it; and the *compassion person* has faith that he can help people work together in love.

In the fourth and fifth verses, we learn that we need to discern the various gifts in the Body of Christ and work together in mutual interdependence.

In this context we can see the importance of using our motivational gifts for the glory of God: This is the only way we will find fulfillment. These gifts—of which we have mostly been unaware—are the motivating forces of our lives, and unless they are channeled properly we cannot help but feel frustrated. But once we discover them, we discover a tremendous potential for happiness.

This book will show you not only how to identify your gifts but also how to release those gifts more effectively. You will see how your particular gifts have been evident in your actions, even from early childhood. You will understand that the gifts provide your basic motivation for what you like to do and they affect the way you do it. You will also find that when you use your special gifts only for your own selfish ends, they tend to become polluted. But when you use your gifts for the benefit of others, cooperating with God's plan for your life, they will produce the greatest joy you can experience.

There is one more list of gifts in the Bible. It is not a new list, but rather a composite of the three lists already mentioned.

> And God has appointed in the church, first apostles, second prophets, third teachers, then miracles, then gifts of healings, helps, administrations, various kinds of tongues. All are not apostles, are they? All are not prophets, are they? All are not teachers, are they? All are not workers of miracles, are they? All do not have gifts of healings, do they? All do not speak with tongues, do they? All do not interpret, do they?
>
> 1 Corinthians 12:28–30, NASB

Here Paul is using as examples gifts from each of the three categories:

Motivational Gifts	Ministry Gifts	Manifestation Gifts
Helps (serving)	Apostles	Miracles
Administrations	Prophets	Healings
	Teachers	Tongues
		Interpretation

The passage is immediately followed by the famous "love chapter," 1 Corinthians 13. Paul is making an important point: Whether or not you are operating in the motivational gifts, the ministry gifts or the manifestation gifts, if you don't do it in love—God's agape love—you are doing nothing! An apt admonition to remember at all times.

Everyone Has a Gift!

Good news: *Everyone has a motivational gift!* No one has been left out. We have tested hundreds of thousands of people and each one has discovered his or her specific giftedness, falling under at least one of the seven categories. (We have never found anyone who fits into an eighth category. In fact, there is no eighth category.)

But don't take our word for it. Look at God's Word:

> As *each one* has received a special gift, employ it in serving one another as good stewards of the manifold grace of God.
>
> 1 Peter 4:10, NASB, emphasis added

> Since we have gifts that differ according to the grace given to us, *each* of us is to exercise them accordingly: if prophecy, according to the proportion of his faith; if service, in his serving; or he who teaches, in his teaching; or he who exhorts, in his exhortation; he who gives, with liberality; he who leads, with diligence; he who shows mercy, with cheerfulness.
>
> Romans 12:6–8, NASB, emphasis added

There you are. Seven motivational (that is, motivating) gifts. And *each one of us* receives one or more. So, what do we do with them?

We Are Commanded to Use Our Gifts to Benefit Others

Scripture stresses that our motivational gifts are given to us *to benefit others*. They are not to be used for selfish purposes. It is only by the grace of God that we are gifted in the first place; therefore we are to use our giftedness to help and bless others.

The contrast of the two seas in Israel shows that an outflow is essential for life. The Sea of Galilee has water flowing not only into it but *out* of it. Therefore the lake is fresh and useful; it supports life. But the Dead Sea has no outlet. It holds in all of the water it receives. Through evaporation, this lake has become the saltiest in the world: There is no life in it at all.

So it is with the motivational gifts. They were designed by the Creator to overflow from us to those around us.

Our Gift Was Built into Us When God Formed Us

Our giftedness was not an afterthought. It was a part of God's plan to shape us for our role in the building of His Kingdom.

One of the most beautiful creation passages in the Old Testament is found in Psalm 139:13–16:

> For You did form my inward parts; You did knit me together in my mother's womb.
>
> I will confess and praise You for You are fearful and wonderful and for the awful wonder of my birth! Wonderful are Your works, and that my inner self knows right well.
>
> My frame was not hidden from You when I was being formed in secret [and] intricately and curiously wrought [as if embroidered with various colors] in the depths of the earth [a region of darkness and mystery].
>
> Your eyes saw my unformed substance, and in Your book all the days [of my life] were written before ever they took shape, when as yet there was none of them.

What a magnificent expression of the design and development of the child in the womb!

God uses what scientists now call DNA in the process. When a child is conceived, half of his DNA inheritance comes from the father and half from the mother. And in that microscopic fertilized egg, joined DNA forms a helix-shaped genetic ladder that is literally six feet long. Yet it is marvelously compacted within that tiny egg. How incredible!

Every detail of our physical being is programmed by DNA. Its intricacies far outweigh the most sophisticated computer system on the market today. The color of your hair was preprogrammed by your DNA. The shape of your nose, your height, your body frame—all your physical characteristics were determined at the moment of conception.

If God has so precisely planned for the development of your physical body—eventually subject to degeneration and death—how much more has He planned for your giftedness? You might call it your spiritual DNA. We believe that our motivational gifts are given to us at conception and that just as our DNA eventually brings forth our physical characteristics, so our motivational gifts bring forth the interests, abilities, enthusiasms and perspectives that make us think, feel and act the way we do.

One of the things that has convinced us that motivational gifts are a part of our initial creation is our study of twins. The first time I tested a twin was nine years ago in Montana. Judy, a young mother in her thirties, commented at the time that she was sorry her identical twin sister, Jane, lived too far away to come to the seminar. Judy scored highest as "exhorter." Other women present who knew both twins insisted that Jane would probably score the same.

A year later I was invited to teach the motivational gift seminar in the Montana town where Jane lived. While she had heard Judy speak of the seminar she had not seen Judy's scores or profile sheet. "I thought it would be best if I didn't see Judy's results until after I had a chance to do the test myself," Jane explained.

After the seminar Jane brought her profile sheet to me. Her primary gift was exhorter! What surprised me more was that her second and third gifts also matched Judy's.

Since then, every time twins have taken the test their primary gifts have been identical.

For instance, one pastor's wife was strongest in the serving gift. Her favorite part of her ministry was hospitality. She loved entertaining people in her home and having houseguests.

Her twin sister had married a wealthy businessman. She could afford domestic help but preferred to take care of her home herself. She loved entertaining her husband's business associates. She, too, was a server.

In another instance, Deanne was tested in Washington state and her identical twin sister, Dianne, by mail on the East Coast. Both proved to be perceivers.

The *Reader's Digest* carried an article on twins that presented even stronger evidence that motivational gifts are wired in us from conception, not added later. One revealing paragraph:

> Identical twin boys, born in Ohio some 40 years ago, were adopted by different families shortly after birth. A year ago, after 39 years apart, they were reunited. It was discovered that each had been named James; that each had had law-enforcement training; that each liked mechanical drawing and carpentry. Each married a woman named Linda, had a son—one named James Alan and the other James Allan— had divorced, and then married a second wife named Betty. Both had dogs named Toy. Also, both favored the same St. Petersburg, Florida, vacation beach.[1]

It is significant for our study that these twins were raised apart in different homes, leaving no opportunity for family or school to influence their identical choices of jobs, hobbies and recreation. Clearly something more fundamental than external influence was involved—something, we believe, built in at conception: our God-given gifts.

Our Gift Can Be Observed in Childhood

Train up a child in the way he should go: and when he is old, he will not depart from it.

Proverbs 22:6, KJV

As we began raising children we took this Scripture seriously, endeavoring to raise our youngsters morally and scripturally.

Then, when the boys were eight and ten years old, we discovered the motivational gifts and began to realize there was more to Proverbs 22:6 than a teaching about discipline and training. The Amplified Bible version of this Scripture gave us new insight: "Train up a child in the way he should go [and in keeping with his individual gift or bent], and when he is old he will not depart from it."

The original Hebrew included the insight that each child has a *gift*—a motivational gift—and a *bent*—a direction to be fulfilled as he uses his motivational gift(s). We as parents, then, have a responsibility to discover our child's giftedness and to "train him up" in it, to encourage the development of that gift, so that when he comes of age he will use that giftedness to achieve God's purposes for him and for his own true fulfillment.

We are grateful that we found this out before our boys were fully grown. We could easily see that Dave was an administrator (with secondary gifts of teaching and exhortation). We could encourage his leadership at school. Dan was completely different from his older brother: a perceiver, with a modifying effect from the gift of compassion. We could encourage him to take strong stands on issues and ideals.

Not only have they expressed gratitude that we encouraged them in their giftedness, but over the years they have brought friends and schoolmates home to take the motivational gift test as well.

Linda was already grown and married when we learned about the motivational gifts. But, in retrospect, we could see that she had a strong gift of compassion with a secondary gift of serving. As a child she was always drawn to others who were hurting or friendless. And her love for animals was exceptional. She wanted to be a veterinarian so she could work with animals, but when she learned they also did surgery she couldn't bear the thought of performing operations. She eventually became a certified nursing assistant.

We Are Not to Neglect Our Gift

> Neglect not the gift [*charisma*] that is in thee, which was given thee by prophecy, with the laying on of the hands of the presbytery.
>
> 1 Timothy 4:14, KJV

Of the fifteen times the word *charisma* is used in the New Testament, we find that it is not uncommon for more than one gift category to be referred to at the same time. (The term, as with any term, must be understood within the context in which it is used.) In this reference, for instance, see the three categories of gifts expressed. First, the supernatural gifts may have been more fully released or manifested by the laying on of hands on Timothy. Second, the manifestation gift of prophecy flowed through an elder who had the ministry gift of a prophet. Third, the motivational gift Timothy had been endowed with was identified and released in greater measure at this special time of his ordination. A careful examination of this verse as given in *The Interlinear Greek-English New Testament* brings out an interesting rendering: "Be not negligent of the in thee gift which was given thee through prophecy with the laying on of the hands of the elderhood."[2]

First of all, notice that the original Greek refers to the "in thee gift," indicating that the gift was already "in" Timothy when the elders prayed for him. The word "given" in the Greek is *didomi*, which has a wide range of meanings according to *Strong's Exhaustive Concordance of the Bible*, including "to be brought forth, shown, and uttered."[3] It is likely that Timothy, being a young man, had not yet identified his primary motivational gift. So, when the elders were ordaining him (utilizing the various manifestation gifts of prophecy and word of knowledge), the gift that was already "in him" was identified verbally. (His primary motivational gift seems to have been that of teacher, as evidenced by many later references to Timothy's ministry of teaching. See 1 Timothy 4:6, 11, 13–16; 2 Timothy 2:2, 15; 4:2.)

That Paul was probably one of those who prophesied over Timothy is indicated by his reference in 1 Timothy 1:18 to "prophetic intimations which I formerly received concerning you, so that inspired and aided by them you may wage the good warfare."

But more important than the timing of the gift is the fact that to neglect it is to neglect God's purpose and plan for our lives. Each of us has an "in thee" gift and, like Timothy, we need to use it for the glory of God and the benefit of others.

Our Gift Colors All That We See

If you put on a pair of sunglasses, all you see will be colored accordingly. So it is with a person's motivational gift. A perceiver will look at life through a perceiver's eyes. Everything will look either good or bad, right or wrong, in God's will or out of God's will. It is impossible for the perceiver to see life in any other way.

A server, on the other hand, will approach reality with the question, "What can I do to help in this situation?" He constantly notices opportunities to do things for others.

A teacher will search for truth in everything she encounters. Like the persistent Diogenes of Greek literature, searching with a lantern for an honest man, the teacher will investigate, seek and research.

An exhorter will see opportunities to encourage people at whatever they do.

A giver will look for ways in which he can invest his time, talent and money in providing for the needs of others.

An administrator, with her broad vision, will grasp the overall dimensions of a situation.

A compassion person will recognize hurts and wounds that need to be healed and see endless opportunities to express love.

And each one may think, *Why don't others see things the way I see them? It's clear to me!*

Our Gift Gives Only One Perspective of the Whole

God has purposely limited and focused our giftedness so that we must work together and remain dependent on each other in order to grasp the whole truth.

Remember the six blind men who went to "see" an elephant? One felt the side and said an elephant was like a wall. The next felt the tusk and claimed an elephant was like a spear. The third felt the trunk and likened it to a snake. The fourth felt a leg and said an elephant was like a tree. The fifth, touching an ear, declared an elephant was like a fan. The sixth felt the tail and insisted an elephant was like a rope. No one was altogether right, yet neither was he entirely wrong. It was only when they got all their observations together that they "saw" the whole elephant.

Thus it is with our motivational gifts. Each of us is somewhat blind to the other perspectives. We are wrong to say our way of seeing is the only true one. We are each partly right. But we are not totally right all by ourselves. We need each other's viewpoints in order to see the complete picture.

In our presentation of the motivational gifts, we not only want to help you to discover *your* gifts but also to become familiar with the *other* gifts: how people with differing gifts think, how they operate and how they benefit the whole Body of Christ. We believe you will be enriched both personally and in your relationships by gaining these insights.

Each Gift Is of Equal Value

Draw a circle in the
space provided at the
right.

Let's suppose the circle represents a pie. Obviously it's easier to cut a
pie into six or eight segments, but we want you to cut the pie above into
seven *equal* slices. A challenge? See how well you can do.

Now, just in case your slices did not turn out symmetrically, write
"These are equal slices" beside the pie. Then label each slice with the
name of a motivational gift: perceiver, server, teacher, exhorter, giver,
administrator, or compassion person.

We want you to grasp the concept of this diagram: all the gifts are
equal. They are equal in the sight of God. They are equal in value in the
Body of Christ. No gift is higher than or better than another gift. They
each contribute invaluably to the collective functioning of the Body of
Christ. If any one gift is not in operation there is a lack, a void.

Whatever motivational gift you have been given is the best gift God
could have given you for the working out of His purposes in your life and
for the benefit of the other people whose lives you will touch. Rejoice in
your giftedness! Use your giftedness! Develop your giftedness! We like
that oft-quoted slogan:

What we are is God's gift to us;
What we make of our lives is our gift to God.

It is true that God bestows some of the gifts more frequently than others. That's because more people are needed in certain functions. There
need to be more followers, for instance, than leaders. From the data we
have compiled,* here is the percentage of people who have each gift:

Perceiver	12%	Giver	6%
Server	17%	Administrator	13%
Teacher	6%	Compassion person	30%
Exhorter	16%		

*This tabulation is based on detailed response sheets from 1000 people over
a ten-year period, representing more than 100 groups in a variety of states,
provinces and countries.

The most prevalent gift is that of compassion—perhaps because there
is so much need for love and compassion in the world.

The gifts of server and exhorter are almost tied for second place. Lots
of servers are needed to get God's work done, and we all need encouragement every day.

But just because there are more individuals with a certain gift does
not mean that gift is more important. Neither does a smaller percentage

mean a certain gift is somehow more special. All the gifts are equally important. All the gifts are necessary. All the gifts, when used properly, are a blessing.

Here's a brief review of the motivational (motivating) gifts and the needs they tend to meet:

GIFT	DEFINITION	NEEDS MET	WHAT IT DOES
PERCEIVER	Declares the will of God	Spiritual	Keeps us centered on spiritual principles
SERVER	Renders practical service	Practical	Keeps the work of ministry moving
TEACHER	Researches and teaches the Bible	Mental	Keeps us studying and learning
EXHORTER	Encourages personal progress	Psychological	Keeps us applying spiritual truths
GIVER	Shares material assistance	Material	Keeps specific needs provided for
ADMINISTRATOR	Gives leadership and direction	Functional	Keeps us organized and increases our vision
COMPASSION PERSON	Provides personal and emotional support	Emotional	Keeps us in right attitudes and relationships

The above chart offers only a bird's-eye view of how the motivational gifts function; there is, of course, the possibility of overlapping and interaction, and secondary gifts will color or modify the operation of a primary gift.

Your Three-Part Nature and the Gifts

One of the most marvelous concepts in the Christian faith is that human beings are created in the image of God. God (Himself triune—Father, Son and Holy Spirit) has made us tripartite in nature: spirit, soul and body.

> God said, Let Us [Father, Son, and Holy Spirit] make mankind in Our image, after Our likeness.
>
> Genesis 1:26

> May the God of peace Himself sanctify you through and through . . . and may your spirit and soul and body be preserved sound and complete [and found] blameless at the coming of our Lord Jesus Christ (the Messiah).
>
> 1 Thessalonians 5:23

The three parts of the human being can be diagrammed like this:

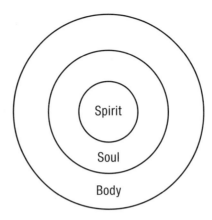

Our Soul Is Triune, Too

In the same way that the human being is made of three parts—body, soul and spirit—our souls are also triune in nature. Jesus pointed out the three areas of the soul when He said:

> You shall love the Lord your God out of and with your whole heart and out of and with all your soul (your life) and out of and with all your mind (with your faculty of thought and your moral understanding) and out of and with all your strength. This is the first and principal commandment.
>
> Mark 12:30

The three parts of the soul are the mind, the will and the emotions. The "heart" in Jesus' statement refers to the seat of the emotions, the "mind" refers to thought and "strength" refers to the will.

Each is also identified in the following passage:

> All that is in the world—the lust of the flesh [craving for sensual gratification] and the lust of the eyes [greedy longings of the mind] and the pride of life [assurance in one's own resources or in the stability of earthly things]— these do not come from the Father but are from the world [itself].
>
> 1 John 2:16

John is describing the negative things that come from the three areas of the soul—the lust of the flesh from the emotions, the lust of the eyes from the mind and the pride of life from the will. Jesus was tempted in these three areas of the soul and passed all tests.

Many good things come from the three areas of the soul. With the mind we think and reason. With the will we make decisions. From the emotions come our feelings. We need all three areas to operate well in order to function normally. But sometimes we are motivated by one area more than the others. Sometimes two of the three areas seem to have greater influence in our lives.

We have discovered that the seven God-given gifts come primarily from one or more of the three areas of the soul. Of necessity we function in all areas. But the way we think, feel and act is colored greatly by our motivational gifting, influenced in turn by the area or areas of the soul that predominate. This helps to explain why God has gifted us in seven specific ways—and why there is no eighth category. Each gift relates to the mind, will and emotions in a specific way.

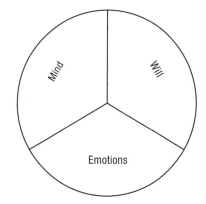

The following diagram helps to explain this:

Note that three of the gifts operate out of and correspond directly to the mind, the will or the emotions:

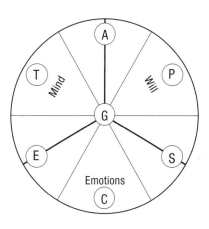

- The teacher gift operates primarily out of the mind area of the soul.
- The perceiver gift operates primarily out of the will area of the soul.
- The compassion gift operates primarily out of the emotions area of the soul.

Three more of the gifts are influenced by and operate out of two of the three areas of the soul:

- The administer gift operates out of the mind and will areas of the soul.
- The exhorter gift operates out of the mind and the emotions areas of the soul.
- The server gift operates out of the will and emotions areas of the soul.
- The seventh gift, the giver gift, operates about equally in all three areas of the soul.

There are no more possibilities. We could call these seven sources the producers of our spiritual DNA: that which causes us to be wired the way we are. Since our gifting begins in our soul at conception, it does not change; it is a given. While it is true that our individual life experiences sculpt our gifting in unique ways, the underlying gifting will always be there.

How Do the Gifts Relate to Each Other?

Because the characteristics of a particular gift extend naturally from the area(s) of the soul that influence it, each gift finds it easier to relate to associated gifts and more challenging to relate to "opposite" type gifts. In general we find it is most difficult to relate to a gift directly opposite to

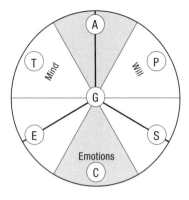

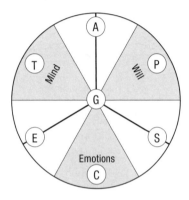

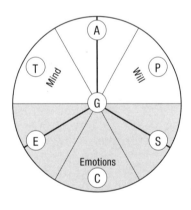

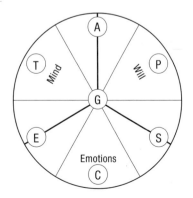

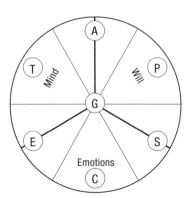

our own. A compassion gift, for instance, sometimes finds it hard to cope with an administrator gift (and vice versa), because the latter operates from the mind and will and the former from the emotions.

The gifts that fall into the triangular arrangement also have some relationship challenges since they are still significantly distinct. For instance the compassion gift, operating primarily from the emotions, finds it hard to understand a teacher gift operating from the mind or a perceiver gift operating from the will.

The easiest relationship for the compassion gift is with a gift that is "next door" and shares some of the same influence from the emotions area. An exhorter (mind/emotions) or a server (will/emotions) therefore has more in common with a compassion person.

The giver gift is unique in that all three areas of the soul are of nearly equal influence. Thus the giver is well balanced, and easily relates to all six other gifts.

The last two diagrams are for you (and your spouse, if applicable) to shade in so you can see the areas of the soul that influence your gifting, perspective and mode of operation. In your strong areas: pray for wisdom and guidance in functioning in all your relationships. In your weak, less gifted areas: seek understanding of others differently gifted and accept and rejoice that you cannot be all things to all people. God has a special plan for you, and He has gifted you accordingly to accomplish that plan.

You can also plot your two or three strongest gifts in one of these circles to see how they strengthen, reinforce, modify, soften, stretch and/or challenge each other. See the combination gift scales in chapter 28 for more information on combination gifts.

3
Placed in His Body

In the two verses of Scripture leading into his description of the motivational gifts, Paul uses the graphic example of the human body.

> For as in one physical body we have many parts (organs, members) and all of these parts do not have the same function or use, so we, numerous as we are, are one body in Christ (the Messiah) and individually we are parts one of another [mutually dependent on one another].
>
> Romans 12:4–5

There are three points from this illustration that apply particularly to our study of the motivational gifts.

First, the body represents completeness, a whole, a totality—but a totality made up of disparate parts. Similarly, we who make up the Body of Christ have different functions. We are not all the same. We are gifted in different ways. Just as a physical body needs hands and feet and eyes and ears to enable it to function properly, so the Body of Christ needs those with different motivational gifts to enable it to function properly. We are to have unity through diversity.

It's good to know we don't all have to behave just alike. It's okay to be different.

Second, we can see in this analogy that we don't have to "do it all ourselves." We do our part. Others do their part. *Together* we get the job done. *Together* we do the work of the ministry of our Lord.

I remember in my teens how I would hear a different sermon each week and try so hard to do what the preacher said. One Sunday he would preach on the importance of prayer, and all the following week I would pray strenuously. The next week he would preach on having a servant's heart, and I'd set out to serve anyone and everyone. Next might be tithing, when I'd determine to increase my giving. Or there'd be a sermon on love and I would wipe my brow from exhaustion, take a deep breath and walk out the church door determined to be more loving even if it killed me.

It almost did. I was trying so hard to be all of these things that I was approaching burnout. I was aiming at some sort of "super-Christian" ideal that was impossible to achieve. I really believed I had to be outstanding in all these areas if I was going to please God. And when I inevitably failed, I was a ripe target for guilt and self-condemnation. I was so relieved when I first discovered the variety of motivational gifts and found that I did not have to be or to do everything well. Rather, I could concentrate on those areas where I had been gifted by God, and I was released to appreciate the very different giftedness in others.

Third, Paul emphasizes our mutual dependence in the Body of Christ. We really need each other. No member of Christ's Body can go off on a desert island and be a victorious Christian all by herself. God has purposely made us so that we are incomplete without the interaction and ministry of our brothers and sisters.

David DuPlessis, who was known internationally as "Mr. Pentecost" for his years of building bridges of understanding between denominations around the world, used to have a wonderful saying: "Whenever I meet someone—anyone—I always ask myself, *What can I impart to benefit this person, and what can he or she impart to benefit me?*"

The Gifts in the Body

One day I said to the Lord, "Since Paul put this analogy of the Body before the list of motivational gifts in Romans 12, is it possible that each gift corresponds to a part of the physical body?"

The Lord not only showed me where each gift might fit in such a scheme, He also gave me Scriptures for each one.

1. Perceiver: the eye of the body.

"But blessed (happy, fortunate, and to be envied) are your eyes because they do see" (Matthew 13:16).

It has become evident to us that perceivers, of all the members of the Body of Christ, are the most gifted with spiritual sight. They see things that the rest of us often miss completely.

> The eye is the lamp of the body. So, if your eye is sound, your whole body will be full of light; but if your eye is not sound, your whole body will be full of darkness. If then the light in you is darkness, how great is the darkness!
>
> Matthew 6:22–23, RSV

Although these words of Jesus may apply individually, they also directly apply to the Body of Christ. The perceiver has the special responsibility of having a clear and sound eye with which to detect God's truth. Of all the members, this is the person who cannot afford pollution or sin in his life—if he does, his sight becomes clouded. The Body counts on perceivers to accurately identify and proclaim the will of God. If the perceiver is not walking in purity of life, his vision is impaired and what he states as truth may, in fact, be error and lead many astray. Then how great the darkness becomes! Jim Jones is a sobering example, leading a thousand people isolated in Guyana to drink poisoned Kool-Aid and die.

2. Server: the hands of the body.

"She opens her hand to the poor, yes, she reaches out her filled hands to the needy [whether in body, mind, or spirit]" (Proverbs 31:20).

Of all the gifted, we notice that servers are literally the most capable with their hands. They have great dexterity. They seem to be able to fix or build just about anything.

This is also referred to in 1 Corinthians 12:28 as the gift of helps. These people love to be helpful, anytime, anyplace—especially if it includes hands-on involvement.

3. Teacher: the mind of the body.

Now these [Jews] were better disposed and more noble than those in Thessalonica, for they were entirely ready and accepted and welcomed the message [concerning the attainment through Christ of eternal salvation in the kingdom of God] with inclination of mind and eagerness, searching and examining the Scriptures daily to see if these things were so.

Acts 17:11

Teachers are exceptionally gifted with intelligence. At first this may not seem fair to the rest of us, but remember that, being the mind of the Body, they need to be so gifted. They are always asking questions. They want to know the basis for everything and they will search until the facts convince them that something is true. Note that these people were commended by Paul for checking out the Scriptures (our Old Testament) to be sure that their acceptance of the Good News had a verifiable foundation.

4. Exhorter: the mouth of the body.

"After the reading of the Law and the Prophets, the leaders [of the worship] of the synagogue sent to them saying, Brethren, if you have any word of exhortation or consolation or encouragement for the people, say it" (Acts 13:15).

Exhorters talk a lot. We have jokingly said that they have the best-oiled jaws of all the gifts. But, seriously, God has endowed them with great facility of speech. How else could an exhorter exhort, console or encourage?

5. Giver: the arms of the body.

"He has shown strength and made might with His arm" (Luke 1:51).

In this New Testament passage, Mary is quoting Old Testament Scriptures that couple strength with the arms (see Isaiah 51:9).

Givers have great strength spiritually, extending the reach of every Christian endeavor.

Remember the story about Moses holding aloft the rod so that Israel might prevail in battle over Amalek? (See Exodus 17:8–16.) When his arms grew weary he lowered them, and the Israelites began to lose. So, God provided two givers: support people, Aaron and Hur, who held up Moses' arms until the battle was won. Givers are a strong support to those who are in spiritual battle or on the "front lines" sharing the Gospel.

6. Administrator: the shoulders of the body.

"For to us a Child is born, to us a Son is given; and the government shall be upon His shoulder" (Isaiah 9:6).

We often say that someone in leadership is shouldering responsibility. Administrators are shoulders in the Body of Christ, carrying the load of leadership. Wise administrators know how to yoke with Jesus so He bears the burden with them.

7. Compassion person: the heart of the body.

"May the Lord direct your hearts into [realizing and showing] the love of God" (2 Thessalonians 3:5).

People gifted with compassion are ruled by the heart rather than the head. They feel deeply, love wholeheartedly and care extensively. They reveal the loving nature of God by showing kindness, concern and mercy to others.

Two Distinctions within the Seven Gifts

When I began my study of the gifts it was 1 Peter 4:10 that helped me identify the gifts we have been given as a lifelong endowment. For a while I was puzzled, however, by the verse immediately following:

Whoever speaks, [let him do it as one who utters] oracles of God; whoever renders service, [let him do it] as with the strength which God furnishes abundantly, so that in all things God may be glorified through Jesus Christ (the Messiah).

1 Peter 4:11

I knew this could, by its context, be referring to the motivational gifts. It seemed that Peter was saying that there are two basic categories of motivational gifts—those that focus primarily on speech and those that focus primarily on service. But which ones were which?

As I studied and prayed about it, the Lord suggested, *Draw the human body and make a horizontal line below the shoulders and above the heart.*

I drew a little cookie-cutter figure and a dotted line.

Now look at the gifts that are represented by the parts of the body above and below the line.

I looked and it suddenly became clear. I could see that the teacher—the mind of the body—must speak in order to teach. The perceiver—the eye of the body—must speak in order to proclaim God's will. The exhorter, being the mouth of the body, obviously had a speaking gift. And the administrator—the shoulders of the body—must have facility of speech in order to lead.

These four, then, were the speaking gifts.

Looking at the gifts below the dotted line, I could see that the compassion person—the heart of the body—is usually not one who likes to get up in front of a group and speak. He would much rather work behind the scenes, serving others through the abundance of love God has given him. The giver—the arms of the body—also has a supportive type of gift, shunning the limelight to serve in the background. And the server—the hands of the body—obviously excels in this area. These three were the serving gifts.

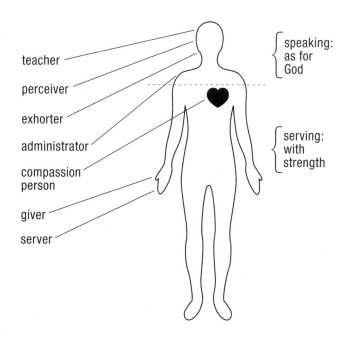

First Peter 4:11 urges those with speaking gifts to speak "as one who utters oracles of God." Such people bear the responsibility of making sure that what comes out of their mouths is what God wants said. What we say has power. God *spoke* the world into existence (see Genesis 1:3). Our words have an impact on others. Anyone with a speaking gift must constantly seek to be led by the Holy Spirit as he speaks.

For those with one of the three serving gifts, the verse contains a tremendous promise. They are to serve "with the strength which God furnishes." God will give them an abundance of strength and energy for their work. We have observed that those with serving gifts seem to have unusual amounts of stamina.

The verse also emphasizes that no matter which category our gift falls into, *all* must be done so that God is glorified.

My husband, Don, has a gift in each category. His primary gift of exhortation enables him to speak and teach well. His secondary gift of giving causes him to enjoy working behind the scenes, encouraging missionaries and seeking ways to get others to support missions. Our daughter, Linda, is a combination of serving type gifts—compassion and server—faithfully helping others and avoiding the limelight.

My strongest three gifts—administrator, teacher and perceiver—have motivated me to be in speaking ministries. I have a keen awareness of the need to be sure that what I teach is scripturally sound. I will often go to great lengths of research to be sure that I only communicate truth.

We Minister in All Areas

Many people asked us, "Is it possible to have all seven of the motivational gifts in my life, to some extent?"

The answer is yes. We will see during the testing process that you will have some scoring, no matter how little, in each gift. We are all endowed with enough of each gift to be able to operate in that area to some degree.

Just because you do not have a particular gift as your primary giftedness does not mean you should shrink from responding to the needs around you.

For example, let's suppose your primary motivational gift is teaching and you scored the least number of points in compassion. In church one Sunday, however, you realize that the woman sitting next to you is crying. You don't know what's wrong, but you can tell she is hurting. Then you remember that compassion was your lowest score, and so you say to her, "Don't expect *me* to help you. Go find someone with the gift of compassion!"

Right?

Wrong!

As part of the Body of Christ we can minister to anyone for any need, anywhere, anytime. *Don't ever let the knowledge of your particular motivational gift keep you from ministering in other areas.*

While it is true that in the above scenario a compassion person would be aware of the hurting person sooner than others and move to meet the need, it does not mean that others are not able to reach out with compassion when it's needed.

We will all minister in the spheres of all seven gifts.

You see, there is a difference between *being* (your motivational gift makes you what you are) and *doing* (your service to Jesus will include a wide variety of activities). That said, the way you minister in any area will always be affected by your primary motivational gift.

Also, remember that God's grace is sufficient for any circumstance we may find ourselves in. He enables. He anoints us for the task at hand. We can count on Him. How do we know that all Christians are enjoined (and enabled) to minister in the areas of all the gifts? The Bible makes it clear.

Perceiving

You are to perceive God's will in various degrees and situations. We should all perceive spiritual truth. "He replied to them, To you it has been given to *know* the secrets and mysteries of the kingdom of heaven" (Matthew 13:11, emphasis added).

We should all proclaim God's will with the help of the Holy Spirit. "And it shall come to pass in the last days, God declares, that I will pour out of My Spirit upon all mankind, and your sons and your daughters shall prophesy [telling forth the divine counsels]" (Acts 2:17).

We should all seek wisdom. "That people may know skillful and godly Wisdom and instruction, discern and comprehend the words of understanding and insight" (Proverbs 1:2).

Serving

You are to serve the Lord and other people in a variety of ways. We should all serve God. "Serve the Lord with gladness! Come before His presence with singing!" (Psalm 100:2). We should all serve others. "Through love you should serve one another" (Galatians 5:13).

We should all serve Jesus.

> If anyone serves Me, he must continue to follow Me [to cleave steadfastly to Me, conform wholly to My example in living and, if need be, in dying] and wherever I am, there will My servant be also. If anyone serves Me, the Father will honor him.
>
> John 12:26

Teaching

You are to teach others in appropriate ways. We should all be prepared to teach.

> Study and be eager and do your utmost to present yourself to God approved . . . a workman who has no cause to be ashamed, correctly ana-

lyzing and accurately dividing [rightly handling and skillfully teaching] the Word of Truth.

2 Timothy 2:15

We should all teach one another.

Let the word [spoken by] Christ . . . have its home [in your hearts and minds] and dwell in you in [all its] richness, as you teach and admonish and train one another in all insight and intelligence and wisdom [in spiritual things].

Colossians 3:16

We should all teach others to obey the commands of Jesus.

Go then and make disciples of all the nations, baptizing them into the name of the Father and of the Son and of the Holy Spirit, teaching them to observe everything that I have commanded you.

Matthew 28:19–20

Exhorting

You are to exhort, admonish and encourage others. We should exhort one another whenever we gather together.

Not forsaking or neglecting to assemble together [as believers], as is the habit of some people, but admonishing (warning, urging, and encouraging) one another, and all the more faithfully as you see the day approaching.

Hebrews 10:25

We should all devote ourselves to exhortation. "Till I come, devote yourself to [public and private] reading, to exhortation (preaching and personal appeals), and to teaching and instilling doctrine" (1 Timothy 4:13).

We should all exhort every day. "But instead warn (admonish, urge, and encourage) one another every day, as long as it is called Today, that none of you may be hardened . . . by the deceitfulness of sin" (Hebrews 3:13).

Giving

You are to give of your resources and energies to God and to others. We should all be generous. "Give, and [gifts] will be given to you; good measure, pressed down, shaken together, and running over" (Luke 6:38). We should all give freely. "Freely (without pay) you have received, freely (without charge) give" (Matthew 10:8). We should all be responsible for the support of ministry. "Contribute to the needs of God's people [sharing in the necessities of the saints]; pursue the practice of hospitality" (Romans 12:13).

Administering

You are to lead as God calls you to do so. We should all lead with a servant's heart.

> You know that those who are recognized as governing and are supposed to rule the Gentiles (the nations) lord it over them [ruling with absolute power, holding them in subjection], and their great men exercise authority and dominion over them. But this is not to be so among you; instead, whoever desires to be great among you must be your servant.
>
> Mark 10:42–43

We should all begin by administering right where we are. "His master said to him, Well done, you upright (honorable, admirable) and faithful servant! You have been faithful and trustworthy over a little; I will put you in charge of much" (Matthew 25:21).

We should all trust God if He wants us in any leadership position. "But God is the Judge! He puts down one and lifts up another" (Psalm 75:7).

Showing Compassion

You are to show love, compassion, and mercy to others. We should all abound in mercy. "Blessed are the merciful: for they shall obtain mercy" (Matthew 5:7, KJV).

We should all be loving.

> Finally, all [of you] should be of one and the same mind (united in spirit), sympathizing [with one another], loving [each other] as brethren [of one household], compassionate and courteous (tenderhearted and humble).
>
> 1 Peter 3:8

We should all show compassion to others. "Thus has the Lord of hosts spoken: Execute true judgment and show mercy and kindness and tender compassion, every man to his brother" (Zechariah 7:9).

In all these ways the Bible admonishes us to minister in all areas of giftedness. This helps to bring balance into our lives. We will still function mainly in our primary motivational gift but we are able to—and we must—minister in the other areas as well.

If I Have a Gift, Why Haven't I Known It?

The best way to measure whether or not you are operating in the sphere of your motivational gift is by this simple test: *Joy* is the byproduct of operating in your motivational gift. *Frustration* is the byproduct of trying to operate outside it.

Joy is always a byproduct of doing the will of God. Joy can never be sought as a goal or an end in itself. But as you function in the giftedness that God has given you, you will have joy.

Why You May Not Know Your Motivational Gift

1. You were never taught about it.

This is probably the major reason for most people. It was certainly true for us. Until 33 years ago, when our friends introduced us to the list of motivational gifts in Romans 12, we knew nothing about them. We had read that passage many times but never recognized it for what it is.

We estimate that fewer than 10 percent of American churchgoers know motivational gifts even exist. Of those, fewer than half have discovered their particular gifts. In many of the other countries where we have taught, we were, to the best of our knowledge, the first ones to teach about motivational gifts.

This is why we feel it is so important to make this information available on a wider scale. We hope you will share the teachings of this book with friends, relatives, study groups, your pastor (or your flock if you are the pastor) and anyone else you think would be helped.

2. You have never received Jesus Christ as your personal Savior and Lord.

While every person is gifted by God whether he or she is a Christian or not, the receiving of Christ releases the motivational gifts in far greater measure and opens the way for the gifts to be used as God intended.

Before a person becomes a Christian, his or her motivational gift will be functioning to some extent, but often in ways that are self-centered and self-serving. Before Christ becomes central in our lives, we are central.

3. You are not being fed spiritually.

Just as a newborn baby needs nourishment, so the person who is "born again" needs spiritual sustenance in order to grow. Many people have been led to Christ but not given follow-up instruction or encouragement. Their ability to recognize their giftedness, like the rest of their spiritual progress, is limited.

4. You have had confusing teaching on the motivational gifts.

Since the same word in English is used to translate the three different Greek words for "gift" in the New Testament, it has led some to suppose that all biblical teaching on gifts should be lumped together.

You may have heard teaching that combines the nine manifestation gifts of 1 Corinthians 12:7–10, the five ministry gifts of Ephesians 4:11, the seven motivational gifts of Romans 12—and a few others, like celibacy, as well. The result? Confusion!

You may have even taken a test made up of as many as twenty-six "gift" possibilities. Yet, when you were finished, you still felt unsure of your giftedness. We continue to meet people who were so puzzled that they gave up the effort to find their giftedness altogether.

It is important to have clear teaching on our gifts so we can identify them and use them for the glory of God and in service to others. It is only when the motivational gifts of Romans 12 are identified as the gifts that we *possess* that the Body of Christ can begin to fully function in them.

Even when we know about the gifts, however, and have singled out our own, we may not be flowing freely in them in our lives.

Obstacles That Block the Flow of Motivational Gifts

1. You may have bondages that hinder the flow of your gifts.

Just as debris in a river can block the flow of the river, so the bondages in our lives may block the flow of our God-given motivational gifts.

The most common bondage we see is that of fear. Incapacitating by its very nature, fear prevents our developing the full potential of our gifts.

Such bondage generally results from negative childhood conditioning. Unfortunately, not every child is brought up in a positive home atmosphere. Divorce, fighting parents, alcoholism, drug usage, occult practices, mental problems, parents who abuse their children with words or actions—all these limit the freedom with which the grown individual will function.

On a survey questionnaire where we ask people to comment on what they were like as children, we'll occasionally get responses like, "I'm sorry, but I could not complete this. Memories of my childhood are too painful."

Happily, a person can be delivered from such bondage with good Christian counseling and ministry.

2. Anger can block the flow of your gift.

Anger is our response to being abused, wounded or rejected. If the anger is not resolved, it is either *expressed* (as in rebellion, retaliation, resentment, hatred, violence and in some cases even murder) or *suppressed* (as in self-pity, self-hatred, depression and even suicide).

Either way, the person winds up in a prison of his own making, described so graphically in Matthew 5:21–26, where Jesus equates the harboring of anger with murder.

In our experience, three steps are necessary to dislodge the obstacle of anger: There needs to be (1) complete forgiveness of all who have angered us in any way, (2) deliverance and (3) inner healing prayer.

3. Trying to be someone other than yourself prevents the natural expression of your gift.

Sometimes other people put pressure on us to conform to a certain image. Or we ourselves may try to imitate someone we admire. Unless this role model happens to have the same motivational gift we do, this can hamper the flow of our own giftedness.

We find that when people take the motivational gifts test, they get really excited as they find out who they are and are released to be themselves and follow God's plan for their lives.

4. Poor self-image can hinder the operation of your gift.

Most people have some degree of a self-image problem stemming from the problems and pressures of childhood. A child is designed by the Creator to be nurtured by two loving parents who will build basic trust and confidence. Not all children are so fortunate. The condition of our fallen race leaves much to be desired; often parents have themselves lacked the nurturing that would have made them confident persons.

But no matter what damage has been done, we can be grateful that we are being transformed into Christ's image as we abide in Him.

5. Irresponsibility can impede the flow of your gift.

Who me? Irresponsible? Only you can check it out. Here is the principle: "Every one to whom much is given, of him will much be required; and of him to whom men commit much they will demand the more" (Luke 12:48, RSV).

Those who have been greatly endowed have a greater responsibility for using all that they have to help others. To neglect to use your gifting is to be irresponsible.

As you discover your motivational gift (or gifts) you may find you have not used them well. Do not let that be a source of discouragement or guilt. It is possible that you did not realize your giftedness was there, let alone what to do with it. So, relax, read on and discover. Then you can become responsible.

6. Sin can block or distort the working of your gift.

There's no doubt about it. Sin pollutes. It pollutes every area of our lives and our motivational gifts are no exception.

In fact, the degree to which we are able to use our gift is dependent upon the degree to which we are in the will of God. Or, conversely, the more we entertain sin in our lives, the more the function of our motivational gifts is polluted.

Sin is missing the mark. God has a plan for each life and our goal should be to discover and cooperate with that plan. Sometimes we commit sins of omission because we are not aware of God's will on a matter. Other times we sin deliberately, doing something we know is wrong. But sin is sin whether it's done knowingly or unknowingly.

The purpose of this book is not to discuss sin. But we do exhort you to get rid of known sin in your life—and ask God to reveal to you any unknown sin so you can get rid of that, too—if you want your motivational gifts to flow freely and beautifully through your life.

The Holy Spirit Empowers the Gifts

You may be doing everything else just right in your life, but if you are not in touch with the power of the Holy Spirit you are missing the great dynamic of the third Person of the Trinity, freely available to every believer. Paul expressed it this way: "But ever be filled and stimulated with the [Holy] Spirit" (Ephesians 5:18). It's part of our inheritance. It's ours for the asking.

God the Holy Spirit wants to be released into our lives to become that well of living water—the sap that flows as we abide in the vine. We have observed that the ongoing flow of the Holy Spirit in a person's life invariably increases the pure and effective flow of that person's motivational gifts.

How to Score Yourself

I recall thinking, when I was first introduced to the motivational gifts concept: *Why hasn't someone come up with a self-testing method to help us discover our gifts?* Then I realized that asking the question itself was my primary motivational gift in action. So I set out to try.

I have always been intrigued with psychological and aptitude tests such as the ones I took in high school and college. I knew something of that nature must be applicable here. I also knew that if God had indeed created seven basic motivational gifts (or what might be called seven basic personality types), then there had to be distinct, consistent characteristics for each. Together Don and I sought unique and strong indicators and designed a testing procedure. We tried our set of testing materials with a number of groups—and it worked! People discovered their giftedness.

Four years later, while I was presenting a motivational gifts seminar in Kansas City, Missouri, before a gathering of the Full Gospel Business Men's Fellowship, I learned that a well-known clinical psychologist, Edward Carr, was present. Feelings of inadequacy swept over me and I found myself making apologies for my "just-a-housewife-and-mom" status.

After the meeting Mr. Carr came over to me. "Don't you ever apologize again for what you are teaching," he admonished me. "What you have presented to us tonight is incredible! You've based your findings on the Bible, but it parallels what clinical psychologists have discovered over many years of research from secular investigation into personality traits. They have categorized characteristics of people in many different ways, and have found that basic personality types can be defined. The research of these secular psychologists simply confirms what you are teaching."

I was grateful to know that what we were teaching was not only biblically sound but also psychologically accurate. What God has created can be empirically discovered and verified, even by those who do not know Him.

For each of the seven motivational gifts, we have developed a list of twenty characteristics typical of that person's personality and approach to life. They are based on:

1. The biblical examples of each gift
2. Some of the initial suggestions of character traits presented by Bill Gothard and Don Pickerell
3. Insight from the input of our brainstorming group
4. Our own research over the years, as we have taught thousands of people in many countries and benefited from their feedback about characteristics consistent in their lives
5. Hundreds of letters of responses and suggestions

We have tried to include only the characteristics unique to each gift. In a few cases, a trait must of necessity overlap another gift. And while each list is reasonably comprehensive, we realize there may be additional characteristics that could be added. We have attempted to include the most indicative qualities, in order to develop an effective method of scoring.

We are indeed wonderfully made and, like snowflakes, no two of us are exactly alike. Even though thousands share your gift, your expression of it will be unique. Even if you are an identical twin, you are going to have differences that affect your individual performance.

These differences come from the influence of countless variables in your life. For instance, your health. While for some the event of sickness or injury may thwart giftedness, for others it may be the very thing that challenges them to rise above limitations and use their gifts in an even greater way. Other variables are heredity, education, culture, economics, marital status, location, talents, self-image—well, the list is endless and each one has an impact on your life and the way you use your gift.

This should help give you some feeling for the magnitude of God's plan in creating such unique individuals—even though, amazingly, we all operate primarily influenced by one of the seven motivational gifts.

Scoring

Here's how the scoring is done: As we present and define each characteristic in the following chapters, ask yourself, *How true is this of me?* Your first response will probably be the most accurate. Don't answer the way you'd *like* to be or the way you think you *ought* to be. Be honest! Remember, there are no right or wrong answers. This is simply a self-discovery process. You alone know yourself well enough to be able to score properly.

It is also important to differentiate, when scoring, between learned behavior and the way you naturally act or think. If you are presently employed, be sure that your current duties do not unduly influence your answers. You may or may not be utilizing your motivational gifts in your job.

If the characteristic is never or almost never true of you, put an "x" (or a check mark) in the box under *never*. Then place a "0" in the points column.

If the characteristic is true of you only occasionally, mark under *seldom* and put a "1" in the points column.

If the characteristic is sometimes true of you (up to 49 percent of the time), score under *sometimes* and give yourself a "2" in the points column.

If the characteristic is true of you 50 to 75 percent of the time, score under *usually*, and write a "3" in the points column.

If the characteristic is true of you most of the time, score under *mostly*, and put a "4" in the points column.

If the characteristic is true of you all or almost all of the time, score under *always* and place a "5" in the points column.

After you have scored yourself on all twenty characteristics, add up your score and transfer it to the tally sheet at the end of each testing chapter. It does not matter whether you score high, low or in the middle. Remember, this is a subjective test. It is the *comparison* of your seven scores that will help you to determine your motivational gifts.

If you were to give yourself a "5" for each of the twenty characteristics of a particular gift, you would receive the maximum score of 100.

Now take a look at the profile sheet at the end of this chapter. Take your total for each gift and transfer it to the profile sheet by shading in the appropriate horizontal column from left (0) to right, stopping where your score corresponds to the number at the top of the chart. (Sample profile sheets are on pages 205 and 206.)

After you have transferred all seven scores you will have a composite profile of yourself. The score that stands out farthest to the right is your primary motivational gift. You will also see at a glance which gift is your second, third and so forth. It is equally important to identify areas where you are the *least* gifted. You need to know this so you can:

1. Recognize areas where it is good to depend on others
2. Rejoice in those who are gifted in the ways you are not
3. Avoid trying to be accomplished in those ways
4. Say, "No, thank you" with confidence when asked to do things (except of course in a general way or to meet an immediate need, as discussed in chapter four) that are outside the sphere of your giftedness

On the other hand, discovering your gifts will release you to accept responsibilities that *will* utilize your giftedness. It will help you use your time and energy in pursuits in which you will tend to be successful and a blessing to others.

Now, move on to your discovery of your motivational gifts!

Adult Questionnaire

ADULT MOTIVATIONAL GIFT PROFILE SHEET

Gift		0	10	20	30	40	50	60	70	80	90	100
*	Perceiver	60										
	Server	32										
*	Teacher	51										
	Exhorter	42										
	Giver	28										
*	Administrator	51										
	Compassion Person	32										

NAME _Ana Bratun_

ADDRESS _044 @ 28TH_

CITY/ST/ZIP _Milwaukee WI 53215_

#1 GIFT _Perceiver_

#2 GIFT _Teacher_

#3 GIFT _Administrator_

material to trusting students. The errors would be multiplied in vast numbers of innocent minds and I'd be responsible. My research had to be *complete*. Besides, I loved doing it.

Because of their love of study and research, teachers also like to have a large personal library of research books.

Dick Mills, a popular speaker with the motivational gift of teaching (and the ministry gift of prophet), has an almost insatiable love for books, especially versions of the Bible (he regularly quotes from 25 translations). He can't pass a Christian bookstore without slipping inside to see if they have any new research books.

One day his wife, Betty, observed that Dick's books had filled all the available spaces around the house and were now spilling over to her kitchen counters. Before long they were appearing on the dresser, then the nightstand, then stacked up in corners. That was it!

"Dick," she announced, "I can't stand it. I can't even clean house without having to move stacks of books. Either they go or I go!"

Well, Dick didn't want to lose his wife, but neither did he want to lose his books. He went to the local lumber store and soon a new addition appeared on their house. You guessed it. He added on a library.

4. Enjoys word studies.

Never	Seldom	Sometimes	Usually	Mostly	Always
0	1	2	3	4	5
			POINTS		

Teachers are fascinated with words. They like to investigate the root meanings and the Greek or Hebrew counterparts. They see words as the building blocks of communication. They want to use words well, and correctly.

They will often check out a word in a reference like W. E. Vine's *An Expository Dictionary of New Testament Words* to determine the precise meaning of the original Greek. They also enjoy topical studies with aids like *Nave's Topical Bible* or *Harper's Topical Concordance*.

Sometimes the study of just one word will lead the teacher into hours of pursuit as one insight leads to another.

When Dick Mills teaches he often will take a single verse of Scripture and spend time explaining the facets of meaning in each major word in it, quoting a variety of authorities. The verse comes alive.

5. Prefers to use biblical illustrations rather than life illustrations.

Never	Seldom	Sometimes	Usually	Mostly	Always
0	1	2	3	4	5
			POINTS		

The Bible is the ultimate authority for teachers. Even if they do not understand a particular verse, they believe that it is their own lack of knowledge, not the Scripture passage, that is the problem. It is a source of new understanding yet to be discovered.

Teachers quote liberally from the Bible, often using stories, parables or characters to prove or illustrate a point. They can trust this source.

Life illustrations are another matter; they are by their very nature subjective. They are not, in the teacher's estimation, a reliable rock upon which to build.

 A teacher may use personal anecdotes to enhance a point, but only *after* the point is well illustrated by Scripture.

I find that this is my tendency. For instance, when I developed a teaching on the subject of anger I first studied what the Bible had to say about it in these passages:

Jesus teaches about it in Matthew 5:21–26.

Paul warns against it in Ephesians 4:26–27.

It was Cain's main problem in Genesis 4:1–12.

It was Jonah's problem in Jonah 4:1–9.

Only then did I add to this what I had learned experientially about anger through the counseling I had done.

Never	Seldom	Sometimes	Usually	Mostly	Always
0	1	2	3	4	5
				X	
POINTS					

6. Gets upset when Scripture is used out of context.

Wow! Does this unpardonable action ever drive the teachers up the wall! To them it is like fingernails across a chalkboard. They are so concerned for the integrity of teaching—be it spoken or written—that they cannot help but lose confidence in any person who proof-texts a point with disregard of the true sense of a passage.

One popular traveling teacher was the rave of many conferences and camps some years ago. He was clever and dramatic in his presentations, keeping his audiences captivated for the most part—except for those with the motivational gift of teaching. When others would leave a session saying, "Wasn't that wonderful!" the teachers would reply, "Not really."

The problem was that the speaker, being blessed with the motivational gift of exhortation, would set out to prove a point and tag on several Scriptures to give it validity. The point itself was usually well-taken but the Scriptures quoted in that context might not be what the biblical writer meant by them at all. It would have been better to have used no Scriptures than to use ones lifted out of context. We noticed that those with the teaching gift quit going to his meetings.

The teacher views *misuse* as *abuse*.

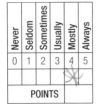

Never	Seldom	Sometimes	Usually	Mostly	Always
0	1	2	3	4	5
				X	
POINTS					

7. Feels concerned that truth be established in every situation.

Whether it's in business, education, religion, human relationships or any other area of life, teachers want truth to prevail. It is the foundation, the anchor, the framework within which they can securely work.

The Berean believers must have had many people with the motivational gift of teaching among them, for they checked out carefully what

Paul said every day to be sure that it lined up with the truth of the Old Testament Scriptures (see Acts 17:11).

Aquila and Priscilla, both teachers by motivational gift, welcomed Apollos, who was also a teacher. But they could see that he was operating on limited knowledge of the Gospel and were quick to instruct him more perfectly in the way of the Lord (see Acts 18:26). With truth fully established in him, Apollos was then able to go to Greece and confound the intellectuals of that day.

8. Is more objective than subjective.

Never	Seldom	Sometimes	Usually	Mostly	Always
0	1	2	3	4	5
POINTS					

In general, men tend to be more objective and women more subjective. There are, of course, exceptions. But when a man has the motivational gift of teaching we see the most objective type of person of all. Such men often become research scientists, business analysts or judges.

Women with the motivational gift of teaching go into similar fields. And it is not unusual for them to hear a shrouded compliment like, "For a woman you are amazingly objective."

Teachers look at life with a certain detachment. They participate, but without their emotions getting in the way. This works as a sort of insulation factor that keeps them from being hurt or emotionally wounded.

Eighteen-year-old Erin, the third of four sisters, attended one of our seminars in her Baptist church. At one point she came to us to share some interesting insights.

"It's been invaluable to discover that my motivational gift is teaching," she told us. "I've always wondered why I could be so detached and objective. Now I see why.

"My parents fight like cats and dogs," she went on. "They love each other, but the fights get pretty bad. My two older sisters couldn't handle it and they both left home when they were sixteen. They're still working through a lot of emotional damage. Now I see that they both have the gift of compassion. They've felt the tension and hurt much more than I ever have.

"My viewpoint has been, if they want to fight that's their business, but I'm not going to waste my time listening to it. So I would just go into my bedroom and read a good book."

9. Easily develops and uses a large vocabulary.

Never	Seldom	Sometimes	Usually	Mostly	Always
0	1	2	3	4	5
POINTS					

Teachers use words well and are fond of learning new ones. Even as children they enjoy word games—Scrabble, Boggle, crossword puzzles. They are good communicators, often eloquent and commanding in their speech.

Several years ago I was one of the speakers at the Billy Graham Writers' Conference in Calgary, Canada. The banquet speaker was Philip

Yancey, author of many books including *Where Is God When It Hurts*. His speech was marvelous. Eloquent! Polished! As an editor I mused that it would be almost possible to take a transcript of what he said and print it without any editing at all.

Later that evening I was talking with Philip. "Your speech was magnificent," I told him. "How long did it take you to prepare it?" I assumed he had worked on it for weeks.

"Well," he confided, "to tell you the truth I put it together on the flight up here this morning. Basically I just jotted some notes on the back of an envelope."

As we talked a bit more I realized that he spoke eloquently *all* the time. Even his casual conversation was polished and impressive. Obviously his motivational gift was that of teacher.

Never	Seldom	Sometimes	Usually	Mostly	Always
0	1	2	3	4	5
POINTS					

10. Emphasizes facts and the accuracy of words.

Teachers are not so interested in opinions; they want facts. Facts are the building blocks of their lives. This combines with their exceptional objectivity and ability to use words well and accurately to make them gifted in editorial work. They make great copyeditors. Like a homing pigeon they readily find their target: misspelled words, improper grammar or inadequate vocabulary.

My Aunt Aleda was one so gifted, much to my dismay as a child. Through my mother's urging I wrote to Aunt Aleda regularly. But she always returned my letters—edited! She'd circle misspelled words and tell me to look them up. She'd correct my grammar, even diagramming sentences to reinforce what I was obviously not learning adequately in school. Needless to say I did not relish the returned epistles. But looking back now, I'm glad she took the time and interest to use her giftedness for my benefit.

In Japan our missionary friend Noel Morris is likewise gifted. Coupled with the detail-orientation of his serving gift, his teaching gift made him meticulous in editing skills. While his main ministry was managing the largest Christian tape loan library in Japan, he helped to support himself and his wife by editing English manuscripts written by Japanese.

Never	Seldom	Sometimes	Usually	Mostly	Always
0	1	2	3	4	5
POINTS					

11. Checks out the source of knowledge of others who teach.

Whenever we teach a motivational gift seminar it is the teachers who come up to us at the close of the session to say, "Now where did you get all this information?" This has happened so often that now we usually include an explanation in the presentation itself.

Teachers are the ones most apt to ask: who, what, where, when and how come? In a young person this can come across as rude or impudent.

Such was the case with the fourteen-year-old grandson of our friends who were living in Munich, Germany. They had invited their grandson to come and live with them for a while and go to a German school. They had not bargained for an adolescent with the motivational gift of teaching, nor did they recognize this as the cause of his incessant questioning.

"He must ask five hundred questions a day," Vi bemoaned. "Some that are none of his business."

"He follows me around asking why I do this and why I do that," Jim said. "And the worst is that he's learned more German than we have, so he's always correcting us."

When we had the opportunity to meet the boy our suspicions were confirmed. He had a teacher gift.

We were able to share with Vi and Jim that this was a giftedness that needed to be channeled, not squelched. Just the simple awareness of their grandson's gift took a lot of pressure off the situation.

12. Prefers teaching believers over engaging in evangelism.

Never	Seldom	Sometimes	Usually	Mostly	Always
0	1	2	3	4	5
				X	
		POINTS			

When it comes to evangelism the teacher keeps a low profile. He or she will lead people to Jesus Christ, but usually in circumstances where a bridge of relationship or friendship has already been built.

Aggressive types of evangelism are not appealing to the teacher. They are definitely not drawn to street witnessing or door-to-door evangelism. But they are glad that others make these efforts. And, once new people have been won to the Lord, the teacher will spend endless hours joyfully teaching the new converts.

Julie Wayner, author of *His Gentle Voice*, is just such a teacher. She confided, "I'd almost rather die than go out door-to-door evangelizing. But give me a group of new believers and I'll commit all the time necessary to train them in the Word of God."

We saw her put this into action some years ago as she faithfully taught the Bible to a group of women (mostly new believers) for six years. I was privileged to continue teaching the group when Julie moved to Michigan and was greatly impressed with the maturity of their faith and the extent of their Bible knowledge.

How fortunate it is that not every Christian is geared primarily to evangelism, for without people to teach the newly evangelized, the Body of Christ would not mature.

13. Feels Bible study is foundational to the operation of all the gifts.

Never	Seldom	Sometimes	Usually	Mostly	Always
0	1	2	3	4	5
			X		
		POINTS			

Teachers cannot imagine anything more important than studying the Bible. They believe it is the foundation upon which all the gifts operate.

Their thinking goes something like this:

How can the perceiver perceive accurately unless she has a solid understanding of the Bible?

How can the server serve well if he is not acquainted with the biblical reasons for service?

How can the teacher teach unless she has studied the Scriptures thoroughly?

How can the exhorter exhort effectively unless he knows the biblical basis for his exhortation?

How can the giver give properly if she is not aware of the biblical guidelines for giving?

How can the administrator be an effective leader unless he understands God's will as revealed in the Word?

How can the compassionate person minister God's love if she does not encounter that love in the Bible?

"Nothing," says the teacher, "is more foundational than studying the Bible!"

14. Solves problems by starting with scriptural principles.

Never	Seldom	Sometimes	Usually	Mostly	Always
0	1	2	3	4	5
				X	
POINTS					

Teachers believe that there is an answer to every problem in God's Word—if not in actual example or principle, at least by implication.

In her book, Julie Wayner describes the problems and challenges she faced as she set out to become a missionary to China. With the closing of that nation to the West, her love for a young man committed to the South American mission field and his subsequent engagement to another woman, she turned at each point to the Bible to give her the principles by which to make decisions.

Julie told us, "I always looked first for the biblical principles that fit the situation. Then secondly for the leading of the Holy Spirit, and thirdly for the juxtaposition of circumstances. If, for any reason, the other two guidelines (as best I could interpret them) did not line up with the first, then I always chose to abide by the biblical principles."

In the end, Julie got her man. They married and went to a mission field in Africa.

15. Is intellectually sharp.

Never	Seldom	Sometimes	Usually	Mostly	Always
0	1	2	3	4	5
	X				
POINTS					

These are the ones you don't want to invite over to play Trivial Pursuit. They'll win for sure.

The fact is that God has gifted these, the "mind" of the Body of Christ, with what they need to be successful in their sphere—a high IQ. They are often brilliant. They were good students in school, loved to study, were self-motivated and often came home with straight As.

The teacher's mind can be likened to a thirsty sponge, soaking up everything it can. As a result he or she is a prolific reader, drawn to

Part II
The Seven Gifts

Characteristics
of the Perceiver *prophet*

We have chosen to call this first gift of the Romans 12 list the gift of perception. The King James Version uses the word "prophecy." But since the same root word is used in the other two lists in the New Testament, it would be easy to confuse it with either the manifestation gift of prophecy or the ministry gift to the Church, the prophet.

Also, the word "prophecy" in our current vocabulary has a variety of connotations, both positive and negative. It seemed to us that a fresh new word would eliminate confusion.

The Greek word for "prophecy" in verse six is *propheteia*, related to *prophets*, which means, according to *Strong's Exhaustive Concordance*, "an inspired speaker." One of its root words is *phemi*, meaning "to show or make known one's thoughts; to speak, say or affirm."

According to biblical scholars, the prominent idea of prophecy in the New Testament is not prediction, but "the inspired delivery of warning, exhortation, instruction, judging and making manifest the secrets of the heart."[4]

In the specific context of motivational gifts, we see that the word refers to one who is especially sensitive to perceiving the will of God and then proclaiming it—or, depending upon the Lord's direction, praying for it to be accomplished.

The perceiver, then, is one who readily perceives, prays about, proclaims and promotes the will of God.

In this chapter we will examine each of twenty characteristics of the perceiver in detail, giving examples from the experience of those with this primary motivational gift.

As you read each section, proceed to score yourself as indicated in the previous chapter.

1. Quickly and accurately identifies good and evil, and hates evil.

Never	Seldom	Sometimes	Usually	Mostly	Always
0	1	2	3	4	5
POINTS					

The perceiver views people or situations as either *in* the will of God or *out of* the will of God. There is no such thing as *sort of* in the will of God or *partly* in the will of God, for in his or her understanding to be not perfectly in God's will is to be out of God's will.

Perceivers see life as a matter of choices. They view the option to choose right as imperative: not to choose right is by default choosing wrong. Compromise is not an option.

They have intense hatred for evil. They want to see evil overcome and eliminated and the Kingdom of God evidenced here on this earth.

A biblical figure with the gift of perception is John the Baptist. From the beginning of his public ministry he exposed evil, identifying with and expressing God's hatred of it. He publicly denounced Herod's adulterous relationship with his brother's wife, even when it meant prison and death.

Spokesmen for righteousness and just causes are frequently perceivers. Their giftedness equips them to be bold and outspoken without regard for either public esteem or their own advantage.

We asked our perceiver friend Vicki why she spent so much of her free time campaigning against abortion.

"Why," she replied emphatically, "abortion is murder! Murder is wrong! How can anyone observe such an evil in our society and *not* speak out about it?"

Our youngest son, Dan, has the gift of perception. At age ten he was somewhat overweight and becoming concerned about it. One day he asked me what he could do to lose weight. I explained to him that sugar was the biggest culprit and that it would help to cut out desserts and sweets.

Sugar immediately became his "public enemy number one." He determined to rid his diet of this evil once and for all. During the next few months his weight dropped until he was slim and trim. Even when he went to birthday parties he refused to eat ice cream or cake.

2. Sees everything as either black or white; no gray or indefinite areas.

Never	Seldom	Sometimes	Usually	Mostly	Always
0	1	2	3	4	5
POINTS					

Perceivers make decisions easily. They form quick evaluations. They see things as right or wrong, appropriate or inappropriate, true or false. They don't see how there can be anything in between. They tend to answer yes or no. They seldom say maybe. They are people of extremes in feelings, words and actions.

Most of us think in terms of a scale from black through many shades of gray to white. We could say, "I'm not doing as well as I might, but at least I'm doing better than I did yesterday." Not so the perceiver. No halfway measures.

Emily Binning, author of *Gordon Takes a Wife*, had been fighting a weight problem most of her life without much permanent success. One day the Lord told her to submit everything she ate to her perceiver husband's approval.

These were the ground rules: she could put anything she wanted on her plate and then ask Gordon what she could eat—a daring thing to submit to the decisions of an uncompromising perceiver! In her book she wrote:

> A couple of nights after this decision, we were invited out to dinner. It was our first experience away from home in submitting my food for Gordon's evaluation. It took quite a bit of whispering back and forth during the meal, during which time I lost a half a potato, one slice of meat, and a roll with butter. Dessert was served: pumpkin pie with whipped cream. I carefully spread the whipped cream over the entire piece before asking Gordon how much I could have, so there would be whipped cream on whatever portion was to be mine! Gordon looked at the pie and said out loud, "You can't have *any* pie."[5]

Gordon saw the situation the way a classic perceiver does: If you are going to do it, let's do it right. (Emily got her weight down and kept it down.)

3. Easily perceives the character of individuals and groups.

Never	Seldom	Sometimes	Usually	Mostly	Always
0	1	2	3	4	5
		✳			
POINTS					

It's easy for perceivers to "get the feel" of individuals and groups—not by any outward analysis, but by the intuitive perception that is their gift.

John the Baptist did not need to ask questions of the group of Pharisees that came out to watch him baptize. "You brood of vipers!" he accosted them (Matthew 3:7, NASB). John knew that the Pharisees had not come to repent but rather to judge, criticize and condemn.

A perceiver can go into a church, a prayer group, a healing service or any group for that matter, and soon tell how spiritual it really is. He or she also has keen sensitivity to what is going on in an individual's life.

During a Canadian seminar we met Bea, a mature perceiver. Later she wrote us, saying:

> I was one of those who scored 100 percent on the perceiver gift. During a coffee break I was talking with a minister I was acquainted with and began to be aware that there was something more going on in his life than he was expressing. I suddenly perceived that he was going through a mid-life crisis. I don't know how, but I just *knew* it. I didn't say anything, but prayed

for him for several days. Two weeks later the minister resigned from his position and confided in me that it was due to a *mid-life* crisis!

It's not that perceivers know everything about a person; God shows them only what He wants them to see—and always for a purpose, usually so that the perceiver can effectively pray for that person.

Never	Seldom	Sometimes	Usually	Mostly	Always
0	1	2	3	4	5
					X
POINTS					

4. Encourages repentance that produces a change of heart.

After challenging the spirituality of the Pharisees and Sadducees, John the Baptist went on to say, "Bring forth fruit that is consistent with repentance [let your lives prove your change of heart]" (Matthew 3:8).

John was well aware of these "religious" individuals' claims to be spiritual leaders, but he was also aware of their hypocrisy. John knew that only a genuine and evident change in their behavior would prove the inward condition of a repentant heart.

We do a lot of personal counseling and have learned to observe the fruit in a person's life in order to help diagnose underlying problems. Evidence of bad fruit means bad roots. We pray for the exposure of the cause of those bad roots, help the person identify all of the hatred and judgment against the one who hurt him or her and then help the person repent of it. If there is genuine repentance there is a change of heart, and his or her life begins to bear good fruit.

Never	Seldom	Sometimes	Usually	Mostly	Always
0	1	2	3	4	5
		X			
POINTS					

5. Believes accepting difficulties can produce positive personal growth.

Most of us avoid problems. We do not view trials as friends or see trauma and tragedy as stepping-stones to maturity. Not so the perceivers! They rejoice in negative events as being the greatest opportunities to work brokenness and consequent maturity into their lives.

By brokenness we mean that experience of once again coming to the end of ourselves, where we say, "God, I can't handle this. I can't do anything without You. Help, Lord!" Then we are ready to receive His help and grow.

Perceiver, prophet and author John Sandford says that two-word cry is the most spiritual prayer a person can utter.

Perceivers welcome the difficulties that press a person into brokenness because they feel it to mean God loves them enough to deal with another area of their lives.

It seems God sifts and sifts the perceivers. He wants to do a thorough and deep work in them so they will be tools well-fitted for accomplishing His purposes here on earth. Years ago I heard Iverna Tompkins say, "God is not letting me get by this year with what He let me get by with last year." She said she often argued with the Lord that "everyone else seems to be getting away with it," and He would gently but firmly tell her that she was not "everyone else"—that He had a plan for her life and it was a narrower way.

Perceivers also rejoice to see evidence of brokenness and growth in others. Have you ever shared a difficult thing you were going through with a perceiver only to have him exclaim, "Praise the Lord! I know God's going to bring forth some great things in your life through this!"

And you say, "Thanks a lot!" That was not what you wanted to hear; you wanted some sympathy. You won't get it from a perceiver! These people know that difficulties and brokenness not only do them good—they do you good, too.

6. Has only a few or no close friendships. _Manny_

Never	Seldom	Sometimes	Usually	Mostly	Always
0	1	2	3	4	5
POINTS					

Often perceivers go through childhood with only one or two good friends—or none at all. Some worry about this, wondering why they don't want to reach out more to kids their own age. Others instinctively know that it's okay—that God made them this way. They feel comfortable in their aloneness.

Most often it's the parents of the perceiver who get overly concerned, feeling that the child should be friendlier and more involved with others.

We faced this with our younger son, Dan, before we understood about gifts. During his primary years Dan seemed to prefer playing alone after school, or just with his older brother, Dave.

"Why don't you invite the boy down the street to come over and play with you, Dan?" we would ask.

"I don't want to."

"But why?"

"He's dishonest. I've seen him steal things from other kids at school."

"Then why not ask the boy up the hill to come over?"

"Not him! He's mean."

"How about Johnny, then?"

"No way. He lies. I don't like to be around him."

And so it would go. Dan couldn't seem to find a friend who lived up to his standards.

Dave was, in many respects, just the opposite of Dan. Dave always brought friends home after school—usually a bunch. It seemed logical to push Dan into friendships so he "wouldn't feel left out." Then we learned about the motivational gifts and recognized that Dave was an administrator child, naturally drawn to a wide range of broad friendships. Dan, as a perceiver child, would tend to be a loner and have highly selective friendships.

Interestingly, when we put our boys in a Christian school Dan made several close friends who had similar standards within the year. For our perceiver son, this was a more congenial atmosphere in which to develop friendships without compromising his values.

Just as the Levites were uniquely set apart from the rest of the twelve tribes of Israel to minister to the Lord in the Temple, so, we believe, perceivers have been called apart to spend much time in prayer, to bring God's Word to the Body of Christ and to uphold God's highest standards. They will not have the luxury of broad friendships for several reasons:

Time for friendships is limited since their call to a ministry of prayer requires a significant time commitment.

Broad friendships require a degree of tolerance for people with differing standards and beliefs. Perceivers do not want to compromise.

God's gifting draws the perceivers to enjoy being "alone with Him."

Never	Seldom	Sometimes	Usually	Mostly	Always
0	1	2	3	4	5
POINTS					

7. Views the Bible as the basis for truth, belief, action and authority.

Perceivers are in the Word a lot. They love to study the Bible and find that God often speaks to them through specific Scriptures. They believe there isn't any other dependable basis for truth but the Bible.

John the Baptist's call was based on the Word of God. He knew Isaiah 40:3 well, and that his was the long-awaited voice of one crying in the wilderness.

Desiring to assure John that He was indeed the Christ, Jesus said to the Baptist's disciples, "Go and tell John what you have seen and heard: the blind receive their sight, the lame walk, the lepers are cleansed, the deaf hear, the dead are raised up, and the poor have the good news (the Gospel) preached to them" (Luke 7:22).

John saw the scriptural evidence in that answer, since he knew the prophecies about the Messiah and what he would do.

Perceivers also depend on the Holy Spirit to illuminate the Word. Our friend Steve Lightle, a perceiver/prophet, describes such an experience:

While I was sitting in a chair, the power of God came into the room. . . . Things began to happen to me spiritually of such a deep nature that I wondered what was going on. For the first time in my life, I had such an intimate and personal time with Jesus, that I could say with Paul, "I . . . heard inexpressible words, which a man is not permitted to speak" (2 Corinthians 12:4, NASB). During these days, the Lord was taking me mainly through the book of Isaiah. This was where I was reading almost constantly for the six and a half days. The Lord would make everything so real to me. It was an ongoing process of revelation.[6]

8. Boldly operates on spiritual principles.

	Never	Seldom	Sometimes	Usually	Mostly	Always
	0	1	2	3	4	5
POINTS			✳			

From the Bible, perceivers are able to extract principles that they apply to daily life. In fact, they are often very demanding of themselves about this. Children who have this gift are incredibly strict with themselves. They usually develop into the kind of teenagers who don't have to have parental restrictions imposed on them because they are already setting their own high standards.

One parent related how her perceiver teenager keeps her honest:

> One day I was talking on the phone to a friend who wanted to borrow our utility trailer. Feeling inwardly irritated because this particular person was always borrowing things, I made up an excuse. "Sorry, the trailer's being used right now," I said.
>
> "Mom!" my daughter said in a shocked tone of voice after I had hung up the phone. "The trailer's just sitting there! It's *not* being used. We're supposed to give to those who ask of us and not turn away from those who would borrow from us."
>
> She was right. . . . She had quoted a principle from Matthew 5:42. Feeling reproved by a daughter I had grown to respect for her principled life, I called my friend back and told her the trailer was available.

The perceiver is a person of principle in all aspects of life: the way he runs his home, business and personal relationships. Perceivers are truly the standard-bearers of Christianity. They are the ones who hold up God's righteousness and say, "This is what we ought to aim for!" If there weren't any perceivers many of us would settle for less. We *need* these people in the Body of Christ.

While perceiving is my third motivational gift, it often pops up in my life. I find I can't get around it, even when the circumstances are to my disadvantage.

For example, 22 years ago I held a big garage sale—many years of accumulated stuff to turn into cash to help pay college tuition for our sons. Among the items was a doll I had played with as a child. Having no little girls in our family to pass it on to, I propped up the doll on one of the sale tables with a $10 sign on her. Halfway through the day she had not been sold, so I marked her down to $8. Shortly afterward a woman picked her up and handed her to me, saying, "I'll take this doll, but I want to look around a bit more."

"Okay," I said, "I'll hold her for you."

Before I could set the doll down another lady, who had just arrived, said, "I'll give you twenty dollars for that doll."

"I'm sorry," I replied, "but I just told that other lady she could have her."

"I'll give you fifty dollars for her," she urged me.

"But I've given my word to the other lady," I said—by now regretting that I'd done so!

"I'll give you a hundred dollars. I've got to have her."

I realized I was being tested, not by the woman, but by God. One hundred dollars would go a lot further on college bills than eight dollars. I could feel the temptation but I could also feel an even stronger pull on my heart. The Lord reminded me of His words: "Let your Yes be simply Yes, and your No be simply No; anything more than that comes from the evil one" (Matthew 5:37). The principle was clear.

Even though the second woman explained that this was a collector's item, a Shirley Temple doll worth $150 or more, I knew what I must do. The doll went for eight dollars.

9. Is frank, outspoken and doesn't mince words.

Never	Seldom	Sometimes	Usually	Mostly	Always
0	1	2	3	4	5
POINTS					

This characteristic sometimes gets perceivers into trouble. One woman who came to work at the Aglow International office had this gift but didn't know it. She was a fairly new Christian who was always criticizing people and telling them what she thought. It wasn't long before most of the people at the Aglow office were upset with her—as her schoolmates and associates had been, all her life.

I started teaching the motivational gift seminar during Carol's third week there. She came up after the very first session and said, "Katie, I know my gift already! For the first time ever I feel I can begin to understand and accept myself," she added, brushing away the tears.

"I've had so much self-hatred because I was always hurting people with my mouth. I didn't know what else to do with what I *saw*," she said, "except to blurt it out. Now I can see that it is wrong to do it that way. I want to grow in my gift so it will help people, not hurt them."

I shared with Carol how perceivers are allowed to *see* many things that are out of God's will, but that God's plan for them is usually to *pray* about it, not to talk about it or confront it.

I saw Carol change into an increasingly sensitive Christian. She has learned how to mitigate her frankness.

We have found that a *mature* perceiver is the most exciting person in the world to be around. You can count on his or her being honest, up-front and candid—yet guided by wisdom and love. We love to talk with perceivers. They are so transparent. They never beat around the bush.

John the Baptist is again a good example. He warned of judgment. He told selfish people to share. He told tax collectors to be honest and soldiers not to misuse authority. And so electrifying were his words that thousands flocked to the wilderness to hear him.

10. Is a very persuasive speaker.

Never	Seldom	Sometimes	Usually	Mostly	Always
0	1	2	3	4	5
POINTS					

Perceivers' persuasiveness stems from the fact that they have such strong convictions about everything. Things are either right or wrong and they will speak out accordingly.

Our perceiver son, Dan, sang in the Living Faith Ensemble during his senior year at Kings, a Christian high school. At the beginning of one church concert the mike partners introduced each other to the congregation. Ursula Rueb, Dan's partner, said with a twinkle in her eye, "This is Dan Fortune, and he's *always* right!"

Peals of laughter broke out among the eighteen members of the group who loved Dan but were often also painfully aware of his strong opinions and persuasiveness.

Phil, a perceiver, shared how important he felt it was to be persuasive: "Even in high school I was aware that some of my friends were aimless, with a lack of ambition to do anything constructive with their lives. I would spend hours urging them to make their lives count. Today they are people of influence with a strong Christian witness."

11. Grieves deeply over the sins of others.

Never	Seldom	Sometimes	Usually	Mostly	Always
0	1	2	3	4	5
POINTS					

These are people who will (inwardly and even outwardly) weep when they see someone involved in serious sin. They know that sin carries within itself the seeds of destruction. They—feeling the heart of God—would spare the person the inevitable consequences of such sowing, but they also know that it is only through repentance that it can be so. Thus they pray for the convicting power of the Holy Spirit to bring the person to repentance.

An assistant pastor's wife, a perceiver we will call Nancy, looked up at the end of the service as the senior pastor was leaving the pulpit and heard God clearly speak to her that he was involved in adultery with a certain woman in the church.

Deeply grieved over the situation, Nancy went home and interceded for them both. For days she wept before God, pleading with Him to change the pastor's heart, to change the woman's heart, to bring them both under conviction of their sin and to stop the affair. After a week of earnest daily prayer, the Lord told Nancy He wanted her to go and confront the woman.

"How did you find out?" the startled woman asked.

"God revealed it to me," Nancy replied. "He wants you to end the affair."

"Well, I won't!" the woman snapped back. "Stay out of my life!"

Nancy went back home and for another week she prayed and wept. At the end of the second week the Lord told her to go again and confront the woman. It was not a pleasant prospect, yet Nancy was obedient. Still the woman refused to listen.

At that point, Nancy reported, the burden abruptly lifted from her shoulders. There was still a human grief for the situation but the godly grief and burden was lifted from her. God calls upon perceivers to intercede but the free will of the sinner can still thwart His will.

We would like to report a happy ending to the story, but tragically sin took its course: Two families were destroyed and many friends and church members were wounded and disillusioned, some even falling away in shock and bitterness.

Never	Seldom	Sometimes	Usually	Mostly	Always
0	1	2	3	4	5
POINTS					

12. Is eager to see his or her own blind spots and to help others see theirs, too.

All of us have blind spots. That's what Jesus was talking about when He asked:

> Why do you look at the speck of sawdust in your brother's eye and pay no attention to the plank in your own eye? How can you say to your brother, "Brother, let me take the speck out of your eye," when you yourself fail to see the plank in your own eye?
>
> Luke 6:41–42, NIV

That plank is our blind spot.

One time my friend Marcia was driving me to the airport when a woman just ahead and to the right of us suddenly started to move over into our lane. If she had continued, we would have had a collision. Marcia honked and the woman quickly swerved away. "We were in her blind spot," Marcia said to me.

It's true. There's an area just over the driver's left shoulder that is not visible in the rearview mirror.

How true this is in life, too, I thought. If we don't sound a warning where there is a blind spot and the person keeps on his or her predetermined course, not seeing the danger, eventually there will be a collision—some sort of crisis.

When we are ready for God to deal with us in the area of our blind spots, we can do nothing better than find a friend with the gift of perception and request his or her discernment.

Never	Seldom	Sometimes	Usually	Mostly	Always
0	1	2	3	4	5
POINTS					

13. Desires above all else to see God's plan worked out in all situations.

Perceivers discern God's plan, and will never let personal desires get in the way of that plan for themselves or others. When a perceiver counsels another person, a characteristic phrase is: "You need to let go of *your* plans and discover what *God's* plan is for your life."

When working with an organization, the perceiver will encourage the individuals in it to sacrifice their own ideas and desires for the good of God's plan for the group.

Often, perceivers are given insights, visions and revelations so that they will know God's will on a matter. Simeon was a devout man, rigorously observing the Law while he waited for the Messiah. The Holy Spirit revealed to this perceiver that he should not see death before he had seen the Lord's Anointed.

How excited Simeon must have been to be let into the very heart of God's plan! Led by the Holy Spirit, he came into the Temple just as Mary and Joseph brought their Son for His dedication. Recognizing Jesus, Simeon took Him in his arms and praised God saying:

> And now, Lord, You are releasing Your servant to depart (leave this world) in peace, according to Your word. For with my [own] eyes I have seen Your Salvation, which You have ordained and prepared before (in the presence of) all peoples, a Light for revelation to the Gentiles [to disclose what was before unknown] and [to bring] praise and honor and glory to Your people Israel.

> Luke 2:29–32

14. Strongly promotes the spiritual growth of groups and individuals.

Never	Seldom	Sometimes	Usually	Mostly	Always
0	1	2	3	4	5
			POINTS		

Perceivers want to see spiritual growth. They view themselves as ever-growing and are eager to help others grow, too.

A perceiver/evangelist ministering in Africa trains young men for mature ministry of their own. As he puts it, "It's the way to multiply my ministry. As I help them grow, the Gospel is spread more widely and effectively."

Perceivers view the spiritual growth of groups as the product of positive changes in individuals. Just as the weakest link in a chain determines the strength of that chain, so they see that in a group the person who is weakest spiritually limits the whole group's effectiveness.

Therefore the perceiver realizes that he or she has to work on a one-on-one basis, helping individual members in order to see the whole group become stronger.

Kit, a perceiver missionary with Youth With A Mission, wrote to us from Montana, "I have enjoyed working with groups during these last years and especially individuals within those groups that needed to grow spiritually. My joy is in helping to mature the saints and to see them operate more effectively in the Body of Christ."

15. Is called to intercession.

Never	Seldom	Sometimes	Usually	Mostly	Always
0	1	2	3	4	5
			POINTS		

This is perhaps the most important characteristic of the perceiver. We have yet to find an adult Christian with the gift of perception who has not been called to intercession. We have found a few who have not yet taken the time to *listen* to discover if they are so called. But the call is there—it's just a matter of tuning in to hear it!

Most perceivers are aware of the importance of intercession. They have an innate sense that it is the most important aspect of their life and ministry. They realize that "mountains are moved" and more can be accomplished through prayer than any other way.

One perceiver said, "About ninety percent of my ministry is in intercessory prayer. Only ten percent of the time do I work directly with people. Usually after I've prayed through on a matter I see the results manifested in the situation. Seldom do I have to take any specific action other than prayer."

Another perceiver said candidly, "Perceivers should be slow to speak but quick to pray!"

Good advice. Perceivers "see" many things that are not in God's will. They may be given revelations about other people's problems and needs. If they don't take it to prayer they can become negative criticizers or obnoxious meddlers. God's purpose in giving them insight is so that they can intercede effectively.

Perceivers are key people in prayer groups. They motivate others to pray. They have the most powerful prayer ministries of all seven gifts. (The giver and the person of compassion are also especially effective in this area—but with different emphases.) Perceivers often fast along with their ministry of intercession.

16. Feels the need to verbalize or dramatize what he or she "sees."

Never	Seldom	Sometimes	Usually	Mostly	Always
0	1	2	3	4	5
POINTS					

Hosea is a biblical example. Remember how he took a harlot for his wife, to demonstrate Israel's faithlessness? Hosea heard the Lord say, "Go, take to yourself a wife of harlotry and have children of [her] harlotry, for the land commits great whoredom by departing from the Lord" (Hosea 1:2).

It was a pretty dramatic move but it got the nation's attention. And when his wife, Gomer, left him to return to prostitution, Hosea sought after her, to demonstrate how God will go out of His way to seek those who have turned their backs on Him.

Sometimes perceivers will use the stage as a vehicle for getting across the message of God. We find that these people are often drawn into the field of drama. It enables people with this giftedness to graphically present what God wants communicated.

Another perceiver friend, Diana, said, "During my late teen and young adult years I was involved in drama groups because I loved to dramatize things I felt strongly about. Once I met the Lord, my interest transferred to Christian drama groups."

The perceiver may have a dramatic flair for illustrating God's truth when teaching, preaching or just talking.

Many Old Testament prophets also had a dramatic flair. Some dressed in sackcloth and ashes when they wanted people to repent. Elisha told leprous Naaman to dip seven times in the Jordan River. Elijah called down fire from heaven. Nathan used a dramatic story of a poor man with only one lamb to touch David's conscience.

In the New Testament, John the Baptist dressed in rough garments of camel's hair and ate insects and wild honey. A prophet named Agabus warned Paul of impending imprisonment by taking off Paul's belt, binding his own hands and feet, and saying, "The Holy Spirit says, 'In this way the Jews of Jerusalem will bind the owner of this belt and will hand him over to the Gentiles'" (Acts 21:11, NIV). Jesus rode a donkey into Jerusalem in an enactment of ancient prophecy.

17. Tends to be introspective.

Never	Seldom	Sometimes	Usually	Mostly	Always
0	1	2	3	4	5
POINTS					

Perceivers know the meaning of the Scripture "Search me [thoroughly], O God, and know my heart! Try me and know my thoughts! And see if there is any wicked or hurtful way in me, and lead me in the way everlasting" (Psalm 139:23–24).

Getting rid of imperfections is a top priority for perceivers. They want God to bring forth that pure gold in their lives, to refine them and make them what He wants them to be. Therefore, they are not afraid to look within and identify those things with which they need to deal. They know the importance of pure motives prompted by the Holy Spirit and not the desires of the flesh.

Howard Pitman describes how he died medically on the operating table and was taken in spirit to the gates of heaven. Thinking his life of "good works" entitled him to come before God with a request, he was shocked to find that God was not pleased with him.

> The sound of His voice came down on me from over the Gates even before the words hit me. The tone of His anger knocked me on my face as God proceeded to tell me just what kind of life I had really lived. . . . He pointed out that my faith was dead, that my works were not acceptable, and that I had labored in vain. . . .
>
> All of these years I thought I was doing those works for God! Now He was telling me that what I did, I did for myself. Even as I preached and testified about the saving grace of Jesus Christ, I was doing that only for myself in order that my conscience might be smoothed. . . . This made my priorities out of order and unacceptable.[7]

Howard had some soul-searching to do! He saw that only what was *prompted by the Spirit* would be of value to God.

Helen, another perceiver from Montana, wrote to us recently: "Introspection has always been a problem in my life. I thought I took myself too seriously. How glad I was to know that this is part of my giftedness—that it's okay to be introspective."

18. Has strong opinions and convictions.

Never	Seldom	Sometimes	Usually	Mostly	Always
0	1	2	3	4	5
POINTS					

Perceivers have an opinion on just about everything. And if you happen to bring up a subject they have never thought about—guess what? They form an opinion on the spot!

Fortunately perceivers usually seek God's help in forming their convictions; thus the perceiver's opinion often carries with it the ring of truth.

But perceivers don't necessarily present their opinions gently. They can be the proverbial "bull in the china shop" and leave a trail of destruction behind them.

Don ran painfully up against the characteristic thirty years ago when he was responsible for a home meeting of twenty-five people. After just a few meetings he could see that five of the women were perceivers. "Lord," I remember hearing him pray, "what are You trying to do to me? Five at once!"

At first, he reports, the sparks used to fly. Each of the five had such strong opinions! Often the opinions did not coincide, and needless to say, there were never any lukewarm discussions. Don was fascinated to watch the Lord at work in the hearts of all five perceivers. The more mature ones tended to be more open to the opinions of others, and the less mature ones were more argumentative. But there was growth for all of them—and for the rest of the group—as they interacted.

19. Has strict personal standards.

Never	Seldom	Sometimes	Usually	Mostly	Always
0	1	2	3	4	5
				✳	
POINTS					

Perceivers are never satisfied with less than their best effort. Unless they are out of fellowship with God, they have impeccable morals. Even teenagers with this gift will seldom compromise their standards. In fact, they are usually more strict with themselves than their parents are with them.

One young man with this gift found out that his older sister had moved in with her boyfriend. At first he was angry because his sister's behavior was reflecting on himself and his family. Then he was angry because it was an offense to God. Then he was angry at Satan for prompting her to immorality. At this point he channeled his anger into prayer and spiritual warfare on her behalf. Three weeks later his sister moved back home.

While some can live their lives heedless of God and the fact that He is aware of all they do, the perceiver cannot. He or she is keenly aware of the Lord's constant presence, and wants to live in a way that is consistently pleasing to Him.

Perceivers are honest. Integrity is their byword. Carolyn came home from the grocery store one day to discover that the clerk had not charged her for a case of canned goods she had placed on the lower shelf of the grocery cart.

"Never mind," her husband said. "They'll never know it."

"But I know," Carolyn replied, her gift going into action. "I'm going back to pay for it."

The grocery store clerk was amazed when Carolyn explained the situation. "You're really honest!" he exclaimed.

"Shouldn't everyone be?" Carolyn asked. "I wouldn't be able to live with myself unless I was.'"

20. Desires to be obedient to God at all costs. _(add)_

Perceivers recognize the importance of obedience. The opposite, in their estimation, is rebellion—a sin described in the Old Testament "as the sin of witchcraft" (1 Samuel 15:23, KJV).

One perceiver did a study of obedience in the Bible. In her words,

I became aware that being obedient to God [1 Peter 1:14] also meant that I was to be respectful to and obedient to others. Starting with Jesus, I am not only to obey Him in everything He tells me to do [James 1:22], I must also bring every thought into obedience to Him [2 Corinthians 10:5]. Then I saw that I must be obedient to secular rulers [Titus 3:1], to leaders [2 Corinthians 2:9], to my parents [Colossians 3:20], to my husband [Ephesians 5:22] and even to my employer [Ephesians 6:5–8]. It's a big order, but with His strength I can do it.

Jesus is my pattern. He was obedient to God in all things, even to His death on the cross.

We often urge parents of young perceiver children to teach these children to be obedient to *them*, so that as they mature they can also be obedient to *God*. We speak from experience. Dan, our perceiver child, was not at all easy to discipline. While he wanted to obey us, his own will and stubbornness would sometimes get in the way.

Fortunately when Don and I got married we found that we agreed on discipline. We also believed the warning, "Spare the rod and spoil the child" (see Proverbs 13:24). We read a powerful little pamphlet presenting the Christian perspective on discipline, *Children, Fun or Frenzy?* and promptly went to the local lumber store. We bought a 36-inch dowel, cut it in half, and strategically placed the two 18-inch rods for quick access when needed.

It worked! The children soon learned that we did indeed wield the rod of authority. After a spanking for disobedient behavior we would scoop them up in our arms, love them, explain why they were being disciplined in that instance and then forgive them. It was clear that this approach made them feel loved and secure. ✳

In fact, one day when David was three he brought the rod to us, saying, "Spank me, I did something wrong." He had broken something he'd been told not to touch and he knew he'd feel better after being disciplined. He did.

Dan was not so eager to be disciplined. Perceiver children are typically strong-willed and hardheaded. They are a challenge to parents, and must be taught obedience or their gift will remain polluted for the rest of their lives.

Dan always tried to justify his actions. He would argue with us. Often we had to send Dan to his room after a spanking while Dave quickly repented, asked for forgiveness and went merrily on his way to play. We remained consistent with Dan and eventually he began to be obedient without arguing. He became a delightful child—internalizing the learned discipline and developing into a youngster of high standards. He grew close to the Lord and grew in his desire to be obedient to Him.

Today Dan understands why we had to discipline him more than we did his brother, and appreciates it. "I would never have been able to obey my heavenly Father," Dan says, "if I had not learned to obey my earthly father."

Dan went on to get his degree in missions, and became a missionary leader on the Island of Roatan (Helene) in Honduras for nine years.

"God said to go and so I went," Dan says.

Now Score

Transfer your scores to the perceiver scoring sheet on page 71. Add all twenty numbers and record your score in the total box. Then transfer that total to the profile sheet on page 52.

Remember, there are no right or wrong answers. This is a subjective self-discovery test. Do not try to compare your scores with anyone else's scores. What is important is the relationship of *all seven* of your *own* scores, revealing your personal profile.*

---

*Additional sets of the seven scoring sheets along with the profile sheet are available from the authors in 8½ x 11 inch size. Scoring sheets are also available in a randomly arranged form that allows identification of the gifts only after the testing is completed and in sets designed for youth, for children, for secular users and in many other languages. See the back of the book for details.

THE GIFT OF PERCEPTION

Characteristics

	Never	Seldom	Sometimes	Usually	Mostly	Always	POINTS
	0	1	2	3	4	5	
1. Quickly and accurately identifies good and evil, and hates evil.				X			
2. Sees everything as either black or white; no gray or indefinite areas.			X				
3. Easily perceives the character of individuals and groups.			X				
4. Encourages repentance that produces a change of heart.						X	
5. Believes accepting difficulties can produce positive personal growth.				X			
6. Has only a few or no close friendships.				X			
7. Views the Bible as the basis for truth, belief, action and authority.				X			
8. Boldly operates on spiritual principles.				X			
9. Is frank, outspoken and doesn't mince words.				X			
10. Is a very persuasive speaker.				X			
11. Grieves deeply over the sins of others.				X			
12. Is eager to see his or her own blind spots and to help others see theirs, too.				X			
13. Desires above all else to see God's plan worked out in all situations.				X			
14. Strongly promotes the spiritual growth of groups and individuals.				X			
15. Is called to intercession.				X			
16. Feels the need to verbalize or dramatize what he or she "sees."				X			
17. Tends to be introspective.				X			
18. Has strong opinions and convictions.			X				
19. Has strict personal standards.					X		
20. Desires to be obedient to God at all costs.				X			
						TOTAL	60

8

Problems of the Perceiver

Each one of the seven motivational gifts has its own set of problems.

We have found it helpful for people to know that their gifts will bring specific challenges. One woman said to us, "It's a relief to know that my problems are typical for my gift. I thought I was the only one in the world wrestling with these things. Now I have hope and direction."

Without problems there would be no opportunity for spiritual growth! As you take an honest look at the problem areas:

1. You will be relieved that you are not alone.
2. Your identification of the problems will assist you in discovering specific solutions.
3. You will know better how to pray for God's help and grace in overcoming the problems.

The scoring is the same as it was for the twenty positive characteristics, but you will *not* fill out a negative profile on yourself! You'll just use the negative scores to see how your maturity level is coming along. The scale goes something like this:

0 to 5 points	=	mature
6 to 10 points	=	growing in grace
11 to 15 points	=	average
16 to 20 points	=	immature
21 to 25 points	=	needs help!

We made initial tests on various people many years ago, and again more recently. Often, their negative score was significantly reduced, although they typically still had higher negative scores in their primary gift compared to their negative scoring in the other gifts (those scores improved as well). We can all heed Paul's exhortation in Philippians to "work out" our own salvation with fear (awe) and trembling.

Here are the five typical problem areas of the perceiver:

1. Tends to be judgmental and blunt.

Never	Seldom	Sometimes	Usually	Mostly	Always
0	1	2	3	4	5
		POINTS			

Perceivers have what one of them calls "a severe case of foot-in-the-mouth disease."

Jonah is the biblical example here. God told Jonah to go preach repentance to Nineveh. Jonah didn't like the assignment because he knew they were wicked and he couldn't imagine how God could forgive them. So he took off in the opposite direction.

You know the story. God appointed special transportation to get him to the right beach at the right time. Jonah decided he'd better get on to Nineveh, where he did preach on the need for repentance. And the people repented.

Well, Jonah hadn't counted on that. He had already judged these people in his own heart and decided they deserved God's punishment. You see, he had a critical spirit. He never got around to praying for Nineveh. Instead he went up on the hillside and waited for judgment to fall. When it didn't, he got angry and God had to deal with Jonah's judgmental attitude.

Perceivers will find that God will deal firmly, even sternly, in their lives if they don't learn to pray more and criticize less. Prayer is the safeguard that prevents a perceiver from developing a critical attitude. Perceivers are called to intercessory prayer. *There are no exceptions!*

A lady in Kansas City came up to me after a seminar and said in a huff, "Well, I'm a perceiver according to the testing, but I'm not an intercessor."

"Have you been called to intercede?" I asked.

"Well, I don't really know," she replied, "but I don't have time for that. I find I can get things done so much faster if I go right to the person and confront them with what they're doing wrong."

"You can get the job done faster than God?" I marveled.

"As a matter of fact, sometimes I can. He takes so long."

I thought to myself, *This is sheer ego!*

"You must always start with prayer," I urged her, "and only go to someone if the Lord tells you to. If you're not careful you could become a critical person that nobody is going to like."

A couple of her friends overheard. "She's already that way," they confided later. "Lots of people can't stand her *now!*"

Well, the Lord dealt with her that night. She couldn't sleep for a long time. The next morning she said to me, "Katie, last night God told me that He had called me to intercession a long time ago, but that I'd been refusing to listen. I realized I've been making a mess of things."

Since then she's grown as an intercessor and has become sensitive rather than blunt. People love her now.

If you discover that you have the gift of perception and you have not yet heeded the call of intercession, watch out! God won't let you off the hook.

We like to share this with perceivers: While in the natural world the shortest distance between two points is a straight line, that's not true in the spiritual world. The shortest distance between you and another person (especially a problem person) is a line of prayer straight up to God, trusting God to deal with the person and the situation and to work out the solution to the problem.

You see, no one likes to be told by someone else that he or she should change. But when you give the problem to God, He can speak directly to the person's heart. He can surmount walls of resistance that we can't get past.

The only time a perceiver should confront someone is after praying about it, giving it to God and receiving a direct instruction to do so. Even then, unless God first softens the person's heart, the confrontation may not be well received. But the perceiver's job is not to change others; he or she is only to deliver the message. It's the Holy Spirit's job to do the convicting and changing.

2. Forgets to praise partial progress due to goal consciousness.

Never	Seldom	Sometimes	Usually	Mostly	Always
0	1	2	3	4	5
POINTS					

The perceivers' desire is always to get themselves and others to that place of perfectly following the will of God. They focus on the fact that Jesus said we are to "be perfect."

When counseling, for instance, the perceiver may be so eager for the counselee to come to perfection in Christ that expectations are too high. He or she pressures the person to change—faster than is possible.

The perceiver needs to learn how to look at a step of progress as being valid in itself. He or she needs to be able to say, "Hey, I'm really glad that you took this step this week. That's good! Now, let's work on the next step."

Lem, a perceiver husband and father, came to us for advice. He complained that his wife was just not making progress spiritually.

We spoke to his wife. Hers was a different story. She was upset because Lem was always expecting her to be spiritual in the same way he was, which meant to spend lots of time in prayer, fast often and follow Lem's rigid rules for the family. She was also frustrated because he was critical of the children to the point that they felt he didn't love them. She said Lem never praised any of their spiritual efforts.

Since his wife had the gift of administration, we explained to Lem that he could not expect her to think and act just like him: She was never going to be one to fast and pray a lot, but she was able to see the unique differences in their children and allow each to develop at his or her own rate.

Lem has taken some of the pressure off and is allowing the progress of his family members to take its course more naturally. He is also learning to compliment and encourage his wife and children along the way.

3. Is pushy in trying to get others and groups to grow spiritually.

Never	Seldom	Sometimes	Usually	Mostly	Always
0	1	2	3	4	5
		POINTS			

There's nothing wrong with wanting people to grow spiritually; the problem is the pushiness.

Jill was thrilled when her husband finally committed his life to Jesus. But a polluted perceiver gift caused her to try to push him into spiritual growth. She would insist that he be at church every time the doors opened. She laid out "the right books" for him to read. And she let him know every time he did something that wasn't "Christian."

Of course it backfired. He dug in his heels and refused to have anything more to do with "that religious stuff."

Jill was deflated and discouraged. But an older woman in her church saw what she'd been doing and gave her some helpful counsel. "Look, Jill," her friend said, "you need to pray more for your husband and talk less. Let him make his own discoveries and decisions."

As soon as Jill stopped pushing, her husband started attending the men's early morning prayer meeting. Today he's the mature Christian Jill wished for.

4. Is intolerant of opinions and views that differ from his or her own.

Never	Seldom	Sometimes	Usually	Mostly	Always
0	1	2	3	4	5
		POINTS			

Perceivers are always convinced that their views are right—and most often they are. But sometimes truth has various facets to it. The perceiver may see one facet of a truth while those with different motivational gifts see other facets. Get all the facets together and you see the whole. Perceivers need to learn to value an encompassing perspective.

We came across an extreme case of this intolerance when we were asked to counsel a couple having serious marriage problems. We'll call them Sam and Sue. Sam was an opinionated perceiver and Sue an intimidated person with a strong gift of compassion.

As soon as they sat down Sam said, "I want you to know that Sue is the one who needs help. There's nothing wrong with me. She's the problem." Obviously *he* was more of a problem!

Then he proceeded to tell us what was wrong with her and how we were to fix it. At that point we wondered why they'd even come for counseling since he had all the answers! According to him a wife was to have no ideas of her own but was to be in an unquestioning servant's role to her husband. He was upset because Sue had recently dared to question his orders.

When we tried to suggest that his view of the marriage relationship was unbalanced, he came back with, "But I *know* I am right. Sue is being rebellious and she must obey me!"

We never saw them again.

5. Struggles with self-image problems.

Never	Seldom	Sometimes	Usually	Mostly	Always
0	1	2	3	4	5
				✳	
POINTS					

Since perceivers have such an inner drive to do what is right, and since they are introspective and readily aware of their own shortcomings, they are quick to judge themselves as inadequate.

Of all the motivational gifts, these people seem most relieved when they discover that the things they've wrestled with internally are indicative of divinely ordained giftedness rather than a testimony to shortcomings and failures. It is not at all unusual for perceivers to come to us at the close of a seminar to tell us how thrilled they are to know that who and what they are is part of God's plan.

We often hear comments from perceivers like, "I always thought I was a misfit, but now I see that God has made me see things the way I do."

One time we noticed tears welling up in the eyes of an older woman while we were teaching on the gift of perception. "If only I had heard this fifty years ago," she told us afterward. "I have lived all my life with a torturing awareness of what was wrong in people and situations. But I didn't know what to do with it, so I criticized. Then I criticized myself for being critical. All my life I've wanted to be different. Now I see that God gave me perception for a reason—so that I could pray for people."

Three weeks later we returned to do another seminar. At the first coffee break this woman came over to us with joy written all over her face.

"These three weeks have been the best in my whole life!" she exclaimed. "Every day I'm interceding for the needs that God is showing to me. It's wonderful. I'm seeing so many answers to prayer. And I like myself now. I'm so glad I learned about my giftedness while I still have some of my life left to live."

We wish that every perceiver could say that. So many are bound up in self-condemnation and self-rejection because they don't understand their giftedness.

If you know any perceivers, please share this good news with them!

**Typical problem areas
of the gift of perception**

	Never	Seldom	Sometimes	Usually	Mostly	Always	POINTS
	0	1	2	3	4	5	
1. Tends to be judgmental and blunt. 1.			✗				
2. Forgets to praise partial progress due to goal consciousness. 2.	✗						
3. Is pushy in trying to get others to grow spiritually. 3.	✗						
4. Is intolerant of opinions and views that differ from his or her own. 4.	✗						
5. Struggles with self-image problems. 5.					✗		
						TOTAL	6

growing in grace

Biblical Perceivers

We have been fascinated to discover the motivational gifts of biblical characters. Recognizing the specific giftedness of these biblical personalities has made Scripture come alive for us. We find ourselves saying things like, "Oh, that's why David did that," or "So that's what motivated Barnabas." They are no longer one-dimensional historical figures who lived "way back when," but rather real people we can relate to and appreciate with new depth.

Identifying their motivational gifts helps us to see why God chose them for their particular tasks. He gifted them, knowing them from before the foundation of the world (see Ephesians 1:4) in accordance with His purpose for each life. We see a wide spectrum of giftedness, all the way from Jonah's stubborn critical spirit—a manifestation of a polluted gift of perception—to beloved disciple John's faithful and loving detailing of the life of Jesus—a manifestation of a mature gift of compassion.

For some biblical characters there is such a wealth of recorded information that we can see the person's gift in full breadth of action. For others, the details are limited. We get only a glimpse of their gifts. And for some we can make only an educated guess. But all through the Bible we now see living people with distinct needs, desires, motivations and abilities.

We have written seven chapters highlighting biblical characters that exemplify the seven motivational gifts. This chapter will deal with the perceiver.

We'd like to challenge you (our gifts of teaching and exhorting are coming through here) to read for yourself the following Scriptures about biblical perceivers:

John the Baptist: Matthew 21:32; Luke 3:2–20; 7:18–29

Anna: Luke 2:36–38

Mary: Matthew 1–2; Mark 6:3; Luke 1:26–56; John 2:1–5; Acts 1:14

Ananias: Acts 9:10–17; 22:12–16

Hosea: Hosea 1–14

Jeremiah: Jeremiah 1–52

Isaiah: Isaiah 1–66

Jonah: Jonah 1–4

See how many perceiver characteristics you can find in these biblical characters as you read these passages. You'll be amazed! And the person will become far more understandable to you.

To get you started, we are printing out the first Scripture here for you to work on. We've used the Amplified Bible, which captures more nuances from the original Greek.

The right-hand column is for your comments. Simply jot down the number of the characteristic, or describe it if you prefer. If the characteristic is from the problem list, identify it with a minus (-) before the number.

Some characteristics will be obvious, others only implied. Ask the Holy Spirit to guide you in this discovery process—to give you eyes to see and help you to read between the lines. You will have fun!

Scripture: Luke 3:2–3, 7–20	Your Comments:
2 In the high priesthood of Annas and Caiaphas, the Word of God [concerning the attainment through Christ of salvation in the kingdom of God] came to John son of Zachariah in the wilderness (desert).	
3 And he went into all the country round about the Jordan, preaching a baptism of repentance (of hearty amending of their ways, with abhorrence of past wrongdoing) unto the forgiveness of sin.	
7 So he said to the crowds who came out to be baptized by him, You offspring of vipers! Who secretly warned you to flee from the coming wrath?	
8 Bear fruits that are deserving and consistent with [your] repentance [that is, conduct worthy of a heart changed, a heart abhorring sin]. And do not begin to say to yourselves, We have Abraham as our father; for I tell you that God is able from these stones to raise up descendants for Abraham.	
9 Even now the ax is laid to the root of the trees, so that every tree that does not bear good fruit is cut down and cast into the fire.	
10 And the multitudes asked him, Then what shall we do?	

Scripture: Luke 3:2–3, 7–20	Your Comments:
11 And he replied to them, He who has two tunics (undergarments), let him share with him who has none; and he who has food, let him do it the same way.	
12 Even tax collectors came to be baptized, and they said to him, Teacher, what shall we do?	
13 And he said to them, Exact and collect no more than the fixed amount appointed you.	
14 Those serving as soldiers also asked him, And we, what shall we do? And he replied to them, Never demand or enforce by terrifying people or by accusing wrongfully, and always be satisfied with your rations (supplies) and with your allowance (wages).	
15 As the people were in suspense and waiting expectantly, and everybody reasoned and questioned in their hearts concerning John, whether he perhaps might be the Christ (the Messiah, the Anointed one).	
16 John answered them all by saying, I baptize you with water; but He Who is mightier than I is coming, the strap of Whose sandals I am not fit to unfasten. He will baptize you with the Holy Spirit and with fire.	
17 His winnowing shovel (fork) is in His hand to thoroughly clear and cleanse His [threshing] floor and to gather the wheat and store it in His granary, but the chaff He will burn with fire that cannot be extinguished.	
18 So with many other [various] appeals and admonitions he preached the good news (the Gospel) to the people.	
19 But Herod the tetrarch, who had been [repeatedly] told about his fault and reproved with rebuke producing conviction by [John] for [having] Herodias, his brother's wife, and for all the wicked things that Herod had done,	
20 Added this to them all—that he shut up John in prison.	

Now that you've gotten to know John the Baptist, perceiver, we'll share what we found:

Scripture: Luke 3:2–3, 7–20	Our Comments:
2 In the high priesthood of Annas and Caiaphas, the Word of God [concerning the attainment through Christ of salvation in the kingdom of God] came to John son of Zachariah in the wilderness (desert).	#13 desires God's plan #15 receives revelation through intercession
3 And he went into all the country round about the Jordan, preaching a baptism of repentance (of hearty amending of their ways, with abhorrence of past wrongdoing) unto the forgiveness of sin.	#1 identifies evil #3 sizes up character #4 encourages repentance #9 is frank, outspoken #11 grieves over sins #20 obedient to God

Scripture: Luke 3:2–3, 7–20   **Our Comments:**

7 So he said to the crowds who came out to be baptized by him, You offspring of vipers! Who secretly warned you to flee from the coming wrath?

#1, 3, 4, 9 (as above)
#12 sees blind spots
#16 dramatizes
#18 has strong opinions

8 Bear fruits that are deserving and consistent with [your] repentance [that is, conduct worthy of a heart changed, a heart abhorring sin]. And do not begin to say to yourselves, We have Abraham as our father; for I tell you that God is able from these stones to raise up descendants for Abraham.

#4 wants evidence of repentance
#8 operates boldly on spiritual principles
#9 is frank, blunt
#10 speaks persuasively
#12 reveals blind spots
#16 dramatizes
#18 has strong opinions

9 Even now the ax is laid to the root of the trees, so that every tree that does not bear good fruit is cut down and cast into the fire.

#4, 8, 9, 10, 16, 18 (as above)

10 And the multitudes asked him, Then what shall we do?

#10 is persuasive

11 And he replied to them, He who has two tunics (undergarments), let him share with him who has none; and he who has food, let him do it the same way.

#2 allows no gray areas
#4 demands fruit
#8 has spiritual principles
#14 promotes growth

12 Even tax collectors came to be baptized, and they said to him, Teacher, what shall we do?

#10 has evidence of persuasiveness

13 And he said to them, Exact and collect no more than the fixed amount appointed you.

#2 has black and white standards
#8 has spiritual principles

14 Those serving as soldiers also asked him, And we, what shall we do? And he replied to them, Never demand or enforce by terrifying people or by accusing wrongfully, and always be satisfied with your rations (supplies) and with your allowance (wages).

#1 identifies evil
#2 has black and white standards
#3 perceives character
#4 demands fruit
#9 is frank, outspoken
#10 is persuasive
#14 promotes growth
#18 has strong opinions

15 As the people were in suspense and waiting expectantly, and everybody reasoned and questioned in their hearts concerning John, whether he perhaps might be the Christ (the Messiah, the Anointed one).

(This shows evidence of the operation of all of the above characteristics in the response of the listeners.)

16 John answered them all by saying, I baptize you with water; but He Who is mightier than I is coming, the strap of Whose sandals I am not fit to unfasten. He will baptize you with the Holy Spirit and with fire.

#13 focuses on God's plan
#14 promotes growth of others
#20 is obedient to God's (lesser) plan for him

17 His winnowing shovel (fork) is in His hand to thoroughly clear and cleanse His [threshing] floor and to gather the wheat and store it in His granary, but the chaff He will burn with fire that cannot be extinguished.

#1 identifies good and evil
#2 allows no gray areas
#9 is frank, outspoken
#13 desires God's plan
#20 is obedient to God by revealing His plan

18 So with many other [various] appeals and admonitions he preached the good news (the Gospel) to the people.

#4 encourages repentance
#10 is persuasive
#13 wants God's plan
#20 is obedient to God

Scripture: Luke 3:2–3, 7–20	Our Comments:
19 But Herod the tetrarch, who had been [repeatedly] told about his fault and reproved with rebuke producing conviction by John for [having] Herodias, his brother's wife, and for all the wicked things that Herod had done,	#1 identifies Herod's evil #3 perceives his character #4 calls for repentance #9 is frank, outspoken #18 has strong convictions #20 obeys God
20 Added this to them all—that he shut up John in prison.	#2 is uncompromising #10 is persuasive

We may have listed some perceiver qualities that you did not discover, and you probably detected others that we missed. But you can see that John is a magnificent example of this motivational gift.

Characteristics of the Server

The second of the seven gifts listed in Romans 12:6–8 is the gift we call server. The King James Version uses the word "ministry," the New International Version—as well as most other modern versions—uses the word "service," and the Amplified Bible the words "practical service." The Greek word is *diakonia*, which conveys the idea of doing practical things in order to be of service to others.

The server receives joy in helping, assisting, carrying out instructions and being of use in a wide variety of ways. As you consider each characteristic, score yourself, then transfer your scores to the final page of the chapter and tally the points for recording on your profile sheet.

1. Easily recognizes practical needs and is quick to meet them.

Never	Seldom	Sometimes	Usually	Mostly	Always
0	1	2	3	4	5
		POINTS			

A server can spot a need a mile away. It's as though he or she has built-in radar geared to others' necessities, and high motivation to do something about those needs.

You can spot these servers easily at a church potluck dinner. Check who is regularly out in the kitchen making the preparations, or setting up tables and chairs or doing the cleanup afterward.

All our married life, our home has been a center for youth meetings, Bible study groups and potlucks. We used to wonder why some of the women quickly migrated to the kitchen to help out while others stayed in the living room to chat. Now we know it's the natural inclination of servers to help in that way. And the server men are the ones who put away the folding chairs, push the furniture back into place and pick up the Styrofoam cups still sitting around the room. The important thing is that servers enjoy doing it.

Iverna Tompkins, author of *How to Be Happy in No Man's Land*, was the main speaker at a convention where I was doing a workshop on the motivational gifts. I was seated to her left at the closing banquet and her secretary, Shirley Green, was to her right. As we started to eat, Iverna commented, "Cool in here, isn't it?" Shirley excused herself, went to the cloakroom, retrieved Iverna's shawl, returned and placed it around her shoulders. A servant's heart! The need was so obvious to her.

How sensitive! I thought. It had never dawned on me that Iverna's casual remark was an expression of practical need.

2. Especially enjoys manual projects, jobs and functions.

Never	Seldom	Sometimes	Usually	Mostly	Always
0	1	2	3	4	5
				X	
		POINTS			

Of all the motivational gifts, it is the servers who have the greatest dexterity—the ability to work well with their hands. That's why we call them the hands of the Body. They can do just about anything that involves manual skill: artistic endeavors, repairs, carpentry, plumbing, electrical work, sewing, cooking or gardening.

One time, five server men from our church volunteered to take a week off from their jobs and go to Guatemala to do repairs on a children's orphanage. They loved every minute of it and got twice as much done as those with any other gift could have.

We often find that servers are not interested in college. They prefer trade schools, beauty schools, art schools and other technical training.

An item in "Dear Abby" a few years ago was so appropriate that we've shared it at all our motivational gift seminars.

College Dropout
Son's choice upsets mother

DEAR ABBY: Our middle son, Greg (made-up name), is our problem. He is a very intelligent young man of 19 who went to college for one year just to please us, then he quit.

"Why waste your money and my time?" he asked.

His grades were above average and he could have continued. His reason for quitting? He likes to work with his hands. He is now going to a trade school, and we are so disappointed in him.

I'm not putting down people who work with their hands, but it seems to me that a man works with his hands only because he isn't smart enough to work with his mind. Greg's father and grandfather are physicians, and both Greg's brothers are lawyers.

Please put something in your column stating that a college degree is absolutely necessary these days. After Greg graduates from college, he can do anything he chooses, but we want him to finish college first. Thank you.

—Greg's Mother

DEAR MOTHER: College is not for everybody. If Greg likes to work with his hands, that's what he should do. It's not true that those who work with their hands aren't smart enough to work with their minds. Handwork done well requires as much skill, talent and brains as [any other] profession.[8]

To which we say, "Amen, Abby!"

In addition to "Mother's" intellectual snobbery, it is probable that the other men in the family had different gifts—they were teachers, exhorters and administrators, perhaps. To insist that a server follow in their footsteps is sheer folly. Not only would Greg not have done well in such pursuits, but he would also have been constantly frustrated and probably resentful that his parents pushed him into a career for which he was not suited.

3. Keeps everything in meticulous order.

Never	Seldom	Sometimes	Usually	Mostly	Always
0	1	2	3	4	5
POINTS					

Servers cannot stand clutter, dirt or disorganization. Women with this gift often dust every day. There are no dirty dishes left in their sinks, their laundry is folded and put away the day it is washed and the beds are made before nine A.M. You can drop in on them at any time of the day and the house will be ready for company.

Men with the serving gift keep their closets in order, their socks never get thrown in the shirt drawer, you can always see the top of their desk and every tool is hanging on the right hook on the pegboard. What's more, the lawn is mowed on schedule and weeds don't have a chance to grow in the flowerbeds.

We stayed in a home in Scotland where the lady was a classic server. When we ate meals in the big family kitchen she would clear the table after each course, quickly wash the dishes and place them in a drainer before serving the next course!

4. Is a detail person with a good memory.

Never	Seldom	Sometimes	Usually	Mostly	Always
0	1	2	3	4	5
POINTS					

Servers have a computer-type memory for details. They can remember where they filed away an article they clipped out of the newspaper three years ago. They remember that you like cream in your coffee, but not sugar. They remember all the birthdays on both sides of the family (and remember to send cards) and they can relate an episode from the thirteenth chapter of the book they read last week with amazing accuracy.

I was so grateful, during the years I was an international vice president of Women's Aglow Fellowship International, for secretaries who were servers. They could actually find things in the files! I could look for hours without locating something. (The most difficult were things I had filed myself.) On the other hand, Susan Duncan could find a filed item in ten seconds or less.

When I was in charge of television production, one of the tasks was to circulate our videotaped programs to cable and UHF stations. With dozens of stations using our thirteen-week sets it was a challenge to keep track of them. Lois McGrew was wonderful. She kept such detailed accounts that we always knew where every tape was, where it was going next and when it would come back to us. I could not have survived without her.

Never	Seldom	Sometimes	Usually	Mostly	Always
0	1	2	3	4	5
		✗			
POINTS					

5. Enjoys showing hospitality.

When the pastor announces that a place is needed for the visiting missionary, it will likely be the servers who offer their homes first. They love to entertain people.

They look for opportunities to invite others over for dinner or dessert, and they do a terrific job of making their guests feel welcome.

There's a couple in our area we are sure must both be servers. When they got married Alice said, "John, let's build a big house so we can entertain lots of people." John, being an excellent carpenter, obliged by building a house with nine bedrooms. They had only two sons but all the rooms were often filled.

At one point they became acquainted with the singing Cameron family from Scotland and became headquarters for them whenever they came to Seattle. There were three Cameron men, and each had a family group. Usually just one of the families came at a time, but one year all seventeen of the clan came at once. Alice and John put them up in style.

The families stayed for three weeks and Alice thought it would be nice to make a new dress for each of the women and girls, which she did in her "spare time." She was also holding down a full-time job. "I've never had such a good time in my life," Alice confided to me. "I just love having company!"

Never	Seldom	Sometimes	Usually	Mostly	Always
0	1	2	3	4	5
		✗			
POINTS					

6. Will stay with something until it is complete.

Servers finish what they start. They have wonderful stick-to-it-iveness. When they say they will do something they will do it. The only thing that produces frustration is when you give them something to do in too short a time. You see, they not only want to finish a task, they want to do it well.

My friend Claudia has all the earmarks of a mature server. She served on our church's women's council and usually volunteered for registrar responsibility for retreats and conferences. Within a day or two—and usually way ahead of schedule—she had all the forms and sign-up sheets designed, printed and ready to go. She followed through on every detail during the registration process, then patiently kept all the necessary records in incredibly neat order.

7. Has a hard time saying no to requests for help.

Never	Seldom	Sometimes	Usually	Mostly	Always
0	1	2	3	4	5
		POINTS			

Because servers are naturally geared to be helpful, and because they know that they are good at it, it is difficult for them to turn down a request for help. As a result they tend to get overinvolved. Even a simple question like, "Do you know what to use for a clogged drain?" will elicit a response like, "Let me come over and look at it." Before he or she has time to think, the server is under the person's sink with wrench in hand and the drain apart.

I was teaching the motivational gift seminar at an Aglow convention in San Diego when a woman came up to me during the morning coffee break, looking as though she had the weight of the world on her shoulders. "What's the matter?" I asked.

"I scored ninety-five on server," she replied, "and it's true. I can't say no to anyone. Would you believe I'm currently on twenty committees between church, PTA, community groups, Cub Scouts, Campfire Girls and Aglow?"

I nodded, indicating I could well believe it.

"I'm exhausted. I can't even get my housework done."

"How many of those committees did the Lord tell you to serve on?" I inquired.

"Oh!" she exclaimed, looking surprised. "I never thought to ask the Lord about any of them."

"I suggest you do," I said. "We can be out of His will by doing too much as easily as by doing too little."

At the lunch break she returned. "I asked Him," she said, her face beaming. "He said five. And He showed me which ones. I'm going home and resigning from the other fifteen. And I'm never going to say yes again without praying first."

That's good advice for all servers. Learn to check with the Lord so you won't get overloaded. It *is* okay to say no.

8. Is more interested in meeting the needs of others than his or her own needs.

Never	Seldom	Sometimes	Usually	Mostly	Always
0	1	2	3	4	5
		POINTS			

Servers are such caring people. When we were in New Zealand we stayed for a week with a lovely Christian family. Two of the Eynons' four girls were still at home: Greta, eighteen, and Aly, sixteen.

We were struck by how much Greta seemed to enjoy preparing meals.

"Mum," she'd say, "let me fix the dinner. You spend time with the Fortunes." She'd put on a beautiful meal and when her mother would get up to clear the table Greta would say to her, "No, you stay there and talk, I'll take care of the dishes."

Aly would take a few dishes to the kitchen, then say, "Please excuse me but I've got to run. I'm setting up the school's talent show and we've got a meeting tonight."

A similar scene would take place each evening with Greta serving dinner and doing the dishes and Aly running off to organize something else. Their parents worried about the situation. They felt that Aly was running out on domestic responsibilities while Greta was overly conscientious around the house. They wished Greta would have more outside interests.

We were able to help them to see that Greta was a server and Aly an administrator. It was predictable that Aly's interests would lean toward group involvement while Greta's giftedness would cause her to focus on meeting other people's needs even to the neglect of her own. We encouraged the parents to let Greta concentrate on the domestic needs of the family for the time being, for that was bringing her joy.

			Never	Seldom	Sometimes	Usually	Mostly	Always
			0	1	2	3	4	5
						✗		
POINTS								

9. Enjoys working on short-term goals rather than long-range goals.

Servers prefer short-term projects. They like something that takes two hours better than something that takes two weeks, and prefer a two-week or two-month project to a two-year project. They enjoy something they can get their teeth into and finish in a foreseeable amount of time. They leave long-range goals to the administrators.

A server would enjoy providing food for the family of a woman who is temporarily in the hospital, but would not necessarily want to take on that kind of service on an ongoing basis. He or she would be glad to work one day a week at the food bank, but would not want to manage the project.

Martha saw the immediate goal: Jesus needed a meal. Mary saw the long-range goal, her need to learn from Him.

Stephen was appointed a deacon, with responsibility for providing for widows, while the apostles saw to the long-range spread of the Gospel.

If you have a server child, here's a formula for getting him to be productive. Never give a server child a list of fifteen jobs to do on a Saturday. It would look overwhelming to him or her. Instead, provide one job to do. When it is completed, show your appreciation and then ask if he or she would like to help with another job. This process can continue all day.

10. Shows love for others in deeds and actions more than words.

Never	Seldom	Sometimes	Usually	Mostly	Always
0	1	2	3	4	5
		✳			
POINTS					

Servers believe actions speak louder than words. They express their love by what they do.

One server said to us, "It's easy to say, 'I love you,' but the other person may never really know if you mean it. I believe that when I do something for someone he *knows* how I feel."

One day when I was working at Aglow International I found a freshly baked loaf of bread on my desk. It was tied attractively with a bow and a few silk flowers. A little note attached to it read: "Dear Katie, I'm not very good with words but I hope this loaf of home-baked bread will say that I like you and would like to get to know you better. Love, Lorene."

What a joy to be the object of her love in action!

One woman complained to me that her husband never said the words "I love you."

I knew her husband and had observed many ways in which he showed his love. "But he's a server," I reminded her. "Think how often he takes you out for dinner so you won't have to cook. He buys you unbirthday presents. He makes you all kinds of things in his workshop. He fixes things that break. He helps you clean house. I wish my husband did half as much!"

The woman had to admit she was blessed to have a server husband.

11. Needs to feel appreciated.

Never	Seldom	Sometimes	Usually	Mostly	Always
0	1	2	3	4	5
			✳		
POINTS					

It's not that servers serve in order to be praised, but appreciation assures them that they've done well. It builds up a positive self-image. It is the culmination of their joy in serving.

In the early days of *Aglow* magazine we were entirely a volunteer staff.

I remember when *Guideposts* editor Len LeSourd visited our Aglow Publications editorial offices in Edmonds, Washington. As we introduced him to our various department heads he was impressed with their enthusiasm. "It's good you could hire such dedicated people," Len commented. "It's impossible to run a publishing house with volunteers. You can't count on them."

"Then it's nice to know we're doing the impossible!" I told him.

"You mean you do have volunteers on your staff?" he asked.

"I mean our staff is *all* volunteers."

"I can't believe it!" he said with astonishment.

"But it's true," I replied. "We have sixty-five workers, and none of them are paid. Some give as much as three or four days a week. We probably have less absenteeism than the average business—and when one of them does have to miss a day for some reason he or she arranges for a substitute from our volunteer substitute list."

"Incredible!" he said. "How is it possible?"

"Well," I said, "we pray in each new staff member. Also, we find that a lot of our volunteers have the motivational gift of serving. We've learned to express appreciation to them regularly for what they do. They know they are important, needed and valued."

Never	Seldom	Sometimes	Usually	Mostly	Always
0	1	2	3	4	5
		✷			
		POINTS			

12. Tends to do more than asked to do.

Servers so enjoy the doing that they often don't want to stop.

When Berta gave birth to twins, the family had five children under the age of six. Her server mother-in-law told her she would be glad to keep all five of their baby books up to date. Berta was delighted because she'd only had time to throw items into a box.

As the years passed Berta continued to forward photos, drawings and miscellaneous mementos to her mother-in-law. Then, when her oldest child graduated from high school, his grandmother presented him with his completed book. Not only were the usual milestones recorded, there were detailed accounts of his growing up. She had chronicled every event, both the great and the seemingly insignificant, with photos, quips, comments, candid descriptions and quotes. The book had been extended to almost one hundred pages of "this is your life" in incredible detail.

What a gift! The son was delighted. Everyone in the family was amazed. The kids knew that Grandma always did more than expected, but this was something else. She assured them that a similar chronicle was in process for each of the others, to be received on his or her graduation day.

Never	Seldom	Sometimes	Usually	Mostly	Always
0	1	2	3	4	5
		✷			
		POINTS			

13. Feels greatest joy in doing something that is helpful.

Don's mother was a classic server. Every time she came to our home for dinner, the first thing she would ask as she came in the kitchen door was, "What can I do to help you?"

Now I do just fine in the kitchen if people leave me alone to concentrate. So my usual answer to her was, "Nothing, thanks, I've got everything under control."

One Thanksgiving she arrived a whole hour early. I had been working on the dinner since eight that morning and had timed everything to finish just on schedule. "I came early to see if I could help you," she offered.

"Thanks anyway," I responded. "Everything's under way."

I could tell she was disappointed as she sat down at the kitchen table to watch me work. She began to talk and the distraction was more than I could handle. "Why don't you go and chat with Don awhile?" I suggested.

She found Don deeply engrossed in the Thanksgiving Day football game on TV. The boys were also watching the game.

Meanwhile in the kitchen the Lord spoke to me: *Katie, you are being selfish.*

"How?" I asked with astonishment.

You're so busy functioning in your gift that you are not making room for your mother-in-law's gift.

The words cut deeply into my heart. I *was* being selfish. She wanted to help and I wouldn't let her. That was downright unkind of me. I repented and realized I needed to do something about it. I called into the rec room. "Mother, I could use your help now!"

She was there in a flash, her face bright.

"Could you make the tossed salad?" I asked.

"I'd love to."

She chatted merrily as she tore up bits of lettuce. It distracted me as usual, but I knew that was okay, too. I needed to learn to cook and carry on a conversation at the same time.

After that I always set something aside for my mother-in-law to do when she came for dinner. I can't say I ever learned to love having her help me but I learned to adapt to it and our relationship improved. Learning to give place to her gift blessed me, too.

14. Does not want to lead others or projects.

Never	Seldom	Sometimes	Usually	Mostly	Always
0	1	2	3	4	5
		POINTS			

Servers are not leaders; they are followers. God made them that way. If a leadership position is forced on them they are frustrated.

It is tempting to turn leadership over to servers. Because they do such a good job at whatever they do, it may seem that they are the natural ones to take charge. But when this happens, they lose their joy. They've been placed in a situation for which they are not equipped. The result is frustration for them, and probably (eventually) frustration for those they try to lead.

Our friend Glenn Koontz, who originally introduced us to the concept of motivational gifts, is a server. He is gifted with his hands and developed hand-tooled parts and equipment that sold very well. Soon Glenn's business outgrew his backyard facility and he moved to larger industrial quarters, continuing to grow until he had eighteen employees.

Now Glenn found himself in a supervisory position as head of his own company. His frustration grew in proportion to the company's growth. As he would observe the work of the people he hired, he realized he could do the jobs faster and better, but his time was no longer available for that. So he put into practice what he had learned about the gifts and hired a foreman who had the gift of administration and left the supervisory work to him. Result? Glenn's frustration disappeared. A wise man, indeed.

15. Has a high energy level.

Never	Seldom	Sometimes	Usually	Mostly	Always
0	1	2	3	4	5
POINTS					

Servers have one speed: *fast forward.*

They seem to have boundless energy. First Peter 4:11 urges them to serve "with the strength which God furnishes abundantly." And indeed servers seem to have unusual endurance and often get by with less sleep than the average person.

We can only surmise that God has endowed servers with all this energy because they are the doers and there's so much that needs to be done.

Don's mother was such a prime example of this high energy level. She worked until forced retirement at 65, then got involved in all kinds of activities through her church.

Even at eighty (she would never admit her age) she would leave us huffing and puffing in a shopping mall trying to keep up with her. We'd often lose her only to find her a dozen counters ahead of us. After two hours of this we'd suggest that we find somewhere to sit down and take a coffee break. "You can't be tired already!" she'd exclaim.

16. Cannot stand to be around clutter.

Never	Seldom	Sometimes	Usually	Mostly	Always
0	1	2	3	4	5
POINTS					

We've heard servers say things like, "I can't leave the office until my desk is clear." Or: "It's only after I have the house picked up that I can sit down and watch television." Or: "I can't stand to go over to my neighbor's house. I feel like I want to dig in and put things away, but I don't think she'd appreciate it."

Servers are the ones who straighten crooked picture frames on your walls.

This trait can be seen even in server children. One pastor shared how his three-year-old grandson gave evidence of his giftedness whenever he went to another child's home to play. Finding the other's room in disarray he would always proceed to tidy it up, line up all the toys and only *then* relax and play.

17. Tends to be a perfectionist.

Never	Seldom	Sometimes	Usually	Mostly	Always
0	1	2	3	4	5
POINTS					

Whatever servers do they want to do *well.* They want things to be just right and are willing to work toward that end.

For other gifts perfectionism could be a sign of abnormal behavior. But the server has been created a perfectionist for God's purposes. Someone in the Body of Christ needs to exhibit this trait in a positive and balanced way.

Our friend Dr. David Stewart of Everett, Washington, is a heart surgeon with the motivational gift of serving. His work requires precision. Fortunate is the patient whose surgeon is a perfectionist.

One time we were visiting a friend, Bob, who is a perfectionist server. He was building some stools in his garage-workshop. "I've got to go to town to get some screws," he announced. (They live way out in the country.) "Would you believe with all the screws I have on hand [he must have 3000] I don't have the right ones? I could get by with what I have—but I want the stools to look perfect." They did.

18. Views serving to be the top priority in life.

Never	Seldom	Sometimes	Usually	Mostly	Always
0	1	2	3	4	5
POINTS					

One server said to us, as he was stacking up the chairs after a meeting at church, "I just can't understand why the other men don't chip in and help."

Serving seems to the server to be the essence of Christianity. To him or her, the rest is mere words. Certainly Jesus' example and teaching on the importance of having a servant's heart reinforces his or her conviction that serving is the greatest activity of all.

But servers need to be careful not to insist that others feel the same way. Each gift thinks its type of functioning is the most important of all.

19. Prefers doing a job to delegating it.

Never	Seldom	Sometimes	Usually	Mostly	Always
0	1	2	3	4	5
POINTS					

Not only do servers prefer to do the job themselves, they also have a sense of guilt when they don't. One man said, "I find it very hard to delegate messy or menial types of work to my kids. I generally end up doing those jobs myself."

Don recalls growing up with a server mother. "She would give me a job to do," he says, "and when she would see that I was doing it too slowly, or with difficulty, she would take the job back and do it herself. I guess I learned that I could get out of various responsibilities that way. But, unfortunately, there were a lot of skills I should have learned at home that I'm now having to learn as an adult. I wish my mother had delegated more to me during those growing-up years."

20. Supports others who are in leadership.

Never	Seldom	Sometimes	Usually	Mostly	Always
0	1	2	3	4	5
POINTS					

Servers make wonderful secretaries, vice presidents or committee members. They have incredible loyalty to those they serve under. It is not unusual for a server to burn the midnight oil to bring a project to culmination. Servers want to see those they support succeed.

A large accounting firm in downtown Seattle invited us to teach the motivational gifts seminar to their employees. The staff members were Christians and wanted to utilize their giftedness more effectively within the business context. It was amazing how many of the group were already functioning in areas that made good use of their gifts. Of the four owners, three had the gift of administration. Very appropriate.

Two weeks later Don Kurth, one of the owners, called me to find out what motivational gift would be most suitable for the secretary-receptionist position they needed to fill. "Find a server," I said, "and you will find the best possible secretary. She will be supportive of the leadership, loyal, detailed, accurate and a joy to work with."

They interviewed three women for the job. When one turned out to be a server with a secondary gift of exhortation, she was hired.

A month later Don called us to report, "We took your advice and hired a server. She's the best secretary-receptionist we've ever had. She's all you said she'd be and more. And her secondary gift of exhortation gives her the friendly, people-oriented qualities that the receptionist part of the job requires. She's perfect for the position."

An Exception to the Rule

This is a good place to point out an important exception to the rule that people will function best in the motivational gift(s) that God has given them. Here it is: *When God calls you to do a job outside the sphere of your motivational gift, He will also give you an anointing that will enable you to do the job.* The anointing supersedes the giftedness.

We continue to emphasize that this teaching on motivational gifts is not designed to put you in a box labeled "All I Can Do." Be led by the Holy Spirit in everything. Be open to a special call from God—and the subsequent provision—at any time in your life.

For a biblical example of this, consider Moses.

If you were God and wanted to deliver several million people from slavery, you would probably choose someone with the gift of administration. He'd organize the exodus in super-efficient fashion.

But that's not what God did. He called a server, Moses, to do the job. How do we know which gifts Moses had, and which he lacked?

Firstly, what was Moses' response when God called him?

"But Moses said to God, 'Who am I, that I should . . . bring the sons of Israel out of Egypt?'" (Exodus 3:11, NASB).

Now if Moses had been a natural leader he would have been excited about the prospect: "Great, Lord! When can we get started?" But as a server Moses had no desire for leadership. He had no confidence in his own ability to tackle the job.

Secondly, Moses was not so much giving an excuse as stating a fact when he went on, "O Lord, I am not eloquent or a man of words . . . for I am slow of speech and have a heavy and awkward tongue" (Exodus 4:10).

Moses was well aware of his own limitations. His natural capabilities all worked *against* his succeeding at the task to which God was calling him. The server usually has little capacity for speaking in front of a group.

But God had a solution to the problem. "He said, Is there not Aaron your brother, the Levite? I know he can speak well. . . . He shall speak for you to the people, acting as a mouthpiece for you" (Exodus 4:14–16).

Undoubtedly Aaron had one of the "speaking gifts."

Thirdly, the people were unable to recognize any natural leadership qualities in Moses. They did not always follow him eagerly, as evidenced by their constant murmuring and complaining. They grumbled that Moses had "brought us out into this wilderness to kill this whole assembly with hunger" (Exodus 16:3).

Now an administrator with a charismatic personality would have been able to rally their wholehearted allegiance. One need only remember the tragedy at Jonestown, where hundreds drank Kool-Aid laced with deadly cyanide at Jim Jones's instruction, to realize how compelling a smooth-talking, clever leader can be. Moses was none of that.

Fourthly, Moses, like so many servers, tried to do the job all by himself. It was his administrator father-in-law, Jethro, who bailed him out of the predicament.

> Moses sat to judge the people, and the people stood about Moses from the morning until the evening.
> Now when Moses' father-in-law saw all that he was doing for the people, he said . . . "Why do you alone sit as judge?"
>
> Exodus 18:13–14, NASB

It never dawned on Moses that there might be a better way to organize the handling of all the cases that were brought to him. But Jethro, who had an astute administrator gift, saw it immediately. "You will surely wear out, both yourself and these people who are with you, for the task is too heavy for you; you cannot do it alone" (Exodus 18:18, NASB).

Jethro told Moses to instruct the people clearly about God's statutes and laws and then to select godly men and delegate the cases to them. He laid out a specific organizational plan with leaders over thousands, hundreds, fifties and tens—the plan upon which the judicial system of the United States is based—leaving only the most difficult cases for Moses himself. "And let it be that every major dispute they will bring to you, but every minor dispute they themselves will judge. So it will be easier for you, and they will bear the burden with you" (Exodus 18:22, NASB).

Fifthly, a good administrator would have led the children of Israel from the land of Goshen to the Promised Land in eleven days—the time it takes to walk between those two places. The administrator, operating in his own strength, would have gotten the job done too quickly. For God not only wanted to get the children of Israel out of Egypt, He also wanted to get Egypt out of the children of Israel. That took forty years—two generations!

Their ancestors had been living in a pagan culture for four hundred years—that's twenty generations. Ungodly aspects of the Egyptian culture had rubbed off on them over the years. Moses, being a server, simply followed God and His timing. God needed obedience more than ability. But God also gave Moses an anointing to be able to do the job.

There may be times in your life when God calls you to do some task and your first response is, "Lord, You know I am not gifted in that area." No matter. God will equip and anoint you for the job; you'll be able to do with His help that which you'd never be able to do on your own.

Don't ever use the knowledge of your motivational gift(s) as an excuse to not do what God calls you to do. Remember, *the anointing supersedes your giftedness.*

THE GIFT OF SERVING

Characteristics

	Never	Seldom	Sometimes	Usually	Mostly	Always	POINTS
	0	1	2	3	4	5	
1. Easily recognizes practical needs and is quick to meet them.			X				
2. Especially enjoys manual projects, jobs and functions.			X				
3. Keeps everything in meticulous order.		X					
4. Is a detail person with a good memory.			X				
5. Enjoys showing hospitality.			X				
6. Will stay with something until it is complete.			X				
7. Has a hard time saying no to requests for help.			X				
8. Is more interested in meeting the needs of others than his or her own needs.	X						
9. Enjoys working on short-term goals rather than long-range goals.				X			
10. Shows love for others in deeds and actions more than words.			X				
11. Needs to feel appreciated.				X			
12. Tends to do more than asked to do.			X				
13. Feels greatest joy in doing something that is helpful.			X				
14. Does not want to lead others or projects.			X				
15. Has a high energy level.	X						
16. Cannot stand to be around clutter.		X					
17. Tends to be a perfectionist.		X					
18. Views serving to be the top priority in life.	X						
19. Prefers doing a job to delegating it.	X						
20. Supports others who are in leadership.			X				
						TOTAL	32

Problems of the Server

The server, like each recipient of motivational gifts, has his or her own typical problem areas. Remember, you are to score these five characteristics just to discover any areas where you may need improvement or growth. *They do not go on your profile sheet.*

Never	Seldom	Sometimes	Usually	Mostly	Always
0	1	2	3	4	5
POINTS					

1. Is critical of others who do not help out with obvious practical needs.

The classic example is Martha, the sister of Mary and Lazarus. In Luke 10:38–42 we see Mary sitting at Jesus' feet, listening to His teaching. Meanwhile, back in the kitchen, Martha is preparing food to serve their hungry guests. To her, Mary's obliviousness to a practical need is incomprehensible.

> But Martha [overly occupied and too busy] was distracted with much serving; and she came up to Him and said, Lord, is it nothing to You that my sister has left me to serve alone? Tell her then to help me [to lend a hand and do her part along with me]!
>
> Luke 10:40

To Martha, getting that meal ready is the most important thing in the world. Jesus loves the server gift in her, of course, but also identifies the servers' problem and speaks kindly correction. It is always a temptation for servers to feel put upon by those who ignore "obvious" practical needs.

For many years we were in a church that met in a school gymnasium. Our services usually ran to about 12:30, and we had to be entirely out of the area by 1:00 since another group rented the space then.

Several servers regularly took down the platform, put away the PA system, folded up the chairs, etc. Other people stood around to fellowship, oblivious to the activity around them. Sometimes, when time was especially short, an announcement would be made, requesting additional help to get the job done.

"Why should we have to ask for it?" we overheard one server say. "Can't people see what needs to be done?"

"How can they be here every Sunday," another agreed, "and never lend a hand?"

2. May neglect own family's needs by being too busy helping others.

Never	Seldom	Sometimes	Usually	Mostly	Always
0	1	2	3	4	5
		POINTS			

The typical example is that of the server husband who so enjoys helping out the neighbors that he never has time to fix things around his own house.

Then there's the wife who does so much volunteer work that soon the laundry is stacking up and dinners are getting later.

Betty, a server, wrote us: "I'm *always* behind at home because I'm so involved doing things for others. When I'm baking, the kids ask, 'Who is that for?' They're surprised when I say, 'For us.' They're used to its being for someone else."

Because servers can so easily get overextended they need to be sure of their priorities.

One server (we'll call him Jack) loved to do volunteer work at his church. When the new building project started he threw himself into it. Soon it was a hit-and-run situation. He'd hit the house after work, grab a quick bite and run to the church to work until it was time to retire in the evening.

"Jack," his wife pleaded, "I never see you anymore! The kids hardly know they have a father. I know the building project is worthwhile, but you *do* have a family."

Jack's priorities had gotten out of order. They should be (1) God, (2) family, (3) job and only then (4) church. In his eagerness to serve Jack had them (1) God, (2) job, (3) church and (4) family if there was any time left over.

Although written about a woman, Proverbs 31:16 is good advice for all, especially the servers: "She considers a [new] field before she buys or accepts it [expanding prudently and not courting neglect of her present duties by assuming other duties]."

3. May become pushy or interfering in eagerness to help.

Never	Seldom	Sometimes	Usually	Mostly	Always
0	1	2	3	4	5
		POINTS			

Servers can sometimes "help" where help is not wanted.

One time we had a server who wanted to be helpful all the time stay at our home for two weeks. She would become restless if her hands were not busy, so she'd do things without asking.

Sometimes she was truly helpful, but other times she just made more work for us. When we'd be gone she'd empty the dishwasher and put the contents away in places we'd never think to look. Months later we were still finding dishes and pans in the most surprising places.

A lady from one of our motivational gift seminars shared this example with us. It seems that there was a server in her church who noticed that one of the Sunday school rooms needed painting. She went to the pastor about it and he assured her that the deacons would take care of it. After several weeks when nothing seemed to be happening she decided to take matters into her own hands.

She went to the local paint store, bought supplies and painted the whole room.

Later she discovered that the deacons had decided to remodel that room, knock out one wall to enlarge it and build floor-to-ceiling cupboards on another wall. As the paint that she had used was a dark color, on the remaining walls they had to put on two extra coats of the lighter paint the deacons had chosen.

Never	Seldom	Sometimes	Usually	Mostly	Always
0	1	2	3	4	5
	✗				
POINTS					

4. Finds it hard to accept being served by others.

Because servers so love to do the serving, they can feel awkward when someone else serves them. But the fact is they need to learn to receive as well as give. Otherwise they rob others of the joy of serving.

Barbara told us she really loved doing things for others but she felt unworthy and uneasy when someone did something for her. "I would immediately look for something to do for them," she recalled, "like bake them a batch of cookies or take them flowers. Then I'd feel better."

Then Barbara's church started a "secret pal" program. "Mine kept doing all these wonderful things for me and I couldn't find out who it was. I was terribly frustrated until I realized this might be the Lord's way of showing me that I needed to be willing to be served, too."

Never	Seldom	Sometimes	Usually	Mostly	Always
0	1	2	3	4	5
		✗			
POINTS					

5. Is easily hurt when unappreciated.

The need for appreciation is so deeply built into the server that some hurt is almost inevitable.

Gloria wrote to say, "I love to be appreciated. I'm highly motivated to do more when people are grateful. But frankly, it really hurts me when I put myself out to help someone and they never even say, 'Thanks.' That seems to be happening a lot lately. What should I do? Should I just quit helping those people who don't seem to appreciate my efforts?"

"Dear Gloria," we responded. "First of all, check your motives. Are you helping others just to get their thanks? We know that your gift motivates you to be helpful, but you need to learn how to be helpful without expecting any thanks. We find it's important to look to the Lord for appreciation. He always gives it even when others don't. Let His love and appreciation be enough for you, and then if a person thanks you, too, that's the frosting on the cake! Keep on serving!"

If you know any servers, appreciate them. They'll love you for it.

Typical problem areas of the gift of serving	Never	Seldom	Sometimes	Usually	Mostly	Always	POINTS
	0	1	2	3	4	5	
1. Is critical of others who do not help out with obvious practical needs.		✳					
2. May neglect own family's needs by being too busy helping others.			✳				
3. May become pushy or interfering in eagerness to help.	✳						
4. Finds it hard to accept being served by others.	✳						
5. Is easily hurt when unappreciated.			✳				
						TOTAL	6

Copyright © 1987 Don & Katie Fortune, P.O. Box 101, Kingston, WA 98346

12

Biblical Servers

It's a little harder to identify servers in the Bible since their ministries are apt to be behind the scenes—not the kind of thing that is usually recorded for posterity. But we do have a very clear example in Martha.

Poor Martha has had an unfair share of detractors. How we wish more had been recorded about her, especially about Jesus' responses to the normal functioning of her motivational gift of serving. Had we been there in person on any of the occasions when Jesus visited her home, we're sure we would have heard the Lord say something like, "Martha, dear Martha, thank you for that marvelous meal. I want you to know that I appreciate all your work and effort."

Maybe as you ponder the following scene, the setting and the fact that Martha was a server, you will see how much her actions demonstrate her gift.

Scripture: Luke 10:38–42; John 12:2	Your Comments:
Luke 10	
38 Now while they were on their way, it occurred that Jesus entered a certain village, and a woman named Martha received and welcomed Him into her house.	
39 And she had a sister named Mary, who seated herself at the Lord's feet and was listening to His teaching.	
40 But Martha [overly occupied and too busy] was distracted with much serving; and she came up to Him and said, Lord, is it nothing to You that my sister has left me to serve alone? Tell her then to help me [to lend a hand and do her part along with me]!	

Scripture: Luke 10:38–42;
John 12:2   Your Comments:

41 But the Lord replied to her by saying, Martha, Martha, you are anxious and troubled about many things;

42 There is need of only one or but a few things. Mary has chosen the good portion [that which is to her advantage], which shall not be taken away from her.

John 12

2 So they made Him a supper; and Martha served, but Lazarus was one of those at the table with Him.

Please note that Jesus never criticized or called to account Martha's gift of serving in its appropriate form. In fact, we read again and again about Martha showing hospitality to Jesus. But when negative characteristic number one, "Critical of others who do not help out with obvious practical needs," came to the surface, Jesus addressed the problem.

Martha had become a fusser. She couldn't see the forest for the trees. Her focus was so much on the meal preparation (no packaged foods or TV dinners then!) that she missed the priceless opportunity to sit at the Master's feet and learn.

Scripture: Luke 10:38–42;
John 12:2   Our Comments:

Luke 10

38 Now while they were on their way, it occurred that Jesus entered a certain village, and a woman named Martha received and welcomed Him into her house.

#5 shows hospitality
#10 shows love with actions

39 And she had a sister named Mary, who seated herself at the Lord's feet and was listening to His teaching.

40 But Martha [overly occupied and too busy] was distracted with much serving; and she came up to Him and said, Lord, is it nothing to You that my sister has left me to serve alone? Tell her then to help me [to lend a hand and do her part along with me]!

#1 recognizes practical need
#12 does more than needed
#17 is a perfectionist
#18 sees serving as all-important
#-1 is critical of Mary

41 But the Lord replied to her by saying, Martha, Martha, you are anxious and troubled about many things;

#12 is overextended
#17 is a perfectionist
#-5 feels unappreciated

42 There is need of only one or but a few things. Mary has chosen the good portion [that which is to her advantage] which shall not be taken away from her.

#4 allows details to get in the way
#-2 is too busy

John 12

2 So they made Him a supper; and Martha served, but Lazarus was one of those at the table with Him.

#5 shows hospitality
#10 shows love with actions

Perhaps one of the reasons Jesus went so often to the home of Mary, Martha and Lazarus was because Martha's gift made Him feel so at home.

Jesus had no place to call His own, but we can easily imagine that this was the nearest place He had to an earthly home.

Now read about some other biblical servers (including another reference for Martha). See how many motivational-gift characteristics you can see in each of them:

Martha: John 11:1–40

Phoebe: Romans 16:1–2

Stephen: Acts 6:1–15; 7:1–60

Philip (the deacon): John 1:43–45; 6:5–7; 12:21–22; 14:8; Acts 6:5; 8:5–40; 21:8–9

Onesimus: Philemon; Colossians 4:9

Peter's mother-in-law: Matthew 8:14–15

Jacob: Genesis 25–30

Characteristics of the Teacher

13

The third motivational gift listed in Romans 12:6–8 is the gift of teaching. The Greek word here for a person who teaches is _didasko_, which means, simply, "to teach or to give instruction."

The person with this gift then should be functioning—at least to some degree—in the area of teaching others. Actually we were tempted to use the word "researcher" because we found that many with this gift were especially drawn into fields of research and may or may not be overtly involved with the function of teaching. Or they may do their teaching through writing (papers, articles, dissertations or books) rather than in person.

But we found that the majority of people with this gift were also involved in some form of in-person teaching, so "teacher" stands.

Proceed through the following twenty characteristics of the teacher, scoring as you go, then transfer the total to your profile sheet.

1. Presents truth in a logical, systematic way.

Never	Seldom	Sometimes	Usually	Mostly	Always
0	1	2	3	4	5
		✗			
		POINTS			

Looking back over school days you can always tell the teachers who had this gift because their lectures were in outline form: points 1, 2, 3, a, b, c. The procedures were systematic. It was easy to take notes.

Derek Prince, renowned author and scholar, is a classic example of a person with the motivational gift of teaching. We have file folders full of notes taken at his lectures. The notes are rich in facts, Scriptures and conclusions, all nicely organized by virtue of the fact that Derek speaks that way. It's easy to look up information from these notes since they are so logically arranged.

We will find that exhorters are actually the most interesting and popular teachers, but they may teach for an hour and make only one significant point. You'll have hardly any notes—and those not in any particular sequence. But a speaker with a teacher gift will give you a rich and organized treasure of facts and information.

2. Validates truth by checking out the facts.

Never	Seldom	Sometimes	Usually	Mostly	Always
0	1	2	3	4	5
POINTS					

A family in our church recently got a ferret for a pet. He's an animal who seems to be actively looking for something all the time—in corners, under chairs, in jackets. The word *ferret* has come to mean "to search out," and that is what the teacher is doing all the time: ferreting out the truth.

Teachers want to be sure that what they believe and accept is based on fact. This was the case with doubting Thomas. Being motivated by his teaching gift he did not want to trust what he heard about Jesus' resurrection and so it was natural for him to respond: "Unless I see in His hands the imprint of the nails, and put my finger into the place of the nails, and put my hand into His side, I will not believe" (John 20:25, NASB).

However, when Jesus did appear to him eight days later, Thomas could only respond, "My Lord and my God!" (verse 28).

If you have the motivational gift of teaching you have probably been called a "doubting Thomas" from time to time. Count it an honor. You were designed by God to investigate the facts and you are doing a good enough job of it that others are noticing. That's great!

Don calls teachers "spiritual detectives." Perhaps that's why so many teachers love to read mystery stories. They are armchair detectives at heart.

3. Loves to study and do research.

Never	Seldom	Sometimes	Usually	Mostly	Always
0	1	2	3	4	5
POINTS					

Since teaching is my secondary gift, I can relate thoroughly to this characteristic. I love to research!

When our boys were preschool age I wanted to be at home, but there were spare hours in my day. So I began to do freelance work writing junior high Sunday school materials for both David C. Cook Company and Union Gospel Press. They would send me the assignments and I would get out my commentaries and concordances and begin to research the Scripture. I'd often spend up to twenty hours on one lesson.

"Why do you spend so much time on that research?" Don would ask. "Couldn't you cut it down a bit?"

The thought horrified me. What if I didn't look into the subject thoroughly enough and wound up writing something inaccurate! I could visualize thousands of Sunday school teachers passing on my marred

books filled with facts and accurate information. He or she has a good memory, especially for dates and history.

When we first went to New Zealand in 1979, we traveled around the South Island with our dear friends Rita and Len Restall. Len is a schoolmaster with the motivational gift of teaching. His reservoir of information constantly amazed us. Everywhere we went Len would spontaneously spill out rich and interesting history about each New Zealand town.

Len was like a living, walking and talking encyclopedia. Whenever we brought up a new subject it was like pressing a computer button: out would come his amazing contribution of vast amounts of information to enhance our understanding. He made our trip more interesting than we could have ever imagined.

16. Is self-disciplined.

Never	Seldom	Sometimes	Usually	Mostly	Always
0	1	2	3	4	5
		POINTS			

Mix a good dose of seriousness with a lot of objectivity, add a love for truth and a keen mind, and you have the ingredients for self-discipline.

Teachers can set goals and stick to them, set parameters and work effectively within them and project time schedules and abide by them.

One woman with this gift was amazing to watch in action. Her life was so self-regulated that fellow workers could set their watches by the moment she walked in the office: always at 8:30 A.M., never 8:29 or 8:31. She also exited at 4:30 on the nose! But while some chuckled at this, her punctuality set a good example of putting in a good day's work for a day's wages.

17. Is emotionally self-controlled.

Never	Seldom	Sometimes	Usually	Mostly	Always
0	1	2	3	4	5
	POINTS				

Of all the motivational gifts, this is the one that grants the greatest emotional equilibrium. Some people have emotional ups and downs that track like the pathway of a roller-coaster ride. Others have smoother patterns of ups and downs with only occasional jolting bumps. But the teacher's graph of mood swings looks more like a horizontal line.

Teachers are highly analytical. They believe reasonable choices can resolve potentially volatile situations. When someone's upset, they may advise, "Calm down. You can, you know."

At one of our Prayer Counseling Training sessions we staged a little melodrama to illustrate just that point:

The scene is a home. The wife is stirring the pot, looking again and again at her watch. Furious looks flash across her face. Finally her husband comes in the door, obviously late again. He offers a weak excuse and his wife goes into a tirade of complaints about his inconsiderateness. He retaliates with complaints about her temper. The argument escalates, the wife becoming all but hysterical with rage.

"Get *control* of yourself," the husband demands.

"I *can't!*" she screams.

Burrrrring. The telephone pierces the commotion.

The wife picks up the receiver. "Hellooo," she calmly coos into the phone. "Why Charlotte, how good to hear from you. No, I wasn't doing a thing. Yes, we're both fine. How about you?"

On and on she goes. Completely in control.

The point is: It's not that she *can't* control her emotions when arguing with her husband—she *won't*. It's a matter of choice.

Never	Seldom	Sometimes	Usually	Mostly	Always
0	1	2	3	4	5
		✗			
POINTS					

18. Has only a select circle of friends.

Common interests seem to be the prerequisite for the development of close relationships. Teachers are seldom drawn into superficial friendships. They tend to be aloof or uneasy in unstructured social situations and they hate meaningless chitchat. They prefer friends with whom they can discuss ideas and concepts. Sometimes they are loners. More often they are comfortable with just a few close friends.

Teachers often tell us, "Some interaction with people is okay, but, quite frankly, I'd just as soon curl up with a good book." Books are often their "best friends."

Our niece, Gayle Hansen, is that way. We spent summers at our cabin on Puget Sound right next door to my sister's cabin. From the time Gayle was old enough to read we noticed that she often preferred being inside with her nose in a book to playing outside with the other kids, even on nice days. We often wondered why this attractive girl seemed so antisocial. When we gave her the motivational gift test (in her teens) we were not surprised that she came out a teacher.

Once when she visited us from California, she said "I'm still a bookworm, Aunt Katie," she said. "I don't go out much. I like to tuck my son into bed early and spend the rest of the evening with a good book."

Never	Seldom	Sometimes	Usually	Mostly	Always
0	1	2	3	4	5
		✗			
POINTS					

19. Has strong convictions and opinions based on investigation of facts.

Teachers have so many areas of interest. They willingly drop what they are doing to investigate a new area of knowledge.

Eadie and Jim Goodboy are both teachers by motivational gift. It is always interesting to visit them in their home, which is loaded with books of every description. We'll be talking and happen to bring up a new subject. Invariably it triggers something in them.

"Just a minute," Jim will say. "I think I have a book that gets into that." He'll quickly retrieve a book from the shelf and flip to the relevant reference.

Or, "I read something about that just the other day," Eadie will say.

Before long the dining room table will be loaded with open books, all contributing to the development of new opinions and convictions.

20. Believes truth itself has the power to produce change.

Never	Seldom	Sometimes	Usually	Mostly	Always
0	1	2	3	4	5
		POINTS			

When teachers teach they present the truth without necessarily explaining to their listeners how to apply that truth to their lives. Teachers believe the application of truth is the job of the Holy Spirit.

"You will know the truth, and the truth will set you free" (John 8:32, NIV) is a favorite verse of teachers. They assume that others will respond to truth in the same way that they do—as being energizing and liberating.

Teachers are even able to teach truth they themselves have not yet appropriated. One summer I worked as a counselor at a private girls' camp on the beautiful wooded shores of Lake Winnepesaukee in New Hampshire. One of my responsibilities was to teach swimming, for which I was provided an instruction manual.

All went well until I got to the lesson on the breaststroke. I had been a reasonably good swimmer all my life, but this was one stroke I was never able to master. I memorized the directions, then walked out on the dock and instructed the girls, step by step. They did it! And I couldn't do it myself. No matter. The instructions worked. Later I slipped into the water myself and, following what I had taught, swam my first breaststroke.

Most with other gifts would have practiced before class. But the teacher has confidence that whatever is truth will be effective.

THE GIFT OF TEACHING

Characteristics

Characteristics	Never	Seldom	Sometimes	Usually	Mostly	Always	POINTS
	0	1	2	3	4	5	
1. Presents truth in a logical, systematic way.				X			
2. Validates truth by checking out the facts.				X			
3. Loves to study and do research.					X		
4. Enjoys word studies.				X			
5. Prefers to use biblical illustrations rather than life illustrations.					X		
6. Gets upset when Scripture is used out of context.					X		
7. Feels concerned that truth be established in every situation.					X		
8. Is more objective than subjective.		X					
9. Easily develops and uses a large vocabulary.				X			
10. Emphasizes facts and the accuracy of words.	X						
11. Checks out the source of knowledge of others who teach.				X			
12. Prefers teaching believers over engaging in evangelism.					X		
13. Feels Bible study is foundational to the operation of all the gifts.					X		
14. Solves problems by starting with scriptural principles.					X		
15. Is intellectually sharp.		X					
16. Is self-disciplined.				X			
17. Is emotionally self-controlled.		X					
18. Has only a select circle of friends.				X			
19. Has strong convictions and opinions based on investigation of facts.				X			
20. Believes truth itself has the power to produce change.				X			
						TOTAL	51

Problems of the Teacher

14

The teacher's problem areas are unique to the teacher gift. But in identifying the problems the teacher will believe that the solutions cannot be far away. (And so it is with each of the motivational gifts—the solutions to the problem areas will come as we see the need for change and cooperate with the work of the Holy Spirit in bringing us into maturity.)

1. Tends to neglect the practical application of truth.

Never	Seldom	Sometimes	Usually	Mostly	Always
0	1	2	3	4	5
		POINTS			

Because teachers believe that their job is to communicate truth and let people make their own use of it, they usually do not give much in the way of practical suggestions. This especially frustrates exhorters. (They focus on the actual application of teaching.) It can also frustrate those with other gifts.

The listener may say, "So we've heard lots of facts, now what do we do with them?"

The teacher responds, "You've got a mind. You figure it out."

But not all minds work with the degree of logic that the teacher's mind does. Many need specific directions—steps one, two, three. A teacher needs to learn how to give at least some measure of practical application to his hearers.

I have the benefit of living with an exhorter. Don keeps me accountable. He's helped me see the need to give practical application when I teach or write and to make my teaching more interesting with anecdotes and illustrations.

We've noticed that when public speakers become known for their style of teaching they tend to draw specialized audiences. Teachers draw other teachers and those interested in gaining knowledge in general. Exhorters draw other exhorters and those interested in gaining practical, life-related knowledge. But if they learn to use both the solid presentation of facts and the practical application of those facts, they will appeal to everyone.

Never	Seldom	Sometimes	Usually	Mostly	Always
0	1	2	3	4	5
		X			
POINTS					

2. Is slow to accept viewpoints of others.

The "know-it-all" attitude can be a real pitfall for people with the motivational gift of teaching. Of course they do know a lot. But no one knows *everything*.

George, now a professor at a university, told us, "I was always dubious about the teaching of other Christians. If they spoke on something I had researched myself and knew was true, that was fine. But if the subject was new I would go home and check out all the Scriptures for myself."

Shawn, who is now attending law school, said he grew up loving to study and learn. But his dedication to this along with his desire to be right caused some strains in his relationships with peers. "They often called me 'Professor Shawn' or 'Mr. Information Booth'—neither meant as a compliment. But as I've learned to be more accepting of others, I've learned to respect their viewpoints, too."

Never	Seldom	Sometimes	Usually	Mostly	Always
0	1	2	3	4	5
	X				
POINTS					

3. Tends to develop pride in intellectual ability.

Pride is probably the number one problem for those with the motivational gift of teaching. It was Lucifer's problem and it changed him from an angel of God into Satan. We know that pride brings downfall. Listen to what Proverbs has to say about it:

> "When pride comes, then comes disgrace, but with humility comes wisdom" (Proverbs 11:2, NIV).

> "Pride goes before destruction, a haughty spirit before a fall" (Proverbs 16:18, NIV).

> "A man's pride brings him low, but a man of lowly spirit gains honor" (Proverbs 29:23, NIV).

In 1 Corinthians 8:1, Paul says that knowledge puffs up, but love builds up. The greatest qualities a teacher can seek are humility and love. These will neutralize the pride problem.

One person who scored very high on teaching wrote to us: "I have always enjoyed learning new things. I couldn't understand why others didn't pursue learning like I did. I thought they were lazy or unmotivated.

I am ashamed to admit that this led me to think I was better than most people. At your seminar I was helped to value the other gifts and the people who so beautifully demonstrate them."

Teachers can indeed develop a superiority complex. The problem is that intellectually they usually are superior. But they need to be careful not to lean on human knowledge and reasoning rather than on the Holy Spirit. The primary tool of the teacher is his or her mind, but Proverbs 3:5 warns us not to lean on our own understanding.

4. Tends to be legalistic and dogmatic.

Never	Seldom	Sometimes	Usually	Mostly	Always
0	1	2	3	4	5
POINTS					

This trait can show up even in children.

Becky, today a young mother, shared how inflexible she used to be. "Even when I played games I insisted that we play strictly by the rules. If someone suggested we take shortcuts in Monopoly I'd tell them to play it right or not at all. Now I see that I was much too legalistic, but at the time I just thought I was being right."

Being right is so important to the teacher that he easily becomes argumentative. The feeling may be "I alone am right and everyone else is wrong." Such lack of checks and balances can expose the teacher to deception. (Perhaps that's why some get into cults.) God's truth is not exclusive; it can be verified by many.

Have you ever been involved in a good group discussion where each person is openly interacting? And then a polluted teacher gift comes along and blurts out, "Well, I happen to *know* that the truth of the matter is . . ." No one can end a good discussion faster.

5. Is easily sidetracked by new interests.

Never	Seldom	Sometimes	Usually	Mostly	Always
0	1	2	3	4	5
POINTS					

Teachers are interested in so many things! Their prolific reading takes them into all kinds of areas. Their research extends to endless subjects. Focusing is not always easy.

We know one man who admits that when he picks up an encyclopedia he seldom gets right to the subject at hand. Just flipping through the pages sends him off on many tangents. "I'll be looking up 'transistors' and on the way I come across 'tape recorders.' Well, I always wanted to know how they came into being so I spend fifteen minutes there. Then I happen to see 'technology.' Another quarter hour goes by. Then I stop at 'television.' Fascinating! After a good look at 'theater' and 'thermometer' and 'thermostat' and 'tide' and 'tornado' I've almost forgotten what I wanted to know in the first place."

Josh, an avid reader, admits that many of the hundreds of books he owns have never been finished. "I've got bookmarks in scores of them," he confesses.

Kathleen hopes she will have a long retirement because she has so many incomplete projects. "I start things, but then if something else comes along that seems more interesting I'll set the first project aside. My attic and closets are full of them."

If you know anyone with the motivational gift of teaching, be patient with them. As the saying goes: God isn't finished with them yet!

Typical problem areas of the gift of teaching

		Never	Seldom	Sometimes	Usually	Mostly	Always	POINTS
		0	1	2	3	4	5	
1. Tends to neglect the practical application of truth.	1.			X				
2. Is slow to accept viewpoints of others.	2.			X				
3. Tends to develop pride in intellectual ability.	3.			X				
4. Tends to be legalistic and dogmatic.	4.		X					
5. Is easily sidetracked by new interests.	5.		X					
							TOTAL	8

Copyright © 1987 Don & Katie Fortune, P.O. Box 101, Kingston, WA 98346

Biblical Teachers

Teachers have a highly visible ministry. However, biblical teachers often have another "public" gift as well, such as perceiver or exhorter, and it's not always easy to tell which is primary. Also, they may have the motivational gift of teaching but the ministry gift of pastor or prophet. To compound matters, they may flow in certain manifestation gifts more than others. How we wish we could ask the writers of the Bible for more information!

Thus, we may identify a biblical character as having a certain gift, while you with equal logic feel that another gift predominates.

We feel, however, that Apollos is a clear example of someone with the motivational gift of teaching. In fact, he's what we call a classic example. It is probable that he also was called of God to the ministry gift of teaching. As you look at the following Scripture passage you will see his giftedness in many aspects of his actions.

Scripture: Acts 18:24–28; 1 Corinthians 3:6	Your Comments:
Acts 18	
24 Meanwhile, there was a Jew named Apollos, a native of Alexandria, who came to Ephesus. He was a cultured and eloquent man, well versed and mighty in the Scriptures.	
25 He had been instructed in the way of the Lord, and burning with spiritual zeal, he spoke and taught diligently and accurately the things concerning Jesus, though he was acquainted only with the baptism of John.	

Scripture: Acts 18:24–28;   Your Comments:
1 Corinthians 3:6

26 He began to speak freely (fearlessly and boldly) in the synagogue; but when Priscilla and Aquila heard him, they took him with them and expounded to him the way of God more definitely and accurately.

27 And when [Apollos] wished to cross to Achaia (most of Greece), the brethren wrote to the disciples there, urging and encouraging them to accept and welcome him heartily. When he arrived, he proved a great help to those who through grace (God's unmerited favor and mercy) had believed (adhered to, trusted in, and relied on Christ as Lord and Savior).

28 For with great power he refuted the Jews in public [discussions], showing and proving by the Scriptures that Jesus is the Christ (the Messiah).

1 Corinthians 3

6 I planted, Apollos watered, but God [all the while] was making it grow and [He] gave the increase.

What a focus Apollos had on knowing the truth! He was a keen student of the Scriptures and an eloquent speaker. He was drawn to Greece, the intellectual capital of the world, where he used his gift to great effect refuting the Jews in public debate and proving that Jesus was the promised Messiah. His was the most appropriate gift for the task.

Scripture: Acts 18:24–28;   Our Comments:
1 Corinthians 3:6

Acts 18

24 Meanwhile, there was a Jew named Apollos, a native of Alexandria, who came to Ephesus. He was a cultured and eloquent man, well versed and mighty in the Scriptures.	**#1** is logical, cultured **#3** is well versed in Scriptures **#9** has an eloquent vocabulary **#15** is intellectually sharp
25 He had been instructed in the way of the Lord, and burning with spiritual zeal, he spoke and taught diligently and accurately the things concerning Jesus, though he was acquainted only with the baptism of John.	**#1** is logical **#2** uses accurate facts **#3** is a student and researcher **#5** has a biblical focus **#13** has a teaching focus **#16** is diligent
26 He began to speak freely (fearlessly and boldly) in the synagogue; but when Priscilla and Aquila heard him, they took him with them and expounded to him the way of God more definitely and accurately.	**#7** is open to new truth **#9** speaks impressively **#19** has strong convictions
27 And when [Apollos] wished to cross to Achaia (most of Greece), the brethren wrote to the disciples there, urging and encouraging them to accept and welcome him heartily. When he arrived, he proved a great help to those who through grace (God's unmerited favor and mercy) had believed (adhered to, trusted in, and relied on Christ as Lord and Savior).	**#12** helps fellow believers **#15** aims at Greek culture **#19** takes along convictions based on facts

Scripture: Acts 18:24–28; 1 Corinthians 3:6	Our Comments:
28 For with great power he refuted the Jews in public [discussions], showing and proving by the Scriptures that Jesus is the Christ (the Messiah).	**#1** proves the truth of the Gospel **#9** speaks impressively **#13** uses biblical base **#15** uses his intellect **#19** has strong convictions
1 Corinthians 3	
6 I planted, Apollos watered, but God [all the while] was making it grow and [He] gave the increase.	**#12** teaches believers **#20** believes truth produces change

How valuable the teaching gift is! How important a role it plays in the lives of those who would take the Gospel into all the world.

Take time to read about some of the other New Testament teachers:

Aquila and Priscilla: Acts 18:1–3, 24–28; Romans 16:3–5; 1 Corinthians 16:19; 2 Timothy 4:19

Timothy: 1 and 2 Timothy; Acts 16:1–3; 1 Corinthians 4:17; 16:10–11

Thomas: John 20:24–28

Luke: Gospel of Luke and Acts

It is very likely that Aquila and Priscilla were a husband/wife team who had the same motivational gift of teaching.

Thomas, famous for his doubting, was simply exercising his teaching gift in wanting to know the facts.

Luke wrote the most systematic account of the life of Jesus and the history of the early Church (Luke and Acts). His being a medical doctor is also compatible with his gift of teacher.

Characteristics
of the Exhorter

The teacher aims for your head; the exhorter aims for your heart. It is not so much the content that the exhorter wants to impart as how that content can be made effective in peoples' lives.

Every one of the gifts can teach, but the exhorter makes the most interesting and palatable teacher. All of his efforts are geared toward edifying and encouraging other people. We could have called this person the encourager. In fact, the Greek word *paraklesis* means "a calling to one's side to aid" denoting both exhortation and encouragement.

As you proceed through the scoring in this chapter (as for all the gifts) remember to score the way you really are, not the way you would like to be.

Even if you do not turn out to be an exhorter you can benefit from observing how they operate. We can all learn qualities of life and action from those who exhibit other motivational gifts.

1. Loves to encourage others to live up to their full potential.

Never	Seldom	Sometimes	Usually	Mostly	Always
0	1	2	3	4	5
POINTS					

The exhorter wants everyone to have a full, meaningful life. Exhorters are builders of people. They want to help people live up to their full potential. Their greatest joy is being an instrument to help another to live victoriously.

The pastor of a church we went to some years ago was an exhorter. His sermons were always vibrant, uplifting and positive. We always left his services encouraged and strengthened. He made people feel expectant and hopeful about their abilities; an I-can-do-it-with-the-Lord's-help type of confidence emerged in many lives.

One young man came out of Bible school eager to become an evangelist. In his first church Martin kept trying to preach soul-winning sermons, but instead he drew in wayward believers who wanted to get their lives right with the Lord. The same thing happened in his second church. Believers were strengthened. Lives were changed. People learned how to overcome problems. Everyone was built up.

"Then I learned about the motivational gifts," he recalls. "I saw that I was not an evangelist at all. I was an exhorter with a teaching ministry. I was gifted to pastor and to build up the flock. They, in turn, could evangelize among nonbelievers and bring them into the church. God had gifted me to edify the believers. What a release it was to go ahead and be what God meant me to be!"

2. Wants a visible response when teaching or speaking.

Never	Seldom	Sometimes	Usually	Mostly	Always
0	1	2	3	4	5
				X	
		POINTS			

Interaction with their hearers is essential for exhorters. They watch the expressions on people's faces, listen for reactions and analyze body language. They need to know that they're *really* communicating. (Perhaps the most frustrating experience for the exhorter is to share something of value with a person and then find out he or she wasn't listening.) Puncho

Since Don is equipped with this gift he can relate to this: "I find I do much better with an enthusiastic and responsive audience. The more people respond the more I feel God's anointing. Lack of response makes me feel flustered. I feel that if they don't want to hear what I'm saying I might as well not say it."

On our third trip to Great Britain we went way up north in Scotland to teach an evening service at the church connected with Faith Bible School in Peterhead. It was cold and windy when we arrived. The wind came right off the ocean, and they don't heat their buildings as we do. They are a hardy bunch.

We had always heard that Scottish people were reserved. But the chill in the room seemed to be coming from both the weather *and* the church members. The first half hour that we spoke was misery for Don. "They didn't laugh at my puns," he recalls. "Their faces were expressionless. I didn't think I'd last an hour. We had found God's frozen chosen.

"Then suddenly I began to see reactions and responses. They were warming up to us. They had sized us up and had accepted us. What a relief! I felt I could have shared all night (but good sense had me stop on schedule). Afterward we had wonderful, warm fellowship with the members of the congregation."

Never	Seldom	Sometimes	Usually	Mostly	Always
0	1	2	3	4	5
POINTS					

3. Prefers to apply truth rather than research it.

Research is not the exhorter's cup of tea. He or she avoids it if at all possible. "Why reinvent the wheel?" they will ask. "If someone else has put together materials on a subject, let's use what's available." It's putting truth to work that the teacher is interested in.

Pat King, an exhorter author and mother of ten who writes at least one book a year, has learned the value of utilizing the research abilities of teachers. When she was preparing to write her book *How Do You Find the Time?* she arranged for her teacher friend Eadie Goodboy to put five hundred hours of research into the field of time management.

"Why should I spend all those hours doing what would be drudgery for me when Eadie, with her beautiful gift of teaching, loves it?" Pat explained. "Together we made a great team, each doing what we do best. She loves the research and I love taking the facts and writing about them in practical ways."

Never	Seldom	Sometimes	Usually	Mostly	Always
0	1	2	3	4	5
POINTS					

4. Prefers the kind of information that has practical application(s).

Notice that Pat King wrote a "how-to" book. Exhorters enjoy that kind of writing. They are "how-to" people.

They also like to read books that focus on practical application. They prefer sermons that reveal how to apply Christian principles to everyday life. Conversely they do not like abstract books or sermons.

Exhorters love to hear other exhorters teach. "Wow! What great teaching," they will say when someone emphasizes the practicality of a principle. On the other hand, they will not be too thrilled at teaching for teaching's sake. Too much *fact* and not enough *act* is, in their estimation, like overloading circuits that have no outlet.

Betty, a Presbyterian friend who loves to teach the Bible to other women, wrote to us, "I try to create Bible studies that help my classes understand how to apply Scripture in the areas where they need help." Her classes are thriving.

Never	Seldom	Sometimes	Usually	Mostly	Always
0	1	2	3	4	5
POINTS					

5. Loves to prescribe precise steps of action to aid personal growth.

Exhorters love to give specific steps for people to follow. They know how to instruct others to get from point A to point C in the best possible way. It's all part of their incredible ability to give constructive and helpful advice.

One of the most visible examples of an exhorter in action is Bill Gothard. Anyone who has taken his Basic Youth Conflicts course is aware of the specific steps prescribed for every subject he teaches. The giant notebook that is part of the course is a practical reference manual for spiritual growth. It is probable that his broad popularity is at least in part due to his very workable approach.

Lorraine, an excellent exhorter counselor, regularly outlines definite steps of action for those she counsels. One young woman had come to her because of a strained relationship with her husband. At the close of the session Lorraine wrote out this simple prescription:

1. Apologize to your husband for *your* wrong attitudes.
2. Cook him his favorite dinner tonight.
3. Shower him with hugs and kisses.
4. Don't criticize anything he says for one week.

The day before her next appointment the young woman called Lorraine to cancel. "I don't need it!" she said excitedly. "The four steps worked so well that it's almost like we're on our second honeymoon."

"I love being worked right out of my job," Lorraine adds. "I wish all my counselees would follow my advice that well."

6. Focuses on working with people.

Never	Seldom	Sometimes	Usually	Mostly	Always
0	1	2	3	4	5
		POINTS			

Exhorters are *people* people. They are not interested in working with things or systems or abstract ideas. They love to be around people, doing things with people or for them.

Ken took a job as a night watchman because it was the only one available. Being an outgoing person he didn't expect to enjoy it, but he was not prepared for the negative impact it would have on him.

His hours were midnight to eight A.M. When he got home his wife was at work and the kids were in school, and by the time they got home he'd be sleeping. He was all alone at work, all alone at home.

After a few months the isolation began to get to him. He started talking to himself just to have "someone to talk to." He became depressed. He lived for the weekends when he could interact with family and friends.

Ken learned about the motivational gifts and found that he was an exhorter, a people person. He began to pray earnestly for a new job. When he found work as a supervisor in a cannery, "it was like coming back to life again," Ken recalls. "What a joy it was working with *people*. I thanked the Lord every day for that job."

7. Encourages others to develop in their personal ministries.

Never	Seldom	Sometimes	Usually	Mostly	Always
0	1	2	3	4	5
		POINTS			

Exhorters want everyone to develop a full and fruitful ministry. They understand well the concept of the Body of Christ with each member functioning to the benefit of the others. They want this ideal realized in practice.

A pastor who is an exhorter will eagerly develop lay leadership and ministries. He or she will sense that everyone needs to be involved in ministry, and will likely test everyone and then enter the data in a computer program so the information can be easily accessed. Ephesians 4:11–13 will be a favorite Scripture, especially the part that talks about *all* the saints doing the work of the ministry.

We have taught in a number of churches where the exhorter pastor invited us specifically to help members of the congregation find their giftedness. He or she would make photocopies of their profile sheets in order to begin to know people's gifts, encourage them and utilize them effectively within the life of the church.

Sometimes we get a call to come back a few years later to do another seminar because, as one pastor said, "There are quite a few new people now and they need to know and function in their giftedness, too."

It's been fun for me to watch Don's exhorter gift in action over the years. Whether leading home meetings, serving as a church elder and staff member, teaching, counseling or just talking with others, Don is always encouraging people to move out into the ministry God has for them. "Don't sit on your hands like I once did," he'll say. "Get involved. Use the gifts God has given you."

Never	Seldom	Sometimes	Usually	Mostly	Always
0	1	2	3	4	5
POINTS					

8. Finds truth in experience and then validates it with Scripture.

Life is so full of lessons and insights to exhorters. That's where they primarily learn. Then they check the Bible to see what it has to say on the subject. They're always glad to find "it's in the Bible, too."

Exhorters discover truth by finding out experientially that something "works." To them there is no more solid basis for truth. If someone hits them and they don't hit back, and this neutralizes the other person's anger and brings him or her to repentance, then "turning the other cheek" is a valid way of life. They may have discovered this truth in practice long before they read Jesus' teaching on it.

An exhorter might be walking by a river and see a large, stately tree. *Ah ha!* thinks the exhorter. *A Christian should be like that tree . . . strong . . . radiating life . . . drawing from the River of Life, Jesus.* The next day his eye happens to fall on the third verse of Psalm 1: "He is like a tree planted by streams of water, which yields its fruit in season and whose leaf does not wither. Whatever he does prospers" (NIV).

"Wow!" he or she exclaims. "How true that is."

Never	Seldom	Sometimes	Usually	Mostly	Always
0	1	2	3	4	5
POINTS					

9. Loves to do personal counseling.

Of all the seven motivational gifts, exhorters are the ones most gifted in and frequently drawn to counseling. They are naturals for it. We have talked with dozens of exhorters who tell us that even in their high school days other students sought them out for counsel. People sense their ability, their caring concern, their interest in helping and their approachability.

One of the most helpful qualities of counselors is the ability to be transparent about their own problems and how they have worked through (or are working through) them. The counselee easily identifies with such a person: "Well, if she's been through this and overcome it, maybe I can, too."

Exhorters have this ability. They are the first ones to admit that they are not perfect, but just another person "on the way." It is easy for them to admit their sins and sorrows, their pains and pitfalls.

Jamie Buckingham, pastor of a church in Melbourne, Florida, and author of many books, is a prime example of this wonderful transparency. His exhorter gift especially comes through in his book *Risky Living*. So many assume pastors are somehow perfect, but Jamie lays bare his struggles and faults and helps the reader to draw upon the resources of the greatest Counselor of all, Jesus Christ.

10. Will discontinue personal counseling if no effort to change is seen.

Never	Seldom	Sometimes	Usually	Mostly	Always
0	1	2	3	4	5
POINTS					

While exhorters are not prone to quitting, there is one situation that will make them give up and move on. If a counselee refuses to implement his or her advice the exhorter may say something like: "I cannot counsel you any further until you have put into action those things we've already agreed on," or "If you cannot follow my advice I cannot help you," or "Look, both your time and my time are being wasted until you are ready to change."

Exhorters realize that their success rests not so much on how much they know or how experienced they are, but rather on how far the counselee is willing to act on the advice given. Without such action the exhorter will feel that his or her efforts are like shoveling against the tide—useless. Exhorters want to make their time and effort count, so they will move on to someone who will act on their advice.

11. Is fluent in communication.

Never	Seldom	Sometimes	Usually	Mostly	Always
0	1	2	3	4	5
POINTS					

Exhorters are the mouth of the body, with the greatest facility in speech of any of the gifts. One of our biblical examples, Peter, was a fluent communicator. Perhaps that's why he was so often the spokesman for the disciples.

Lynn Severance, a gifted elementary teacher, says that communication has always been important to her. "I grew up feeling I had a lot to say and to contribute," she recalls, "but since this was not particularly encouraged in my home, I never felt confident to come forth with it. Now as a teacher, my exhorter gift and especially my communication skills have been released—words roll out as naturally as breath. It's so good not to be burying my gift under a bushel."

Another exhorter friend told us, "My greatest joy has always been to express encouragement to others. If I had no voice I'd probably write prolific letters or emails."

It is not surprising that many exhorters become teachers, preachers, counselors, supervisors—even radio announcers or TV hosts—fields that require giftedness of speech.

12. Views trials as opportunities to produce personal growth.

Never	Seldom	Sometimes	Usually	Mostly	Always
0	1	2	3	4	5

POINTS

Exhorters unquestioningly believe Romans 8:28: "All things work together for good to them that love God, to them who are the called according to his purpose" (KJV).

They also refuse to accept the word *impossible*, preferring to believe what the angel said: "For with God nothing shall be impossible" (Luke 1:37, KJV); and Jesus' words: "If ye have faith as a grain of mustard seed . . . nothing shall be impossible unto you" (Matthew 17:20, KJV).

Exhorters see opportunities, not obstacles. Challenges, not trials. Possibilities, not problems.

For years I worked closely with Marion Shelton, my dear exhorter friend, at Aglow International. We've shared many joys and sorrows together, many high points and low points. But whenever a problem or trial faced us I could count on Marion's saying, "Hallelujah! God is giving us another opportunity to be overcomers."

She kept us focused on the solution rather than the problem. What a blessing that was! What encouragement to get our eyes back on Jesus and to seek out what He wanted us to do.

Whenever Marion heard anyone grumbling or criticizing she'd whisper, "Attitude check. Testing . . . one, two, three, four." Then we'd know it was time to talk to the Lord, not to others or about others.

13. Accepts people as they are without judging them.

Never	Seldom	Sometimes	Usually	Mostly	Always
0	1	2	3	4	5

POINTS

While perceivers see people as either *in* the will of God or *out* of the will of God—with nothing in between—exhorters are just the opposite. They don't see extremes at all—only a vast gray area where everyone is somewhere along the way. No one has arrived. No one is a complete failure. But everyone is at that point in life where a few well-chosen steps will bring him or her that much closer to God's will.

Therefore the exhorter does not see any need to judge people for where they are—or are not—but rather sees the need to help them take those steps in the right direction. It is this nonjudgmental attitude that enables him or her to help people so much.

Have you ever been around a judgmental person? He or she doesn't have to say a word. It emanates, and it erects a silent barrier between you.

You close yourself off from him or her. It is difficult to receive anything at all from such a person, especially advice or admonition.

But an exhorter accepts you as you are. Imperfect? Yes, but a fellow traveler along life's way. A pastor from Portland says that the three basic ingredients for a mature Christian are to be loving, forgiving and accepting. Exhorters are good at all three. It's easy to open up to someone like that.

14. Is well liked because of his or her positive attitude.

Never	Seldom	Sometimes	Usually	Mostly	Always
0	1	2	3	4	5
		POINTS			

There is an old song that goes, "Accentuate the positive, eliminate the negative, latch on to the affirmative, and don't mess with Mister In-Between." It must have been written by an exhorter. They are so positive!

Because of this other people like to be around them. Someone has said you draw more bees with honey than with vinegar. So the exhorter draws people to him or her just by being optimistic and positive.

One pastor from the Bible Belt says some Christians look as though they've been baptized in lemon juice. Not so exhorters. They radiate the joy of the Lord.

When we were traveling around the South Island of New Zealand with Rita and Len Restall (she was then the Aglow national president) we got to see the fruit of the ministry of a mature exhorter. For years Rita had ministered to women throughout her beautiful country. She had poured out her love and encouragement to them and helped them to develop chapters and to train leaders.

Every place we went women greeted Rita with love and honor. They adored her—it showed on their faces and was demonstrated with words and actions. We could not help but think of that marvelous passage about the virtuous woman (the Amplified version says "capable, intelligent, and virtuous") in Proverbs 31, especially verse 28: "Her children rise up and call her blessed." Rita was like a spiritual mother to many of the women. And verse 31: "Give her of the fruit of her hands, and let her own works praise her in the gates [of the city]!" Rita's fruit was made evident by the abundance of love the women had for her.

15. Prefers to witness with his or her life rather than verbal witnessing.

Never	Seldom	Sometimes	Usually	Mostly	Always
0	1	2	3	4	5
		POINTS			

While exhorters can witness verbally (and they do), they believe they must *live* the Christian life in order to be credible. "We need to walk our talk," one exhorter said candidly. To them faith must be demonstrated in practical ways in daily life. They love the book of James, especially these verses from chapter two:

But someone will say, "You have faith; I have deeds."

Show me your faith without deeds, and I will show you my faith by what I do . . .

You foolish man, do you want evidence that faith without deeds is useless? . . .You see that his [Abraham's] faith and his actions were working together, and his faith was made complete by what he did . . .

As the body without the spirit is dead, so faith without deeds is dead.

verses 18–26, NIV

Exhorters believe that it is not enough to know the *logos*—the written Word—but that it is essential to live the *rhema*—the living Word of God. The truth of the Bible must become flesh—in them, here and now. One exhorter says, "I can only teach or witness to that which I've appropriated in my *own* life. If my life is witness, then others will want what I've found—Jesus Christ."

16. Makes decisions easily.

	Never	Seldom	Sometimes	Usually	Mostly	Always
	0	1	2	3	4	5
POINTS						

Decision making comes naturally and easily to most exhorters. For them life is too short to be indecisive. They are action people. They make their decisions based on what they know at the time. *Let's decide and get on with it*, their thinking goes. If more information is needed, they figure it will come.

"If I'm wrong in a decision," Belinda says, "God will correct me. I'm confident in that. I don't mind being corrected. It's better to move ahead and get something accomplished, even if I have to make adjustments later on, than to be paralyzed by indecision."

Since exhorters are such practical people and so life-related in all that they do, we find that their decisions are usually right on target.

17. Always completes what is started.

	Never	Seldom	Sometimes	Usually	Mostly	Always
	0	1	2	3	4	5
POINTS						

Similar to the serving gift the exhorter does not like unfinished work or uncompleted projects. He finishes the letters he starts, she works overtime to complete assignments at the office or he burns the midnight oil to complete a Bible study assignment.

Barb McGriff was in an art class I was taking. She was new at painting but enthusiastic about learning. She and her husband, Mark, are *both* exhorters—something we come across very rarely. They are a delightfully positive couple, great in accomplishments.

Each week our instructor demonstrated how to paint a new subject. Most of us would not get our pictures done and would just leave them until the next week. Not Barb. She always took her unfinished painting home and usually worked on it that evening until it was completed.

"Why don't you come early next week and finish it up?" I asked her one day.

"Oh, I couldn't wait that long," she insisted. "Once I see the picture taking shape I can't wait to see it finished. Besides, I don't like to leave anything half-done."

We've also noted that exhorters need only *one* bookmark. They never read more than one book at one time.

18. Wants to clear up conflicts with others quickly.

Never	Seldom	Sometimes	Usually	Mostly	Always
0	1	2	3	4	5

POINTS

Exhorters do not like strained relationships. They go immediately to the other person to find out what's wrong. If necessary, they will even take the blame in order to build the bridge to a restored relationship.

"This characteristic shows up in my life so often," wrote Kathy from Canada. "I can't stand having anyone angry at me. So, even if I am not the one who caused the problem, I'll take the step to clear up the situation. I'll say, 'I'm sorry,' to get the air cleared. It feels so great to have relationships right again."

She went on to say, "I love to encourage others to clear up such situations as quickly as possible, too."

19. Expects a lot of self and others.

Never	Seldom	Sometimes	Usually	Mostly	Always
0	1	2	3	4	5

POINTS

Don feels that very few people, including himself, live up to their potential. "I expect a lot of myself," he says, "and I guess that keeps me motivated to accomplish more. God has equipped all of us so abundantly. Often we don't recognize this.

"If we set low goals, that's all we'll ever accomplish. If we set higher goals, we'll grow. Often I can see potential in others that they don't see themselves. I enjoy encouraging them to stretch."

Each of us has a comfort zone, an area within which we can operate without being challenged. It's easy just to stay there. The exhorter doesn't believe that's God's perfect will for us. He believes God wants us to venture out into the unknown and do things we didn't think we could.

"There's so much that needs to be done in the Kingdom of God," Don says. "The Gospel needs to be shared at home and abroad, support ministries are needed everywhere, the hurting need to be helped, the hungry need to be fed. Whenever anyone says to me, 'Well, I don't know what I could possibly do,' I say, 'Okay, let me tell you . . .'"

Don admits there was a time when he was just a pew warmer. No more! His only regret now is that there are so few hours in a day. "I want to make the hours I have count," he often tells people. "You have the same twenty-four hours that I have. You can make them count, too. (Oops, I'm sounding like an exhorter—but I'm proud to be one!)"

Never	Seldom	Sometimes	Usually	Mostly	Always
0	1	2	3	4	5
POINTS					

20. Needs a "sounding board" for bouncing off ideas and thoughts.

When Don and I were first married I discovered that one of my roles as a wife was to be his sounding board. Don would bounce ideas off me. I would listen, analyze and then give him my opinion. That's not what he wanted. He wanted me to just listen.

You see, exhorters often think with their mouths. They like to verbalize a thought aloud so they can hear how it sounds. It's as though they're trying an idea on for size—to see if it fits. They can then do their own analyzing. A sounding board is basically passive. So, I've learned there is a reason why God created me with one mouth and two ears! I've learned to *listen*.

While it's common for a married exhorter to use his or her mate for a sounding board, sometimes it is a close friend. Single exhorters rely on friends, relatives, classmates, teachers and sometimes whoever is available at the moment.

THE GIFT OF EXHORTATION

Characteristics

	Never	Seldom	Sometimes	Usually	Mostly	Always	POINTS
	0	1	2	3	4	5	
1. Loves to encourage others to live up to their full potential.					X		
2. Wants a visible response when teaching or speaking.					X		
3. Prefers to apply truth rather than research it.		X					
4. Prefers the kind of information that has practical application(s).		X					
5. Loves to prescribe precise steps of action to aid personal growth.			X				
6. Focuses on working with people.				X			
7. Encourages others to develop in their personal ministries.			X				
8. Finds truth in experience and then validates it with Scripture.		X					
9. Loves to do personal counseling.		X					
10. Will discontinue personal counseling if no effort to change is seen.				X			
11. Is fluent in communication.			X				
12. Views trials as opportunities to produce personal growth.			X				
13. Accepts people as they are without judging them.			X				
14. Is well liked because of his or her positive attitude.			X				
15. Prefers to witness with his or her life rather than verbal witnessing.			X				
16. Makes decisions easily.			X				
17. Always completes what is started.			X				
18. Wants to clear up conflicts with others quickly.			X				
19. Expects a lot of self and others.					X		
20. Needs a "sounding board" for bouncing off ideas and thoughts.	X						
						TOTAL	

Problems
of the Exhorter

Exhorters tend to have a "mouth problem." Since God has made them the mouth of the Body of Christ, they use it a lot, either for good—encouraging others—or in negative ways, as we will examine now.

Consider your scoring prayerfully to see if there are areas in which you need some growth. None of us has arrived. Even Paul, in the later years of his ministry, realized that he needed to press on to the goal of the high calling in Jesus Christ (see Philippians 3:14).

1. Tends to interrupt others in eagerness to give opinions or advice.

Never	Seldom	Sometimes	Usually	Mostly	Always
0	1	2	3	4	5
		✗			
POINTS					

Exhorters have much to say. And, normally, that is not a problem. But when there is an ongoing interchange of conversation, or any kind of structured meeting going on, the exhorter's tendency to interrupt can be a source of frustration for others.

When I was serving on a Christian board there was one member, an exhorter, who was known for her excellent ability to build up people. But in the board meetings she was also known for interrupting.

One day I had tried a number of times to say something but she had repeatedly interrupted me. My frustration level rose.

"You've interrupted me five times," I burst out at last. "Please let me finish what I'm saying."

"I haven't interrupted you," she protested.

"Yes, you have," I insisted.

"You're kidding," she said, with a look on her face that made me realize that she didn't know how often she jumped in to speak before others were finished.

"You *do* interrupt a lot," another member confirmed.

"I don't believe it," she replied. "I'll tell you what," she said to me. "Next time I interrupt anyone, poke me in the side. If I'm doing it I really want to know."

"Okay," I said, hoping her ribs could take it.

During the remaining four hours of the board meeting I poked her fifteen times.

"I'm amazed," she said, still shocked at the revelation. "I had no idea I was interrupting that much. I really want to overcome that habit."

She made excellent progress once she recognized the problem.

2. Will use Scriptures out of context in order to make a point.

Never	Seldom	Sometimes	Usually	Mostly	Always
0	1	2	3	4	5
		POINTS			

The exhorter believes it is the *point* he or she is making that is important. In his or her mind, verifying it with Scripture is secondary. Of those who hear the exhorter, many will not bother to check out the proof text. Not so the teachers and the perceivers. They'll check it out and if the Scripture has been used out of context they may reject the point, or even the one who made the point. They may even try to correct the exhorter.

Exhorters are adaptable. So, if their error is pointed out to them they'll say, "Okay, if that Scripture doesn't fit I'll find another one that does."

Exhorters usually have a good sense of humor, too. We'd like to share some of their on-purpose out-of-context antics:

An exhorter who started a Christian diet class used as her motto: "He must increase, but I must decrease" (John 3:30, KJV).

An exhorter Christian dentist tells his patients that his favorite Scripture is, "Open wide your mouth and I will fill it" (Psalm 81:10, NIV).

An exhorter mom painted the following Scripture in giant letters across one wall of a church nursery in Seattle: "We shall not all sleep, but we shall all be changed" (1 Corinthians 15:51, KJV).

3. May be "cut-and-dried" in prescribing steps of action.

Never	Seldom	Sometimes	Usually	Mostly	Always
0	1	2	3	4	5
		POINTS			

Because those with the motivational gift of exhortation are so good at giving advice they can easily fall into the trap of giving "pat" answers. They may counsel three people in a row with the same basic problem and, after prayer, prescribe the same steps of action. The people are helped. Then along comes the fourth person. Same problem. This time the exhorter doesn't bother to pray about what advice to give since the same counsel worked for the previous three cases. But this time that advice is not what was needed, and therefore is ineffective.

It is very important for the exhorter to consistently rely on the Holy Spirit—the Counselor—for wisdom and guidance in giving advice. Otherwise he or she can develop a cocky I-know-what-to-do-in-every-situation mentality.

Never	Seldom	Sometimes	Usually	Mostly	Always
0	1	2	3	4	5
POINTS					

4. Is outspokenly opinionated.

Exhorters are always glad to tell you what they think. They are not as rigidly opinionated as the perceivers or the teachers, but on matters of life application they have strong opinions. That, coupled with the well-oiled jaw, makes opinions spill out readily.

He or she can also be gossipy, bossy, overtalkative and feisty. Actually, as one exhorter put it, "My mouth often runs ahead of my mind."

The exhorter's bossiness stems from the desire to give advice. Exhorters rather enjoy telling others what to do. Someone once said, "Don't answer questions that haven't been asked and don't give advice that hasn't been asked for." The exhorter could benefit from that wisdom.

Perhaps the most effective prayer for the overtalkative exhorter would be, "Lord, put a guard over my mouth." Jesus warns that we are responsible for every idle word we speak.

Never	Seldom	Sometimes	Usually	Mostly	Always
0	1	2	3	4	5
POINTS					

5. Can become overly self-confident.

In today's world, self-confidence is a sought-after quality. But like the foolish man who built his house upon the sand, it makes a bad foundation. Our basic confidence must be in the Lord. Then, with sober appreciation for the gifts and abilities He has given to us, we can begin to build godly self-confidence.

Joleen confessed to us that she was once an overconfident exhorter. "I figured I had an answer for just about everything," she confided. "I passed out advice like some doctors pass out pills. There were no problems, just challenges.

"I was crushed when I began to see the results of some of my meddling. Sometimes my advice was completely wrong for the person, or got in the way of God's dealing with him or her. God really humbled me and helped me to build my confidence in Him."

She acknowledged that the battle wasn't over—that there was still a struggle with a know-it-all attitude. But she was grateful that she had learned to recognize it and deal with it appropriately.

If you run into any exhorters you will usually be blessed by them. But if you are still a victim of torrents of verbalization, feel free to request: "Please say that in twenty-five words or less!"

Typical problem areas
of the gift of exhortation

	Never	Seldom	Sometimes	Usually	Mostly	Always	POINTS
	0	1	2	3	4	5	
1. Tends to interrupt others in eagerness to give opinions or advice.			X				
2. Will use Scriptures out of context in order to make a point.		X					
3. May be "cut-and-dried" in prescribing steps of action.	X						
4. Is outspokenly opinionated.		X					
5. Can become overly self-confident.	X						
						TOTAL	4

Copyright © 1987 Don & Katie Fortune, P.O. Box 101, Kingston, WA 98346

Biblical Exhorters

Where would we be without exhorters? We know how much they are needed today, and it was the same in biblical days. It's one thing to become a Christian and quite another to live the Christian life. Exhorters have been gifted to encourage believers to appropriate the grace of God in their Christian walk.

Barnabas is a good illustration of the gift of exhortation. Even his name means "son of encouragement." Take a look at what the book of Acts has to say about him and we think you'll be struck by his exhorter characteristics.

Scripture: Acts 4:36; 11:22–26	Your Comments:
Acts 4	
36 Now Joseph, a Levite and native of Cyprus who was surnamed Barnabas by the apostles, which interpreted means Son of Encouragement.	
Acts 11	
22 The rumors of this came to the ears of the church (assembly) in Jerusalem, and they sent Barnabas to Antioch.	
23 When he arrived and saw what grace (favor) God was bestowing upon them, he was full of joy; and he continuously exhorted (warned, urged, and encouraged) them all to cleave unto and remain faithful to and devoted to the Lord with [resolute and steady] purpose of heart.	

Scripture: Acts 4:36; 11:22–26	Your Comments:
24 For he was a good man [good in himself and also at once for the good and the advantage of other people], full of and controlled by the Holy Spirit and full of faith (of his belief that Jesus is the Messiah, through Whom we obtain eternal salvation). And a large company was added to the Lord.	
25 [Barnabas] went on to Tarsus to hunt for Saul.	
26 And when he had found him, he brought him back to Antioch. For a whole year they assembled together with and were guests of the church and instructed a large number of people; and in Antioch the disciples were first called Christians.	

The fact that Barnabas was full of joy indicates that he was functioning in his proper sphere, for joy is the byproduct of operating in one's motivational gift.

Note also that Barnabas went after Saul. Others in the body of believers were not yet ready to trust this one who had persecuted the Church so viciously, but Barnabas could see the potential in Saul and most assuredly contributed to his becoming the mighty Paul that we encounter later.

Scripture: Acts 4:36; 11:22–26	Our Comments:
Acts 4	
36 Now Joseph, a Levite and native of Cyprus who was surnamed Barnabas by the apostles, which interpreted means Son of Encouragement.	**#1** is named encouragement
Acts 11	
22 The rumors of this came to the ears of the church (assembly) in Jerusalem, and they sent Barnabas to Antioch.	**#1** is sent to encourage
23 When he arrived and saw what grace (favor) God was bestowing upon them, he was full of joy; and he continuously exhorted (warned, urged, and encouraged) them all to cleave unto and remain faithful to and devoted to the Lord with [resolute and steady] purpose of heart.	**#1** exhorts faithfulness **#4** has practical faith **#7** encourages ministry **#9** counsels groups **#13** is nonjudgmental **#14** is positive and joyful **#19** expects a lot of others
24 For he was a good man [good in himself and also at once for the good and the advantage of other people], full of and controlled by the Holy Spirit and full of faith (of his belief that Jesus is the Messiah, through Whom we obtain eternal salvation). And a large company was added to the Lord.	**#2** gets a visible response **#6** focuses on people **#7** encourages development **#13** is accepting **#14** is loved by others **#15** has a life of witness **#17** completes what he started
25 [Barnabas] went on to Tarsus to hunt for Saul.	**#13** is accepting
26 And when he had found him, he brought him back to Antioch. For a whole year they assembled together with and were guests of the church and instructed a large number of people; and in Antioch the disciples were first called Christians.	**#1** teaches how to live **#3** helps apply truth **#4** teaches practically **#6** focuses on people **#11** communicates **#17** completes teaching job

Some of the apostles had more than one strong motivational gift. Paul was one of those. While we think his primary gift was giving (making him a mighty missionary), we also see a strong secondary gift of exhortation as well as perceiving and teaching. We see Paul giving practical advice and encouragement—often! There are too many references to list here, but as you read about Paul, or read his writings, observe his gifts in action.

Peter, being the mouthpiece for the disciples, obviously had great facility of speech. We believe Peter was also an exhorter. Consider these passages: Acts 2:14–41; 3:1–4:21.

Also read about:

Silas: Acts 15:22–40; 16:25, 29; 17:4, 10–15; 1 Peter 5:12

Titus: 2 Corinthians 2:13; 7:6, 13–14; 8:6–23; 12:18; Galatians 2:1, 3; 2 Timothy 4:10; Titus

Aaron: Exodus, Leviticus, Numbers

Characteristics of the Giver

Of all the seven motivational gifts, this is the one least likely to be identified by the one who has it. Part of the reason may be that the giver's "left hand" does not know when his "right hand" gives alms (see Matthew 6:3). Another may be the giver's "all-around" personality. The giver shares several traits of the server, can be a leader or a follower and has a love for the Word of God like the perceiver and the teacher. But when it comes to the use of resources, the giver is unique.

The Greek word is *metadidomi* (distinct from *didomi*, "to give") meaning "to give over, share or impart." It is to be done with *haplotetes*—simplicity, sincerity and liberality.

As you score this gift be sure to distinguish between learned behavior and innate tendencies. For instance, you may have been raised and trained by your parents and your church to be generous and to tithe. But has that always been your joyful *inward motivation*? You may need to reflect on your childhood in order to score accurately.

Never	Seldom	Sometimes	Usually	Mostly	Always
0	1	2	3	4	5
	✗				
POINTS					

1. Gives freely of money, possessions, time, energy and love.

Notice that givers give far more than just money. If they have money they will give generously of it, but they also give of anything else they possess. They give comprehensively. They give with abandonment. And, in the more mature stages of givers' lives, they give with absolutely no strings attached and no ulterior motives. They simply become channels for the Lord to use for the distribution of His resources, for they are convinced everything belongs to Him.

Sharon, a young homemaker whose gift of giving was yearning for a way to express itself, was well aware of the family's tight budget. It had been a joint decision that she not go to work but be free to be a full-time mother.

One day she had a bright idea. "Honey," she asked her husband, "could we afford forty-two cents a day, five days a week, for a special project?"

"Well, sure," he replied, "that's only about nine dollars a month."

Sharon was delighted. She bought the first five postage stamps and launched her project. Each day she took one name from her Christmas card list and spent time praying for the person (or couple or family), asking the Lord to bless them and guide them. Often, as she prayed, the Lord would quicken a verse of Scripture for them.

Then Sharon wrote a letter, expressing her love for the person, enclosing the Scripture in the form of a simple bookmark she made using her calligraphy skills.

What a blessing it must have been to be on her Christmas card list, to be the recipient of such a gift at a totally unexpected time of year!

We recently came across this very appropriate quotation: "The best gift cannot be bought or sold. It is giving a part of oneself."

Never	Seldom	Sometimes	Usually	Mostly	Always
0	1	2	3	4	5
		✗			
POINTS					

2. Loves to give without others knowing about it.

Jesus had a lot to say about not broadcasting our good deeds.

"Be careful not to do your 'acts of righteousness' before men, to be seen by them. . . . So when you give to the needy, do not announce it with trumpets. . . . Then your Father, who sees what is done in secret, will reward you" (Matthew 6:1, 2–4, NIV). Giving is to be secret.

Givers do not want acclaim or credit. They just want to please their heavenly Father. That joy is reward enough for them. Often they will go to great lengths to assure that others do not find out about their gifts.

While I was editor of *Aglow* magazine we received a book manuscript by Joanne Sekowsky titled *A Christian Roadmap for Women Traveling Alone*. We felt it would be an excellent resource for singles, but we did not have the one thousand dollar advance the printer required, so we put it on hold.

Penny (a fictitious name) heard about it and came by my office, shutting the door behind her. "Here's a check for one thousand dollars," she said. "That book needs to get out."

"This is wonderful! Thank you," I said gratefully.

"Just one thing," Penny insisted. "No one else is to know about this. It's between the Lord and me."

3. Wants to feel a part of the ministries to which he or she contributes.

Never	Seldom	Sometimes	Usually	Mostly	Always
0	1	2	3	4	5
POINTS					

Givers give to ministries that they believe in—ones that are effectively sharing the Gospel. Therefore they not only give monetarily, but they also get involved in other ways. They will pray for the ministry, write letters of encouragement, send "care" packages and sometimes show up in person to assist in the work.

Weldon, a pastor with a mature gift of giving, had been supporting a ministry in the Philippines. He not only wrote regularly himself, he also encouraged members of his congregation to do so. The children of the missionary were well remembered at Christmas and on birthdays.

Then the Holy Spirit began nudging Weldon about going to help personally. He did, assisting in preaching, ministering to the poor and teaching leaders for a whole month. Afterward he said, "It was the best thing that ever happened to me."

4. Intercedes for needs and the salvation of souls.

Never	Seldom	Sometimes	Usually	Mostly	Always
0	1	2	3	4	5
POINTS					

It is not unusual for givers to be awakened in the middle of the night with a "burden" for someone.

A man with this gift asked a returning missionary, "What was happening to you three weeks ago, on May 6th to be exact?"

"May 6th!" the missionary exclaimed. "Why, that was the day there was an attempted robbery of our compound. But for some reason the thief dropped everything and fled—we don't know why."

"Oh, that explains it," Graham said.

"Explains what?"

"Well, I was awakened out of a deep sleep and sensed great danger for you and the others," Graham explained. "So I prayed for you, for maybe an hour, until the burden lifted. If I'm calculating right, our night is your day, so it all fits. I'm glad the Lord awakened me."

Givers often keep lists of people who need to receive salvation. They will intercede faithfully until with joy they can check a name off the list. When you ask a group to pray for the salvation of your relative or neighbor, the givers will follow through on your request. Others may mean to, but soon forget. Not so the givers. Above all they want people to come into the Kingdom of God.

Never	Seldom	Sometimes	Usually	Mostly	Always
0	1	2	3	4	5
POINTS					

5. Feels delighted when his or her gift is an answer to specific prayer.

Since givers know that the highest and best use of their gift is when they are being led to give by the Holy Spirit, they are especially thrilled when someone says, "How did you know I needed this? It's an answer to prayer."

One time we happened to be right in the middle of such an incident. Annie had come into an inheritance and had $700 she wanted to give to someone who really needed it. She attended a meeting where a missionary couple spoke. Afterward Annie slipped into a chair beside us.

"Do you think they could use $700?" she asked. "As I listened to them I felt God was telling me to give it to them. But I don't know if they really need it."

"Oh, they do," we assured her. "In fact, we happen to know that they have been raising money to buy video equipment and are exactly $700 short of their goal."

"That's great!" Annie exclaimed, hurrying off to present the missionaries with a check. We don't know who was blessed the most, the recipients or the giver. Annie left the meeting still exclaiming, "Isn't God good!"

Never	Seldom	Sometimes	Usually	Mostly	Always
0	1	2	3	4	5
POINTS					

6. Wants gifts to be of high quality or craftsmanship.

When givers give they give the very best. They are generous, even lavish. They want their gifts to be the highest quality they can afford. If they cannot afford to buy a gift they will make one—with great thoughtfulness and skill.

JoAnn had been attending the Tuesday morning Bible study at our home. She had noticed that my Amplified Bible was falling apart. It was a hardback edition that had seen ten years of extensive use. Whenever I turned to the middle of the New Testament, Ephesians would fall out. I'd just stuff it back in place and go on. Soon Galatians began falling out, too. I put up with it because it was my favorite Bible and had all my markings and marginal notes.

One afternoon JoAnn arrived at our front door. "Here," she said, thrusting a package into my hands, "this is for you." And she walked off.

I opened it. It was a beautiful new leather-bound Amplified Bible, the most expensive and durable edition available. JoAnn had gone out and purchased the very best for me. I have used that Bible for forty years and guess what? None of the pages have ever fallen out.

7. Gives only by the leading of the Holy Spirit.

	Never	Seldom	Sometimes	Usually	Mostly	Always
	0	1	2	3	4	5
	✗					
POINTS						

You can't talk a mature giver into giving. They will resist pressure appeals. They give only as the Holy Spirit leads them.

About ten years ago we were getting ready to go overseas to teach the motivational gift seminar. We had just revised the materials and had taken them to Barb, a professional typist, so we would have a neat master copy to take with us for duplication purposes. We'd put off picking up the typing, though, because our account was down so low we couldn't pay for it.

The day before our departure we decided that I should drive over to Barb's and ask if we could take the work now and pay her when we got back. When I arrived I found Barb in pain. Her back had gone out and she was unable to find a comfortable position.

"Let me pray for you," I offered.

"Thank you," she moaned. "Maybe it will help."

I prayed for her lower back to be adjusted and for the Lord to take away all her pain.

"Hey!" she exclaimed. "It's gone! The pain is gone!" She got up and bent in all directions to be sure. "The Lord sent you at just the right time."

Then Barb handed me the bill. But across the bill had been written, "Paid in full."

"What's this?" I asked.

"Oh, that," Barb replied. "The Lord told me this morning that I needed to have a part in your ministry. It's something I can do to help."

"Barb," I said, "you don't know how much this blesses me."

As I drove home I praised the Lord all the way. "Thank You, Lord, that You spoke to one of Your givers on our behalf."

8. Gives to support and bless others or to advance a ministry.

	Never	Seldom	Sometimes	Usually	Mostly	Always
	0	1	2	3	4	5
	✗					
POINTS						

When givers select a ministry to advance with financial support they check it out thoroughly to be sure (1) it gets the Gospel out effectively, and (2) overhead and administrative expenses are not taking too much of a chunk out of the donations.

Sometimes the giver wants to be an anonymous source of blessing for those who have genuine needs.

A man in a small town in Montana is just such a giver. His business is doing well and the more he gives the more it seems to prosper. One day in church his attention was drawn to a young girl with badly protruding teeth. Her mother is a widow and their meager budget did not allow for braces.

The man went to the local orthodontist, gave him three thousand dollars and said, "Call in this girl and see that she gets her teeth straightened. If there are additional costs, let me know. But please, don't tell them, or anyone else, where the money has come from. Just tell them it's the Lord's provision."

Over the next few years this giver had the joy of seeing the girl's bright smile blossom as her teeth came into proper alignment. He was personally blessed in blessing her.

9. Views hospitality as an opportunity to give.

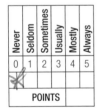

Never	Seldom	Sometimes	Usually	Mostly	Always
0	1	2	3	4	5
POINTS					

Like the server, the giver loves to practice hospitality. Outwardly this characteristic looks the same for both. But the inner viewpoint differs. The server sees hospitality as a chance to serve; the giver sees it as an expression of giving.

I stayed in the home of a giver one time when I was speaking in far northern British Columbia. Charlotte did everything she could think of to make my stay comfortable. She fixed a lovely dinner, then throughout the rest of the evening kept trying to give me something else to eat— another dessert, another cup of coffee, fruit, mints and nuts.

In addition it seemed that hardly a half hour went by that she did not bring me a gift. "Here's a lipstick I think would look good with your coloring," she told me. A cosmetics distributor, she'd looked through her supplies until she found just the right shade for a redhead.

Later she brought me a special cleansing spray for glasses. "I think you'll find this useful," she said hopefully.

Then came some perfume, a box of powder, a pen, pictures of her house and her cat. I felt a bit embarrassed accepting so many gifts but I knew she was loving the opportunity to give.

"We don't get many guests way up here," she explained. "I so seldom get to entertain."

Her stored-up desire to practice hospitality was unleashed and I was the beneficiary!

10. Handles finances with wisdom and frugality.

Never	Seldom	Sometimes	Usually	Mostly	Always
0	1	2	3	4	5
POINTS					

Givers are good at handling money. The best, as a matter of fact. They're careful, cautious, even a little tight with their own spending. They do not squander money.

One couple was in financial difficulty, getting deeper in debt as bills piled up. They went to a church elder for advice. After listening to them awhile he told the husband, "It seems to me that your wife has a natural ability with finances. Why don't you turn the responsibility over to her for six months and see if she can't solve the problem?"

"I never thought of doing that," the husband said. "I always assumed it was the husband's responsibility to handle the money. But I'm not good at it, so I'd love to give it to her."

The wife, a classic giver, immediately established a budget, began making partial payments to creditors and cut out all spending except for absolute necessities. No more restaurant lunches for her husband or school cafeteria meals for the kids. Brown bag would have to do. No more clothes purchases for anyone. She stretched the food budget by clipping coupons and by getting fruits, vegetables and bread at the church's food bank.

By the end of the six months they were almost in the black. "Honey," her grateful husband said, "I'm delegating the family finances to you *permanently*."

Givers also make great treasurers for any kind of group. They are excellent to have on financial committees, and make fastidious book-keepers and accountants.

11. Quickly volunteers to help where a need is seen.

Never	Seldom	Sometimes	Usually	Mostly	Always
0	1	2	3	4	5
POINTS					

Here's another characteristic that the giver has in common with the server. The server, however, is apt to jump in first to meet a need while the giver comes alongside to help once someone else has identified the need.

Announce a church work party some Saturday and it will be the servers and the givers who show up with greatest enthusiasm. They'll work all day and come back again if the job isn't finished.

Ask for volunteers for any worthwhile cause and guess which gifts will respond first.

If someone is sick or hospitalized, the servers and the givers will be taking in meals even before someone thinks to organize such acts of kindness.

12. Seeks confirmation on the amount to give.

Never	Seldom	Sometimes	Usually	Mostly	Always
0	1	2	3	4	5
POINTS					

Steve Lightle shared with us that he and his wife, Judy, always pray about the amount of money they give above their basic tithe to others or other ministries. "We find that at least eighty percent of the time Judy and I feel we should give exactly the same amount," Steve said. "It's so good to have such confirmation."

Steve gave a specific example:

Recently while I was spending time in prayer the Lord kept bringing to my mind a special friend of ours in Israel who has a very vital ministry. After praying for him awhile, the Lord laid it on my heart to give him a specific amount of money. What was unusual was that the amount was not in round numbers like fifty, one hundred or two hundred. It was specifically two hundred and forty dollars.

I told Judy that the Lord was saying to send our friend some money and asked her to pray about it and see what amount it should be. A bit later Judy called to me, "Steve, I believe the Lord wants us to send two hundred and forty dollars."

"Thank You, Lord," I said, "that's confirmation!" And I quickly got the check off to our dear friend in Israel.

We received a letter back. He was overjoyed. Our gift was a specific answer to prayer. He had been in need of an essential piece of equipment costing four hundred dollars. He'd been given two hundred dollars toward it and been praying for the other two hundred and forty dollars so that he could pay a tithe on the four hundred dollars. Our gift had been *exactly* what he had needed. "Nobody knew about my need," he said, "except God."

Never	Seldom	Sometimes	Usually	Mostly	Always
0	1	2	3	4	5
POINTS					

13. Has strong belief in tithing and in giving in addition to tithing.

The person with the motivational gift of giving would never think of withholding part of his or her tithe. That would be robbing God. Givers believe that everything they have—money, home, car and all the other possessions—belongs to the Lord. They see themselves as stewards of God's resources. The tithe is only the foundational aspect of their giving. Givers give beyond that, often up to 20 or 30 percent of their income or more.

In a book about one famous giver, inventor-manufacturer Robert Gilmour LeTourneau, the biographer writes, "In the matter of giving R. G. LeTourneau considers himself merely a steward of the money God has placed at his disposal. His oft-repeated statement is that he gives away 90 percent of his earnings to the Lord's work."[9] At the time the biography was written, 28 years before LeTourneau died, he had already donated twelve million dollars to missions and other Christian work.

Never	Seldom	Sometimes	Usually	Mostly	Always
0	1	2	3	4	5
POINTS					

14. Focuses on sharing the Gospel.

Givers are naturally evangelistic. We've found that even as children (providing they knew the Lord themselves) givers attempted to lead other children to Jesus.

Jerry Raaf, a Canadian Armed Forces chaplain, recalled how strong his desire to share the Gospel had been all his life. Even as a five-year-old he would try to tell his little friends about Jesus. They didn't always want to hear and would run home. But that did not discourage Jerry.

One day his parents searched for him and finally found him out in the chicken yard. He had locked the gate so the chickens couldn't get away and was preaching his heart out to his captive audience.

Giver-evangelist Rod McDougal held 57 "miracle crusades" throughout the Philippines over a period of seven years. (We've known Rod and his wife, Trena, since they were leaders in the Jesus People movement in

Seattle in the '60s.) After we participated in one of his citywide crusades in Iriga City and saw with our own eyes between seven hundred and two thousand people come to the Lord each evening, we said to Rod, "Why don't you report this in your newsletter? You only speak of a few hundred being reached."

"Those who have not been here cannot believe it," Rod explained. "Some are skeptical even of the numbers we do use; they think we must be exaggerating. It's hard to believe it ourselves. But the harvest fields are white here. It's a joy to help with a harvest that's so plentiful."

15. Believes God is the source of his or her supply.

Never	Seldom	Sometimes	Usually	Mostly	Always
0	1	2	3	4	5
POINTS					

Since, from the giver's viewpoint, everything belongs to God, the Christian's job is simply to distribute money and resources wherever He directs. Therefore, if the supply runs out (he or she reasons), it is God's responsibility to replenish that supply. Meanwhile, the giver is content to get by with whatever he or she has or, as the case may be, has not. Like Paul, the giver knows how to be abased or to abound.

Givers love the Scripture: "But my God shall supply all your need according to his riches in glory by Christ Jesus" (Philippians 4:19, KJV). They have every confidence that if they are being obedient to God's direction in their life, He will indeed take care of their needs.

There is a seeming paradox. On the one hand givers seem most capable of all the gifts of earning a good living, while at the same time they are the ones most likely to be led to "live by faith."

Perhaps the most outstanding example of such faith that we know of is George Mueller, who lived in England more than a hundred years ago. Starting with one children's home, Mueller never asked anyone but God to supply his financial needs, knowing without a doubt that He was the source of supply for the work he was called to do. God met those needs by prompting people from many walks of life to bring or send resources. Eventually five children's homes were built at Ashley Down, caring for 2,050 orphans at a time.

Today the work continues in Mueller's tradition and still conducts no financial campaigns, but trusts God for its support.

16. Is very industrious with a tendency toward success.

Never	Seldom	Sometimes	Usually	Mostly	Always
0	1	2	3	4	5
POINTS					

Whatever givers touch seems to turn to gold. The endeavors they get involved in habitually succeed. True, givers are hard-working, but it's more than that. We believe that God prospers givers so that they can (and they usually do) give even more to the work of the Gospel.

When a giver named Patricia Stamets moved to Seattle, she was a single mother trying to get her kids through college. The economic cycle in Seattle was low but she was thrilled to get a job selling real estate, and was grateful when her mother loaned her enough money to buy a car—a necessity for the job.

One day during the first week Patricia was praising the Lord for His provision of the car when she heard Him ask, *Are you* really *thankful?*

"Oh, yes, Lord," she replied. "I am truly thankful."

Then I want you to show it.

"But how, Lord?"

Then the Lord told her He wanted her to have "The Lord is my shepherd . . ." painted on the side panels and the tailgate of her station wagon in four-inch-high old English letters.

"Okay, Lord, I'll do it," she said.

It wasn't long before word got to the president of the real estate firm and Patricia was called into his office. He told her in no uncertain terms to get that "religious stuff" off her car or she'd lose her job.

The next day, Scriptures still in place, she went to a home to take a listing. And when the client was walking back to the car with Patricia she saw the words. "You know the Lord!" the woman exclaimed. She asked Patricia to come back into the house to pray with her for a desperate situation she was facing. At 10:30 that evening Patricia got a phone call from the woman saying that the crisis had been defused, and in just two days the house sold.

"While I never took the initiative to share my faith," Patricia told us, "day after day people responded to the Scripture, enabling me to pray and minister to their needs. My sales soared and within a couple of months I was a top performer in the industry. The Lord blessed me both financially and in opportunities to be a channel for His purposes. There are no economic down-cycles in God's economy."

She added that the president of the company, impressed with her success, never mentioned the Scripture on her automobile again. Patricia has had three more cars with "The Lord is my shepherd . . ." painted on each of them.

17. Has natural and effective business ability.

Never	Seldom	Sometimes	Usually	Mostly	Always
0	1	2	3	4	5
POINTS					

Givers are good at making money. Even as children they are drawn into "business." They are the ones likely to open up a corner lemonade stand, or go door-to-door distributing homemade "business cards" offering babysitting or lawn mowing or car washes.

Givers also learn to save money at an early age. My nephew Rex, along with his brother and two sisters, lived with my family for a while. Whenever we gave the children spending money, three of them would take off immediately for the grocery store. Not Rex. He would put his in his bank to save until he had enough to buy something he really wanted, rather than spend it on candy.

When the kids were given nuts or candy, Rex would only eat a little piece and then stash the rest away to eat later. Sometimes when I was cleaning house I would find his treasures hidden behind the cups in the china closet or under a sofa cushion. I kept his hiding places secret.

Today Rex continues to exhibit the characteristics of a giver. He works hard in his business, carefully invests his money, is building his own house and takes his wife on an exciting two-week vacation each year.

More than any other gift, the giver is the one most likely to start up his or her own business. These usually develop, grow well and become financially successful.

18. Likes to get the best value for the money spent.

Never	Seldom	Sometimes	Usually	Mostly	Always
0	1	2	3	4	5
POINTS					

Givers don't like to waste money. When they give, they give the best. But when it comes to spending money on themselves, they're frugal. They shop for bargains and sales. One giver said, "I never buy a garment for myself at full retail price. I check the sale racks or wait for post-season markdowns."

Mary Jane is a giver who has always clipped grocery coupons but was delighted to find a few years ago that her local supermarket would accept newspaper ad coupons from other stores.

"I save at least twenty dollars a week this way," Mary Jane revealed. "What with the manufacturer's coupons that I pair up with another store's double-coupon offer, and the freebies and store coupons I clip from the newspaper, I sometimes get about seventy-five dollar's worth of groceries for twenty-five dollars.

"I haven't paid for my weekly dozen eggs for two years, since one store started making them their free incentive item. The other day I got a whole chicken and a sixty-four-ounce apple juice free as well. This kind of couponing only takes about thirty extra minutes of my time each week, and it releases about a thousand dollars a year for the Lord's work."

19. Is definitely not gullible.

Never	Seldom	Sometimes	Usually	Mostly	Always
0	1	2	3	4	5
POINTS					

We think God has supplied givers with this characteristic to protect them from those who would wrongly dissociate them from their money. They are not easily fooled. You can't pull the wool over their eyes.

This clear-eyed quality shows up in other areas besides finances. Lucy, a mature giver who owned a nursing home, demonstrated it every day in her relationships to the elderly people in her care.

A white-haired man wheeled up to her in his chair while I was there and said: "Please tell the nurse at the desk that it's okay for me to go to my daughter's this weekend."

"Now, Mr. Jones," Lucy said, "you know your daughter only has you one weekend a month. You went last weekend."

Next a lady hobbled up complaining that her roommate was stealing her clothes. "No, Mrs. Smith," Lucy assured her, "she couldn't possibly do that. She can't even get out of her bed. You look again. Your clothes are all there, dear."

As we continued down the hall, a half-dozen others reported crises and Lucy quietly defused each one. Some were so convincing that we would have hurried to their rescue. But Lucy explained, "In this work you have to be able to discern the real from the imagined, and the genuine from the attempted manipulation. Many live in the past or in a fantasy world. I'm grateful that God has gifted me with the ability not to be gullible."

20. Possesses both natural and God-given wisdom.

Never	Seldom	Sometimes	Usually	Mostly	Always
0	1	2	3	4	5
POINTS					

Givers are fair and objective. They are often wise beyond their years.

We cannot help but think of King Solomon, a biblical giver who prayed for wisdom and received much. In 1 Kings 3:16–28 we read that two women both claimed to be the mother of a surviving baby. After hearing their claims Solomon asked for a sword and gave the order to cut the living child in two and give half to one and half to the other.

What an awful-sounding command! But it was wisdom indeed, for the true mother cried out to spare the child, while the mother of the dead child agreed: "Neither I nor you shall have him. Cut him in two!" (verse 26, NIV).

Solomon's command had elicited from the women the responses that enabled him to determine the facts. Note the concluding verse: "When all Israel heard the verdict the king had given, they held the king in awe, because they saw that he had wisdom from God" (verse 28, NIV).

THE GIFT OF GIVING

Characteristics

Characteristics	Never 0	Seldom 1	Sometimes 2	Usually 3	Mostly 4	Always 5	POINTS
1. Gives freely of money, possession, time, energy and love.		X					
2. Loves to give without others knowing about it.			X				
3. Wants to feel a part of the ministries to which he or she contributes.		X					
4. Intercedes for needs and the salvation of souls.				X			
5. Feels delighted when his or her gift is an answer to specific prayer.		X					
6. Wants gifts to be of high quality or craftsmanship.			X				
7. Gives only by the leading of the Holy Spirit.		X					
8. Gives to support and bless others or to advance a ministry.		X					
9. Views hospitality as an opportunity to give.	X						
10. Handles finances with wisdom and frugality.	X						
11. Quickly volunteers to help where a need is seen.		X					
12. Seeks confirmation on the amount to give.	X						
13. Has strong belief in tithing and in giving in addition to tithing.			X				
14. Focuses on sharing the Gospel.			X				
15. Believes God is the Source of his or her supply.						X	
16. Is very industrious with a tendency toward success.		X					
17. Has natural and effective business ability.	X						
18. Likes to get the best value for the money spent.				X			
19. Is definitely not gullible.		X					
20. Possesses both natural and God-given wisdom.		X					
TOTAL							28

Problems of the Giver

Quite frankly, we find that givers do not have significant problem areas as frequently as the other motivational gifts, but we do list below the five that occur occasionally. It seems that givers wrestle mainly with the types of problems that all of us have, such as being prideful or lukewarm in their faith.

Score yourself, asking the Holy Spirit to guide you.

1. May try to control how contributions are used.

Never	Seldom	Sometimes	Usually	Mostly	Always
0	1	2	3	4	5
	POINTS				

While givers are generous, they can also give with strings attached. A classic example is the person who donates money for new church carpeting but wants to select the color personally. Or the person who gives to the organ fund but wants to head up the committee that selects it.

We ran into this type of problem in another country, where one of the elders of a small church had donated a building for people to meet in and then insisted on having the final say on what happened there because "after all, I paid for the building." The pastor had to confront him on the matter and ask him to decide whether he actually gave the building to the church or was just letting the church use it, in which case they ought to be paying rent.

Just as parents need to cut the apron strings when their children are grown, so givers need to learn to cut any unseen strings that can remain attached to their gifts.

2. Tends to pressure others to give.

Never	Seldom	Sometimes	Usually	Mostly	Always
0	1	2	3	4	5
	✗				
POINTS					

As do recipients of each of the other gifts, givers see theirs as of primary importance. They don't understand why others don't give as much as they do. And so, consciously or unconsciously, they can be a source of pressure.

Janet had been a generous giver all her life. It was no problem until she got married. Up until then she had earned her own money and given to any cause she liked. Her husband was definitely not motivated in the same way. In fact, he was super-conservative about money. He agreed to tithe, but felt anything over and above that was overdoing it.

Janet found herself pressuring him to give each time a missionary came to the church, each time there was a special project to be funded and each time she heard of anyone in the church who had a genuine need.

"I didn't realize how much strain I was putting on our marriage," she admitted. "At first my husband didn't say much. Then he began to take a defensive stance about money in general. He started snapping at me over all kinds of things. He seemed to resent any suggestion from me, even about nonmonetary matters."

It took awhile for Janet to realize it had been her pushiness about giving that was at the root of the matter. "I asked the Lord to forgive me for pressuring my husband unwisely," Janet testified. "Then I asked my husband's forgiveness. I told him, 'Honey, you know how I love to give, but without you as a balance I might give away everything we have.'

"The most wonderful thing happened. He suggested that whenever either one of us was aware of a need we both pray about it—together— and find out what the Lord wanted. It's added a whole new dimension to our marriage."

3. May upset family and friends with unpredictable giving.

Never	Seldom	Sometimes	Usually	Mostly	Always
0	1	2	3	4	5
	✗				
POINTS					

Since givers depend on the leading of the Holy Spirit, an observer may see neither rhyme nor reason for their pattern of giving. In fact, the seemingly capriciousness can be a source of irritation to loved ones.

Blanche is a joyful giver who has her own source of income from a small home business. One day her daughter Trudy called from Hawaii. "Mom, I'm so depressed. Mark has broken off our engagement. I know it's for the best, but . . . could you come over for a week? I need some cheering up."

"Trudy, there's nothing I'd love more. But my work has piled up and I must meet the deadlines." Blanche felt bad as she hung up the phone.

Three hours later another call came, this time from a close family friend who'd moved to another state. "Blanche, I just had to talk with you. I'm feeling so blue."

"What's the matter, Alice?"

"Well, I know it sounds silly but I'm feeling so useless, so unneeded. I guess I've got the empty nest syndrome."

The Holy Spirit's timing was crystal clear to Blanche! "Alice," she said, "how would you like a week in Hawaii?"

"Who wouldn't?" Alice replied, "but our finances are tight."

"No, I mean I'll pay your way." Blanche went on to outline Trudy's need and her own prior commitment.

"Trudy loves you so much and it would be such a blessing to me if you could take my place."

Blanche wired the money to Alice, who left the next day for Hawaii and did a wonderful job of being a substitute mom for Trudy. All three were blessed. Not so Blanche's husband, who couldn't understand why, if there was money for a trip to Hawaii, he wasn't the one to go.

"At first I was upset with my husband's reaction," Blanche acknowledged. "Then I realized that he did not understand how a girl needs another woman's shoulder to cry on at such a time as this. I could see I needed to share my reasoning with him. And I asked him to forgive me for my unthinking independence."

	Never	Seldom	Sometimes	Usually	Mostly	Always
	0	1	2	3	4	5
POINTS						

4. Tends to spoil own children or other relatives.

Givers love to give so much that they can spoil their children, nieces, nephews or grandchildren.

Georgia admitted that she used to go overboard with gifts for her children on their birthdays and at Christmas.

I so overloaded my kids with presents that they didn't know what to play with first. Worse, they began to *expect* a heap of packages. I saw an attitude of the-world-owes-me-a-lot developing. So my husband and I came up with a plan.

We sat down with the children and explained to them that Christmas was Jesus' birthday and that we could give gifts to Him by giving to those in need instead of each other. We were amazed how the children took to the idea. We "adopted" several needy families, got the names and ages of the children and took our kids shopping with us to help us pick out the presents. The joy on their faces told us we were doing the right thing.

Christmas morning we sang "happy birthday" to Jesus and then gathered up all the presents to deliver to the various families. What a delightful time we all had. We had invited two one-parent families from our church for Christmas dinner; afterward the kids from the three families played games while the adults talked.

When we tucked our oldest daughter into bed she said, "This is the neatest Christmas we've ever had."

5. May use financial giving to get out of other responsibilities.

Never	Seldom	Sometimes	Usually	Mostly	Always
0	1	2	3	4	5

POINTS

Sometimes givers figure that if they provide the money they've done their part.

Jim loved to give, but he also loved to make money. He enjoyed his job and often worked overtime. When his church—which had met for years in an old school—announced plans to build, he contributed a very generous amount to the building fund. But when it came time to put up the structure with mostly volunteer labor, Jim was "too busy" to help.

He rationalized that he'd work overtime at his job on Saturdays during the project so he could make an additional contribution. But it wasn't long before the Holy Spirit brought him under conviction and he admitted to himself that it was simply that he preferred working at his office to physical labor. He repented.

When he showed up the next Saturday at the building site he found it was great fun working with the other men. He decided getting personally involved was an important part of giving, too.

Typical problem areas of the gift of giving

	Never	Seldom	Sometimes	Usually	Mostly	Always	POINTS
	0	1	2	3	4	5	
1. May try to control how contributions are used.	X						
2. Tends to pressure others to give.		X					
3. May upset family and friends with unpredictable giving.		X					
4. Tends to spoil own children or other relatives.			X				
5. May use financial giving to get out of other responsibilities.		X					
						TOTAL	5

Biblical Givers

Givers are noted for their generosity, their ability to multiply assets and their success in business. Abraham, the biblical example that we have selected for study in this chapter, is a prime example of all these qualities.

Givers also have a close walk with God and a great desire to share the Gospel with others. In Old Testament days the Gospel had not yet been given, but Abraham was the champion propagator of monotheism. The closeness of his walk with God enabled him to leave the security of his homeland and follow Him into the Promised Land.

Look for the giver's characteristics in the verses that follow:

Scripture: Genesis 13:2, 9; 14:14, 16, 19–20, 22–23	Your Comments:
Genesis 13	
2 Now Abram was extremely rich in livestock and in silver and in gold.	
9 Is not the whole land before you? Separate yourself, I beg of you, from me. If you take the left hand, then I will go to the right; or if you choose the right hand, then I will go to the left.	
Genesis 14	
14 When Abram heard that [his nephew] had been captured, he armed (led forth) the 318 trained servants born in his own house and pursued the enemy as far as Dan.	
16 And he brought back all the goods and also brought back his kinsman Lot and his possessions, the women also and the people.	

Scripture: Genesis 13:2, 9; 14:14, 16, 19–20, 22–23	Your Comments:
19 And he [Melchizedek] blessed him and said, Blessed (favored with blessings, made blissful, joyful) be Abram by God Most High, Possessor and Maker of heaven and earth.	
20 And blessed, praised, and glorified be God Most High, Who has given your foes into your hand! And [Abram] gave him a tenth of all [he had taken].	
22 But Abram said to the king of Sodom, I have lifted up my hand and sworn to the Lord, God Most High, the Possessor and Maker of heaven and earth,	
23 That I would not take a thread or a shoelace or anything that is yours, lest you should say, I have made Abram rich.	

The giver's heart comes through in Abraham's life again and again. Here's what we saw in these passages:

Scripture: Genesis 13:2, 9; 14:14, 16, 19–20, 22–23	Our Comments:
Genesis 13	
2 Now Abram was extremely rich in livestock and in silver and in gold.	**#1** has possessions to share **#10** is wise in finances **#16** is successful in business
9 Is not the whole land before you? Separate yourself, I beg of you, from me. If you take the left hand, then I will go to the right; or if you choose the right hand, then I will go to the left.	**#1** gives Lot choice of land **#8** blesses those around him **#15** has faith in God's supply **#20** has wisdom
Genesis 14	
14 When Abram heard that [his nephew] had been captured, he armed (led forth) the 318 trained servants born in his own house and pursued the enemy as far as Dan.	**#1** gives energy and time **#11** helps Lot
16 And he brought back all the goods and also brought back his kinsman Lot and his possessions, the women also and the people.	**#1** gives back possessions **#11** helps Lot **#16** succeeds in undertaking
19 And he [Melchizedek] blessed him and said, Blessed (favored with blessings, made blissful, joyful) be Abram by God Most High, Possessor and Maker of heaven and earth.	**#1** prospers **#8** is blessed for blessing others
20 And blessed, praised, and glorified be God Most High, Who has given your foes into your hand! And [Abram] gave him a tenth of all [he had taken].	**#7** gives by God's leading **#13** gives the first tithe **#16** is successful
22 But Abram said to the king of Sodom, I have lifted up my hand and sworn to the Lord, God Most High, the Possessor and Maker of heaven and earth,	**#14** is focused on God
23 That I would not take a thread or a shoelace or anything that is yours, lest you should say, I have made Abram rich.	**#15** knows God is his Source **#20** is wise in decisions

God could trust Abraham with great riches because Abraham was generous and never let possessions become idolatrous. Here we see Abraham giving the choice of land to his nephew. Then he gives his time, energy and personal resources to rescue Lot. After the battle was won he gave a tithe of all the spoils to Melchizedek, thus becoming the first recorded tither.

But the greatest giving of all is recorded in Genesis 22, in the story of how Abraham unquestioningly obeyed God when He asked him to give his only son, Isaac—the son through whom all the promises were to be fulfilled—as a burnt offering. God restrained Abraham from killing Isaac at the last moment saying, "Now I know that you fear and revere God, since you have not held back from Me or begrudged giving Me your son, your only son" (Genesis 22:12).

Read for yourself the whole story of this remarkable giver in Genesis 12 through 25:8. Also read about:

Dorcas: Acts 9:36–42

Cornelius: Acts 10:1–31

Epaphras: Colossians 1:7; 4:12; Philemon 23

Paul: Romans 1:1–20; Acts 9–28 (Note: Paul was also strongly gifted as a perceiver, teacher and exhorter. But his main role was to proclaim the Gospel to all the world.)

Lydia: Acts 16:14–15, 40

Zacchaeus: Luke 19:1–10

Solomon: 1 Kings 1–11; 2 Chronicles 1–9

Characteristics of the Administrator

The administrator is a born leader. He or she will emerge into leadership just as surely as Joseph, our biblical example, did.

We could have used other words for this gift: facilitator, organizer, ruler, leader or superintendent. According to *Strong's Concordance*, in the Greek the word is *proistemi*, from the verb "to stand before" or "to preside."

Score yourself as you go and transfer the total to your profile sheet.

1. Is highly motivated to organize that for which he or she is responsible.

Never	Seldom	Sometimes	Usually	Mostly	Always
0	1	2	3	4	5
		POINTS			

Administrators love a challenge. Don tells me that's why I love him so much, because he's a challenge. (There are times when I can say "amen" to that!)

They also love to "dig in" and develop or organize anything they're in charge of. The natural motivation is there—a creative desire to take "raw materials" and people and produce something that has never been—like organizing an office, setting up a committee or developing a project.

Although I've always been an organizer, from organizing neighborhood playmates to being responsible for nine hundred young people as director of Christian education in a large Methodist church, my favorite project has been developing *Aglow* magazine.

The original challenge was to get the testimonies of Christian women out to those who could not come to our meetings. But as the women passed along the little magazine to friends and relatives, and subscriptions started pouring in, we found that we had an unintended national publication on our hands.

The Lord kept adding competent personnel to our volunteer staff as we increased our vision and enlarged our operation. Every day was exciting. And we saw the magazine develop from 12 black-and-white pages into 32 pages of full color. After seven years, 100,000 copies were going out to 65 nations.

An organizer-leader is by job requirement a "jack of all trades but master of none." He or she must have a wide range of interests and abilities, but those who carry out specific tasks will be more capable and specialized. In order to supervise effectively, he or she needs to know a little bit about a lot of things. I often praised the Lord for those with expertise in their fields. *Together* we made a team.

Never	Seldom	Sometimes	Usually	Mostly	Always
0	1	2	3	4	5
		✓			
POINTS					

2. Expresses ideas and organization in ways that communicate clearly.

Administrators are excellent communicators. They look for ways to express what they want to say clearly and effectively. Believing that a picture is truly worth a thousand words, they like to use charts, diagrams, outlines, graphs and other visual aids.

Guess why you have a profile sheet and a scoring system in this book? Since administrating is my primary motivational gift, the first thing I thought of when I learned about the gifts was, *Why hasn't someone organized them into a systematic assessment so that people can test themselves?* What a joy it has been to see people all over the world use these testing sheets to discover their God-given gifts.

When I was editor of Aglow Publications, I also loved doing flow charts so we could see what happened to an order from the time it arrived to the time the materials were shipped out. In addition I kept an up-to-date progress and sales chart on the back of my office door. At one glance I could see how we were doing financially.

Diagramming came so naturally to me that when Don and I were newlyweds and had our first disagreement I got out a piece of paper, drew a diagram of our differences and outlined a solution. It was not exactly what he wanted to see. I thought it would clear up the whole matter—but I had to learn there was a time and place for such things.

Never	Seldom	Sometimes	Usually	Mostly	Always
0	1	2	3	4	5
		✗			
POINTS					

3. Respects and handles authority well.

Administrators understand, honor and respect authority structures. They feel comfortable with them, whether they are at the top or somewhere within the system.

The centurion who came to Jesus to ask Him to heal his servant probably had the motivational gift of administration. When Jesus offered to go to the sick man's bedside the centurion replied, "Lord, I do not deserve to have you come under my roof. But just say the word, and my servant will be healed. For I myself am a man under authority, with soldiers under me. I tell this one, 'Go,' and he goes; and that one, 'Come,' and he comes. I say to my servant, 'Do this,' and he does it" (Matthew 8:8–9, NIV).

Jesus commended the centurion's confidence in His authority, and the servant was healed.

Administrators want to know how much authority they have and what authority they do not have, for they respect those limits. They like to have exact parameters defined, so they will not inadvertently step outside of them, and they like the freedom, within those parameters, to "be their own boss." They are creative and productive given this situation, stifled and inhibited without it.

4. Will not assume leadership unless it's delegated by those in authority.

Never	Seldom	Sometimes	Usually	Mostly	Always
0	1	2	3	4	5
			X		
POINTS					

Because of his or her keen respect for authority, the administrator will never deliberately usurp it. Therefore, in any situation where authority exists, the administrator will not try to move in to utilize his or her skills—no matter how needed—unless those in authority ask him or her to do so.

Some years ago I was the speaker at a women's retreat in Kansas City. On the last evening a women's quartet sang after my concluding message, then invited people to come up for individual ministry. About fifty women responded. I thought, *This is going to take hours. I'd love to go over and help them.* But I had not been told specifically by the leaders to assist in this prayer time. They had not said that I couldn't, either, but because I always submit my ministry to the leaders of the inviting group I felt I could not go beyond what had already been established.

"Glued" to my chair, I felt torn. I wanted to help but I "couldn't." Later I described my dilemma to the leaders.

"Oh, we simply assumed that you would help with the ministry time," they said in surprise. "We never thought to mention it."

But since they hadn't, I felt I couldn't participate.

There are lots of administrators who are not utilizing their abilities because of this characteristic. We encourage those in leadership positions to search out these facilitators and delegate areas of responsibility to them.

5. Will assume leadership where no specific leadership exists.

Never	Seldom	Sometimes	Usually	Mostly	Always
0	1	2	3	4	5
			X		
POINTS					

In situations where there is no existing leadership or authority structure, it is the administrators who will most naturally step in and take charge. Divide a large group into subgroups and give each a task to do, and it will be those with the motivational gift of administration who emerge as the spontaneous leaders of the individual units. True, they would prefer to be appointed ahead of time to take the lead, but when a group is floundering with no designated leadership, they will take the reins.

Dan, a young man with a degree in business administration, says, "I can't stand lack of leadership in an organization. If no one else will, I usually end up taking control to bring order out of the chaos."

In the early days of Aglow there was no one in leadership in the loosely knit fellowship. So I took the initiative in starting the magazine. But eight years later when the Lord showed me that I was to develop the Aglow television ministry, the organization had a well-established superstructure with a president and six vice presidents (of which I was one). So I waited, without saying anything, until the time came that the whole board recognized it was time to start such a ministry and appointed me to do it.

Never	Seldom	Sometimes	Usually	Mostly	Always
0	1	2	3	4	5
	✗				
POINTS					

6. Especially enjoys working on long-range goals and projects.

While the server enjoys short-term goals—two days or two weeks—the administrator thrives on two-year projects. "In fact," one administrator said confidently, "I really prefer a project that can take several years. I like something I can throw myself into, make long-range plans and establish shorter-range goals along the way."

When you ask a person with the gift of compassion to set a goal he or she says, "Whatever for?" He or she lives one day at a time—or more precisely, one moment at a time. It's the administrators who attend time-management seminars. They want to increase their skills in handling projects of significant size.

Dorothy, a writer from the Pacific Northwest, told us she did not fully realize how much she enjoyed long-range challenges until she was nearly forty years old. "At that time," she explained, "I began to mix with other writers and found myself in charge of a writing group. My job was to encourage new or faltering writers and now it's almost become an obsession. I help them set personal long-range writing goals and keep after them to stick to a program that will enable them to reach these goals, even if it means neglecting my own writing."

Never	Seldom	Sometimes	Usually	Mostly	Always
0	1	2	3	4	5
	✗				
POINTS					

7. Is a visionary person with a broad perspective.

Proverbs 29:18 tells us, "Where there is no vision . . . the people perish." Vision is needed to keep people in focus, whether in business or faith. A good leader is a person of vision, and in upholding that vision for others to see he or she can inspire great accomplishment.

That vision can be anything from a revelation of God as to His particular purposes for a particular group to the simple ability to visualize how people can work together to accomplish a common goal.

Nehemiah had a vision for the rebuilding of the walls of Jerusalem. Joshua held on to the vision of the Promised Land. Joseph had a dream-vision showing how to spare the Middle East from seven years of devastating famine. David had a vision for his role as king but waited for the appointed time. Gideon had a vision of victory. The Bible is full of visionary leaders.

Along with vision comes a specific type of faith. Administrators believe that they can accomplish—with the help of others—what they are able to visualize.

Administrators often have vision beyond the scope of the people they lead, but those who follow are spurred on and kept on course by the vision of the leader. Without this, the people would fail to achieve their potential.

8. Easily facilitates resources and people to accomplish tasks or goals.

Never	Seldom	Sometimes	Usually	Mostly	Always
0	1	2	3	4	5
			POINTS		

Like one who loves to put pieces of a puzzle together, the administrator loves to fit people and resources together to facilitate a task.

Paul is a systems analyst for the Boeing Company. "I have to be an organizer, educator and motivator of various people if I am to accomplish the goals I've been assigned," Paul explains. "I enjoy using organizational ability, logic and persuasion as my basic tools for working with people to get the job done."

In contrast, Julia uses her administrator gift in her home. "First thing in the morning I always make out a list of things to be done during the day," she confides. "Then I think through the jobs, who will do them and when. I schedule tasks for the kids. I get the resources ready—the broom and mop, the garden tools or the bathtub cleaner. I even 'organize' my husband. He's not always so happy about it but he knows if he does his part all the work will get done on schedule."

9. Enjoys delegating tasks and supervising people.

Never	Seldom	Sometimes	Usually	Mostly	Always
0	1	2	3	4	5
			POINTS		

Administrators love to tell people what to do. We mean that in a positive sense. They easily see what jobs need to be done and they seem to know who can do them well. They enjoy distributing work in such a way that it will bring about maximum satisfaction and accomplishment.

Marvin was asked to take over the leadership of a large Christian organization that was bogged down with ineffective workers. Marvin's motivational gift of administration enabled him to trim the staff and place capable people in key positions. Then he delegated lots of responsibility, taught leadership principles to key staffers and trained them to supervise effectively. The organization was turned around from financial failure to an effective ministry.

Our son David also has this gift. We used to chuckle when he'd come home from college on weekends and walk in the door with a string of delegations: "Dad, would you look at the car, it's running kinda funny. Mom, will you do this load of laundry for me, I didn't have time to do it myself this week. Dan, would you mow the lawn for me—I've got to study for a massive exam!" In a moment of time he had us all working on his delegated tasks while he pursued his most important goal. Today David is a top executive in an international company, handling the assimilation of smaller companies and delegating lots of tasks and responsibilities.

Never	Seldom	Sometimes	Usually	Mostly	Always
0	1	2	3	4	5
POINTS					

10. Will endure criticism in order to accomplish the ultimate task.

Leaders get criticized! It seems to be part of the "occupational hazard" of administration. There are always those who feel the leader should do things differently, or slower, or faster, or more carefully, or more daringly or whatever. Administrators will not allow such criticism to sidetrack or stop them. They keep their eyes on the goal.

A variation on Abraham Lincoln's famous statement might be, "You can please all of the people some of the time, and some of the people all of the time; but you can't please all of the people all of the time." However, this will not deter an administrator from his course.

One pastor said, "The problem working with a church is that you have people. When you have people you have problems."

Someone else once answered an outspoken critic of churches: "There are no perfect churches. And if you should find one and join it, it would not be perfect anymore!"

If you know any administrators, pray for them. They are being bombarded with more than their share of criticism.

Never	Seldom	Sometimes	Usually	Mostly	Always
0	1	2	3	4	5
POINTS					

11. Has great zeal and enthusiasm for whatever he or she is involved in.

Enthusiasm emanates naturally from the administrator. The Amplified Bible says that administrators are to do their job with "zeal and singleness of mind." The Greek word is *spoude*, which in the King James is translated "diligence" and by Wuest as "intense eagerness and effort." From *Strong's Concordance* we learn that the word also encompasses the ideas of speed, dispatch, earnestness, haste, intense effort and determination.

It is as if God has given the administrator the ability to throw all of his or her efforts into a situation in order to see it to a conclusion.

Dennis, carrying several types of heavy administrative responsibilities, testifies, "I absolutely love what I am doing. I can hardly wait to get to work each day. I love the demands and challenges of my job. I enjoy seeing how quickly I can accomplish what I need to do and then move on to the next area with just as much zeal and enthusiasm."

Although the administrator's zeal is pure and altruistic, it is so strong that others are often threatened or overwhelmed by it.

"I was responsible for a volunteer organization," Hazel says. "I was really sold on its purposes and threw myself wholeheartedly into the work. But some of the membership seemed suspicious of my enthusiasm and began to resist every idea I presented. I finally set up a teaching session on the motivational gifts so they could learn what to expect from each other's giftedness. It helped. They began to accept my zeal and we worked together much better."

12. Finds greatest fulfillment and joy in working to accomplish goals.

Never	Seldom	Sometimes	Usually	Mostly	Always
0	1	2	3	4	5
POINTS					

Servers work toward immediate goals, experiencing joy as each one is accomplished. For administrators with their longer-range projects, the point of joy is often "way down the road."

Each time I wrapped up an issue of the magazine—all the stories edited, pictures ready, captions and titles written, layout completed—and stuck the package in the mailbox to the printer, that was my major point of joy. (I have to admit that there was also a type of "anticipated joy" along the way.)

Wanda found her gift of administration invaluable in her job as the Christian education coordinator of her church. "The first goal I worked on," she says, "was to organize a resource center that would supply the teachers with the materials they would need in order to do their job well. Then I spent months training them in teaching methods. What a sense of fulfillment there was at last, to see the whole staff working together to make our Sunday school the best it could be."

13. Is willing to let others get the credit in order to get a job done.

Never	Seldom	Sometimes	Usually	Mostly	Always
0	1	2	3	4	5
POINTS					

The mature administrator does not worry about getting credit for accomplishments. Like anyone else, he or she enjoys a pat on the back, but would rather share that credit with the whole group. He or she sees success as a collective achievement. It is not false modesty when administrators refuse accolades, insisting, "None of this could have happened if it had not been for the excellent work of my associates." They really mean it. They see themselves as facilitators, and the others as the real accomplishers.

Roy Burkhart, pastor of a large church in Ohio, when addressing five hundred seminary students on the practical aspects of pastoring, asserted: "It's amazing what you can get accomplished in a church if you don't care who gets the credit."

In the business world Jeff has learned how well his staff operates with the liberal distribution of appreciation. "But I even go beyond that," he admits. "Whenever I drop a hint or an idea and one of my employees picks up on it and develops it, I give him credit for thinking of it. I love to see people feeling useful and valued. It makes me feel good, too."

Never	Seldom	Sometimes	Usually	Mostly	Always
0	1	2	3	4	5
		✗			
		POINTS			

14. Prefers to move on to a new challenge once something is completed.

Once administrators complete a goal, they're ready to move on. Some assume that once an organizer gets a business or a church group functioning, he or she would enjoy staying at the helm and continuing to coordinate. Not so. Once the system is running smoothly he or she would rather turn it over to someone else and move on to new challenges.

After seven years *Aglow* magazine was running smoothly. We finally had paid staff and a good group of editors, and I no longer felt needed. I knew pretty well in advance what each day would hold. There was no adventure left. I longed for something new to do.

Then, at the close of my eighth year, the whole television field opened up for us. It was unmapped, untried territory and I was delighted. I could glimpse the potential for women sharing the Gospel with other women in the privacy of their own homes.

I remember standing on the rooftop of a skyscraper in Chicago that housed a Christian television station and looking out in the darkness at vast numbers of high-rise apartment buildings, visualizing the thousands upon thousands of women in those apartments—some lonely, some abused, some afraid and many without hope. "Oh, God!" I cried. "This is how we can reach them! They probably wouldn't come out to a meeting, but they'll listen to another woman share her heart on their own TV sets."

I loved spending the next three years developing the *Women Aglow* television series.

Never	Seldom	Sometimes	Usually	Mostly	Always
0	1	2	3	4	5
			✗		
		POINTS			

15. Constantly writes notes to self.

This characteristic applies to all with the gift of administration without exception. They daily write reminder notes to themselves and make lists of things to do, calls to make and goals to accomplish.

Administrators tend to have so many things on their mind that if they don't write something down when they think of it, they're apt to forget. At a writer's conference I was talking with the then-new editor of *Decision* magazine. He shared with me some of the things he liked about his new job and I could easily tell that he had the gift of administration. Just for fun I said, "You write notes to yourself, don't you?"

"How did you know?" he asked with astonishment.

"Because," I replied, "I can tell that you are an administrator by motivational gift and they *always* write notes to themselves!"

My friend Adele admits, "I live my life by lists. Sometimes I spend more time making them than it would take to do the job. I have such a tendency to want to organize—but some things would be better left spontaneous."

Another administrator confided in us that whenever she did not have a piece of paper handy she'd jot notes on her hand, and then hope she didn't forget and wash her hands before she got the notes transferred!

16. Is a natural and capable leader.

Never	Seldom	Sometimes	Usually	Mostly	Always
0	1	2	3	4	5
			✳		
POINTS					

Is a bee drawn to honey? Does a cow come back to the barn? Just so an administrator is bound to lead—at least part of the time.

One of the things we have learned about administrators is that they do not do well in any kind of dual leadership. They have strong convictions about the way they lead. Each one has his or her own style and two leaders will clash. They far prefer to be given specific areas in which they are in sole charge than to be placed in what they view as the no-man's-land of tandem leadership. As one man put it, "I'd much rather follow than try to share leadership on an equal basis with another administrator."

One of the rare couples who do share the motivational gift of administration is a young pastor and his wife, Duncan and Judy. Both were raised on farms and loved gardening. So in their first pastorate they decided to plant a vegetable garden in the backyard, and later related this scene to us:

"The rows should go north and south," Duncan declared.

"Oh, no," Judy insisted, "we always planted east to west."

"Well, the tall vegetables need to go over here on the south side to help shade the other crops," Duncan claimed.

"You've got to be kidding," Judy blurted out. "Everyone knows it's best to plant the corn and the beans on the north so the smaller plants get adequate sunshine." They spent the next hour arguing over where each vegetable should go.

"We were getting nowhere," Judy said. "We were both so sure we were right. I don't think we would ever have gotten our garden planted if God had not given Duncan some special wisdom. He got a stick and drew a line right down the middle of the plot and gave me the right side while he took the left. Our rows went in different directions and we each followed the methods we'd been used to. And you know what? We each had a beautiful, productive garden."

There can also be exceptions. My administrator friend Bette Ayers wrote:

Thought you would find it interesting that on occasion two leaders can work together. While I was the chairman of retreats for our church I had JoAnn McMoran as my right-hand gal. I cannot tell you how wonderful it was working with her. I was so blessed to have her to pray with me and seek the Lord's will in every aspect. I found that when two administrators work that well together, it's because they have the Lord as the Administrator!

Never	Seldom	Sometimes	Usually	Mostly	Always
0	1	2	3	4	5
		POINTS			

17. Knows when old methods are working and when to introduce new ones.

In any group or organization where a method of operation has been established, people feel at ease with it. But when an administrator is placed in leadership he or she may see that changes are necessary. Yet it is not easy to move people out of their "comfort zone." The adjustment calls for great wisdom, and administrators have it.

Jesus explained that a leader in the Kingdom of God "is like a householder who brings forth out of his storehouse treasure that is new and [treasure that is] old [the fresh as well as the familiar]" (Matthew 13:52).

In Japan we visited Meiji-Mura, a restored village of the Meiji period. Our host, Pastor Tempei Wada, pointed out a house that had an old-fashioned storehouse out back. "That is like the storehouse Jesus mentioned," he said. "It was where the householder kept his treasure, his money, his silver dishes, anything of value.

"Notice there are no windows," he commented. "When the door was bolted there was no way for a thief to break in. The householder would store his valuables there—new purchases as well as family heirlooms, and bring them into the house to enjoy as he desired."

We thought the parallel was apt. The wise leader introduces new ideas or new ways of functioning one or two at a time, letting people hold on to much of the familiar while adjusting to the fresh. Then another new idea can be introduced, and then another, but not all at once.

Never	Seldom	Sometimes	Usually	Mostly	Always
0	1	2	3	4	5
		POINTS			

18. Enjoys working with and being around people.

Administrators are *people* people. They share this characteristic with the exhorters, except that the motivation in their case is not to encourage but to get to know, to learn from and to interact with. Administrators are great observers of human behavior and are constantly learning how to work with people more effectively.

We've watched our son David focus on people. In high school he loved being a part of a group, whether it was a football team, a Christian singing group, the church youth group, the student body leadership or just his own group of friends.

In his junior year he noted that many of the students were unaware of the problems of people in third-world nations. He was especially interested in the plight of the people of Haiti, and came up with an idea to expose fellow students to the needs of the Haitians.

With the help of a teacher and a staff member of World Concern, he arranged for eight students and two adults to go on a ten-day trip, first to Washington, D.C., to talk with a congressional aide, then on to Florida to visit a refugee camp and finally to Haiti to visit Christian hospitals, schools, churches and orphanages and to get acquainted with the people. "It was a real experience in interpersonal relationships," David said.

During his sophomore and junior years at Seattle Pacific University David became "peer advisor" of a dorm floor. It helped pay for his room and board but more importantly gave him the opportunity to interact with other students and to further develop his leadership skills.

When David told us he was considering running for student body president for his senior year we could encourage him to do so, for with his motivational gift of administration and his love for people we knew he'd do a great job. He was elected—and he did.

19. Wants to see things completed as quickly and effectively as possible.

Never	Seldom	Sometimes	Usually	Mostly	Always
0	1	2	3	4	5
POINTS					

Administrators want to get the job done—fast! They do not like delays, red tape or people dragging their feet.

One administrator mother said, "I get very upset and frustrated when I can't finish a simple project around the home quickly. The greatest obstacle is not knowing where things are. With a family as large as mine [she has six children] it's amazing what disappears or doesn't get back to its rightful place."

Jenni, who has taken on the directorship of a girls' drill team, shared how frustrating it is when the youngsters do not pay attention or apply themselves. "They have the potential to be champions but that takes work. Often they simply play at learning the formations. It's delayed our progress; I wish they wouldn't waste time."

20. Does not enjoy doing repetitive or routine tasks.

Never	Seldom	Sometimes	Usually	Mostly	Always
0	1	2	3	4	5
POINTS					

"Boring!" That sums up the administrator's opinion of repetitive work. No challenge. No interest.

We estimate that an administrator would last no more than one day on an assembly line job. Servers on the other hand might enjoy the security of a work routine where they knew exactly what was expected of them. No wonder administrators love having servers on their team, so they can delegate this kind of work to them.

Susan, an administrator from Kamloups, Canada, wrote us that while she is doing routine tasks around the house she beats the boredom by organizing her current projects in her head. "Not only does the housework become more tolerable," she reported, "but when I'm free to work on the project, most of the planning is already completed and so I save time."

Gladys says she copes with routine housework by listening to teaching tapes. Wilma has a similar system, only with her it's good music. Mark wears his Walkman and headphones when he mows the lawn. Georgia prays as she vacuums and scrubs floors. And Pete memorizes Scripture on his half-hour drive to and from work. All good ideas for administrators!

THE GIFT OF ADMINISTRATION

Characteristics	Never 0	Seldom 1	Sometimes 2	Usually 3	Mostly 4	Always 5	POINTS
1. Is highly motivated to organize that for which he or she is responsible.			X				
2. Expresses ideas and organization in ways that communicate clearly.			X				
3. Respects and handles authority well.			X				
4. Will not assume leadership unless it's delegated by those in authority.				X			
5. Will assume leadership where no specific leadership exists.				X			
6. Especially enjoys working on long-range goals and projects.		X					
7. Is a visionary person with a broad perspective.		X					
8. Easily facilitates resources and people to accomplish tasks or goals.				X			
9. Enjoys delegating tasks and supervising people.				X			
10. Will endure criticism in order to accomplish the ultimate task.				X			
11. Has great zeal and enthusiasm for whatever he or she is involved in.				X			
12. Finds greatest fulfillment and joy in working to accomplish goals.				X			
13. Is willing to let others get the credit in order to get a job done.				X			
14. Prefers to move on to a new challenge once something is completed.			X				
15. Constantly writes notes to self.				X			
16. Is a natural and capable leader.				X			
17. Knows when old methods are working and when to introduce new ones.			X				
18. Enjoys working with and being around people.			X				
19. Wants to see things completed as quickly and effectively as possible.				X			
20. Does not enjoy doing repetitive or routine tasks.						X	

TOTAL 51

Problems of the Administrator

When people with the gift of administration carry their positive characteristics to an extreme, they can *become* problem areas. God has equipped administrators with enablings and giftedness to accomplish tasks and achieve goals. Yet if they don't slow down enough to "smell the roses," their gift scrunches life's priorities into configurations that were never meant to be.

One dear saint from Australia told us that if Satan cannot get a Christian to sin deliberately his next tactic is to push that person to operate in a typical characteristic to an extreme, until everything is out of balance and his or her witness is no longer effective. As you score yourself be aware of the need for moderation in all things.

1. Becomes upset when others do not share the same vision or goals.

Never	Seldom	Sometimes	Usually	Mostly	Always
0	1	2	3	4	5
			✳		
POINTS					

When the administrators find their co-workers have stunted vision that hampers the accomplishment of goals, it is to them as a millstone around their necks.

One administrator, Ed, worked for an organization that was structured so that all seven people who headed up departments also served as the governing board. Their policy was not to move ahead on any project unless *all* were in agreement. It seemed an ideal way to govern, but in practice there were frustrations when the negative vote of one person became the determining factor.

"There were several on the board who were quite conservative and automatically suspicious of any new idea," Ed reported. "Each time I'd present a proposal to increase the organization's effectiveness one of them was sure to dig in their heels and we'd hear, 'Well, we've never tried it before,' or, 'We'd better put that on the shelf for now.'

"I would get so upset," Ed admitted. "Their lack of vision was absolutely frustrating. I finally blew up. I'm not proud of it but I told them we'd never make any progress if they continued to let the person of least vision determine the level of our work.

"The Lord dealt with me about my attitude, but He also showed me that that particular authority structure was not for me. I was able to move on to another job where I didn't feel so many restraints."

Perhaps the most important thing for the administrator to learn is that prayer changes things. Persuasion and the presentation of facts only go so far in changing another's limited perspective. But God can move mountains—and people—and enlarge the vision of others if we just ask.

prayer request

2. Can develop outer callousness due to being a target for criticism.

Never	Seldom	Sometimes	Usually	Mostly	Always
0	1	2	3	4	5
POINTS					

If it is true, as psychologists tell us, that for every negative word spoken against us we need four positive words to neutralize the negative effects, then it's clear why many administrators build up a callousness to protect themselves from the barrage of criticism their position invites.

Malcolm, an administrator with an executive position, is married to a woman who used to pick at him constantly. She majored on his weak points and bombarded him with unkind comments.

"I could take criticism at work," he insisted, "but it was the critical attitude of my wife that defeated me. I built walls of silence and sarcasm and determined I was not going to let her hurt me anymore. We were living in the same house but that was all. Our marriage was falling apart and I kept telling myself I didn't care.

"Fortunately our pastor did. He called us in for counseling and helped me to begin to let down the walls as he also taught my wife how to communicate without criticizing. It took time, but what we both learned was worth it, and now we are helping to counsel others with similar problems."

3. Can regress into "using" people to accomplish own goals.

Never	Seldom	Sometimes	Usually	Mostly	Always
0	1	2	3	4	5
POINTS					

Administrators are so goal-oriented that they can forget people are not pawns to be moved about as in a game of chess. It's not that they mean to do this; it just happens. They can push a good quality to an extreme until they become inconsiderate of—or even hurtful to—others.

I remember how, in the early days of Aglow when our editorial and publishing "office" was in the spacious room over our unusually large two-story garage, I would lapse into this from time to time. Most of our volunteer staff worked just until four o'clock so they'd be home before their husbands were.

One day I could see that we could finish mailing out the magazine if everyone would work only a half hour longer. I asked if they would.

"My husband gets very upset if I'm late," one woman apologized. "He doesn't mind my doing volunteer work, as long as it doesn't interfere with our home life."

"I'd like to stay and help," said another, equally apologetic, "but my babysitter can't stay past 4:15."

"I can stay an extra ten minutes," one person ventured, "but I've got to shop and get dinner on the table or my son will miss basketball practice."

I suddenly realized what I was doing. I'd started looking at them as so many hands to get a job done, rather than seeing them as real people with real families with real needs to be met. *I* was the one who needed to apologize!

Never	Seldom	Sometimes	Usually	Mostly	Always
0	1	2	3	4	5
POINTS					

4. Tends to drive self and neglect personal and family needs.

Priorities! That's what administrators need to keep in mind. As one told us, "I give myself one hundred percent to whatever I do." But this potentially admirable quality can also wreak havoc in other areas of life.

Administrators can get overextended, be too committed to a task, or take on too much for either their own good or their family's well-being. Their zeal for their work or ministry can leave those they love the most feeling neglected.

Some excellent advice is given in the beautiful description in Proverbs 31, "She considers a [new] field before she buys or accepts it [expanding prudently and not courting neglect of her present duties by assuming other duties]" (verse 16). Whenever administrators are considering new fields of endeavor they need to take stock of their present obligations and take on new responsibilities only if they can do so without neglecting spouse, children, job or church commitments—and still have time for devotions, exercise and recreation.

Never	Seldom	Sometimes	Usually	Mostly	Always
0	1	2	3	4	5
POINTS					

5. Neglects routine home responsibilities due to intense interest in "job."

I was tremendously relieved to learn that administrator women do not have to love housework! I used to feel so guilty about it. I do get it done—eventually. But I'll have to admit that our house looks lived in.

I procrastinate. I don't love dusting. I do it and the next day the dust just resettles on everything. I make the bed and then, of all things, we sleep in it and I have to make it again the next day. I wash clothes and soon they need to be washed again. There's no end to routine. (I'm so grateful for the reports that there is no dirt or dust in heaven.)

Housework must be done. But I have a cordless phone, so I can be loading the dishwasher while I talk on the phone. I listen to tapes while I do floors. I watch my favorite TV program while I fold laundry and iron. I've learned to make housework endurable.

And for you administrator men, it's okay to hate yard work, and cleaning out the gutters and repainting the house—but just remember that those things still need to be done. You are the men who, along with career women, are most likely to become "workaholics" or "married to your job." So watch it!

For *all* of us administrators, we need to remember that our love for our job, our volunteer projects, our church work or whatever we're involved in must not make us neglect life's necessary responsibilities.

Typical problem areas of the gift of administration

	Never	Seldom	Sometimes	Usually	Mostly	Always	POINTS
	0	1	2	3	4	5	
1. Becomes upset when others do not share the same vision or goals.				✗			
2. Can develop outer callousness due to being a target for criticism.			✗				
3. Can regress into "using" people to accomplish own goals.			✗				
4. Tends to drive self and neglect personal and family needs.					✗		
5. Neglects routine home responsibilities due to intense interest in "job."					✗		
					TOTAL		16

Biblical Administrators

In the Bible, administrators are often kings, priests or bishops. Such people may assume leadership not only because of their giftedness but also because of the advantages of birth, position or power. The example of the motivational gift of administration that we have chosen to examine, however, is a person who rose to leadership without special status or influence.

Joseph was born into an important Jewish family and he was indeed favored by his father, Jacob. But this was not enough to help him out of trouble. Joseph's mistake was announcing his governing abilities (in his two dreams of leadership) before anyone else was prepared to accept them. Then, after his brothers sold Joseph into slavery, there was nothing in his family ties or credentials that helped him rise to leadership.

See how many characteristics of the gift of administration you can find in the following references:

Scripture: Genesis 37:9–10; 39:4; 41:29–30, 40	Your Comments:
Genesis 37	
9 But Joseph dreamed yet another dream and told it to his brothers [also]. He said, See here, I have dreamed again, and behold, [this time not only] eleven stars [but also] the sun and the moon bowed down and did reverence to me!	
10 And he told it to his father [as well as] his brethren. But his father rebuked him and said to him, What is the meaning of this dream that you have dreamed? Shall I and your mother and your brothers actually come to bow down ourselves to the earth and do homage to you?	

Scripture: Genesis 37:9–10; 39:4; 41:29–30, 40   Your Comments:

Genesis 39

4 So Joseph pleased [Potiphar] and found favor in his sight, and he served him. And [his master] made him supervisor over his house and he put all that he had in his charge.

Genesis 41

29 Take note! Seven years of great plenty throughout all the land of Egypt are coming.

30 Then there will come seven years of hunger and famine, and [there will be so much want that] all the great abundance of the previous years will be forgotten in the land of Egypt; and hunger (destitution, starvation) will exhaust (consume, finish) the land.

40 You shall have charge over my house, and all my people shall be governed according to your word [with reverence, submission, and obedience]. Only in matters of the throne will I be greater than you are.

God had a plan for Joseph's leadership ability. He operated in his gift first in prison, then over the whole of Egypt and surrounding lands. Here are the characteristics we see suggested:

Scripture: Genesis 37:9–10; 39:4; 41:29–30, 40   Our Comments:

Genesis 37

9 But Joseph dreamed yet another dream and told it to his brothers [also]. He said, See here, I have dreamed again, and behold, [this time not only] eleven stars [but also] the sun and the moon bowed down and did reverence to me!

- **#7** is a visionary person
- **#11** has zeal for a dream
- **#16** has leadership capabilities, revealed by his dream
- **#19** wants quick fulfillment of dream

10 And he told it to his father [as well as] his brethren. But his father rebuked him and said to him, What is the meaning of this dream that you have dreamed? Shall I and your mother and your brothers actually come to bow down ourselves to the earth and do homage to you?

- **#10** draws criticism

Genesis 39

4 So Joseph pleased [Potiphar] and found favor in his sight, and he served him. And [his master] made him supervisor over his house and he put all that he had in his charge.

- **#3** works under authority
- **#5** assumes responsibilities
- **#8** has his facilitating abilities recognized
- **#9** enjoys supervising
- **#16** is a leader even in jail

Genesis 41

29 Take note! Seven years of great plenty throughout all the land of Egypt are coming.

- **#7** is a visionary

30 Then there will come seven years of hunger and famine, and [there will be so much want that] all the great abundance of the previous years will be forgotten in the land of Egypt; and hunger (destitution, starvation) will exhaust (consume, finish) the land.

- **#6** sets long range goals
- **#7** is a visionary
- **#14** enjoys a challenge

Scripture: Genesis 37:9–10; 39:4; 41:29–30, 40   Our Comments:

40 You shall have charge over my house, and all my people shall be governed according to your word [with reverence, submission, and obedience]. Only in matters of the throne will I be greater than you are.	**#1** is motivated to organize **#3** accepts authority **#6** gives long-range goals **#7** has a broad perspective **#8** is a facilitator **#16** is a capable leader

Have you ever wondered what would have happened to all of those Middle Eastern countries if a person with such an outstanding gift of administration had *not* been available? Joseph's farsighted leadership saved millions of other people, as well as his family.

Now take time to look up more about Joseph, and some of the other biblical examples of the gift of administration:

Joseph: Genesis 30–40

Nehemiah: Nehemiah 1–7

Deborah: Judges 4–5

David: 1 Samuel 16–31; 2 Samuel; 1 Kings 1–2; 1 Chronicles 10:13–29:30

Annas: Luke 3:2; John 18:13–24; Acts 4:5–6

James, brother of Jesus: Matthew 13:55; Mark 6:3; Acts 12:17; 15:13; 21:18; 1 Corinthians 15:7; Galatians 1:19; 2:9

Jairus: Matthew 9:18; Mark 5:22–43; Luke 8:41–56

Characteristics of the Compassion Person

Of all the gifts, that of compassion is by far the most frequently bestowed. How wonderful that this is so! "What this world needs now is love, sweet love," as the song tells us. Maybe it's because so many people are hurting that God has created such a vast number of compassionate people. On our survey they made up 30 percent of the primary gifts. That's almost one-third of the population.

"To have mercy" in Greek is *eleeo*. *Strong's Concordance* defines it as "to *compassionate* (by word or deed, specifically by divine grace); have compassion, (pity on); have (obtain, receive, show) mercy (on)." (We have elected to use the word "compassion," rather than "mercy," because the latter can carry a negative connotation of weakness.)

The compassion person is to show his or her compassion with cheerfulness, *hilarotes* in the Greek, according to Vine, signifying "that readiness of mind, that joyousness, which is prompt to do anything; hence, cheerful." Wuest notes that our word *hilarity* comes from this Greek word. Vincent defines it as "the joyfulness, the amiable grace, the affability going the length of gaiety, which make the visitor a sunbeam penetrating into the sick-chamber, and to the heart of the afflicted." The Amplified Bible states that our acts of mercy or compassion are to be done "with genuine cheerfulness and joyful eagerness" (Romans 12:8).

Remember there is no eighth gift type. This is the final gift in the list. So, complete the adventure of discovering your giftedness. When you've transferred your compassion total to your profile sheet, you'll see the whole picture of your giftedness. As we reach the close of this section, we'll take a look at what your profile sheet indicates and how to evaluate it.

Never	Seldom	Sometimes	Usually	Mostly	Always
0	1	2	3	4	5
		✳			
POINTS					

1. Has tremendous capacity to show love.

Of all the motivational gifts, this is the one with the greatest capacity and ability to show love to others. Reflecting the nature of their heavenly Father, compassion people seem to be an unending source of *agape* love. The more opportunities they have to give love, the more joyful and fulfilled they are.

I was teaching the motivational gift seminar at a women's retreat in western Pennsylvania some years ago when I noticed a woman on the first row with tears rolling down her cheeks. I wondered if I had said something to upset her. At the next break she came up to me.

"I just wanted you to know those were tears of joy you saw," she told me. "I've been sitting through all the sessions saying, 'This doesn't fit me, nor does this,' and getting pretty discouraged. I said, 'Lord, am I going to fit into any of these gifts?'

"Then as you started to share about the gift of compassion the Lord spoke to me and said, *This is the gift I've given you and now I'm going to enlarge your heart so that you can give more of My love to others.*

"Katie, I felt a sensation in my physical heart, just as if it were being stretched, and then I felt the love of God pour into my heart and I could see how He truly loves and cares for everyone in the world. I was overwhelmed with the greatness of His love and with the fact that He had gifted me in such a way that I could be a channel for His love. I couldn't help crying for joy."

Never	Seldom	Sometimes	Usually	Mostly	Always
0	1	2	3	4	5
	✳				
POINTS					

2. Always looks for good in people.

Compassion people are noncritical. It's almost as if they have built-in blinders that keep them from seeing bad things in others. Their focus remains on the good, both realized and potential. Neither do they want to hear others talk about the negatives in people.

Barbara Ann Chase, who served as an international officer of Aglow for several years, was an excellent example of this characteristic. Whenever she would hear any of us talking about someone's negative traits she would interject with, "But that person has so many *good* qualities. Why just the other day I saw her . . ." and she would go on to list all the positive things she knew about the person.

Her beautiful focus on the good qualities of others was an important check on the rest of us, for we can always find bad points in anyone if we look hard enough.

Dixie Choyce, a lovely senior citizen in our former church with a spontaneously flowing gift of compassion, shared this memory with us: "I decided at about age eighteen that there had to be something good about everyone no matter how unpleasant the person was to get along with. So I tried to find that positive quality and value it." She's spent a lifetime looking for, and finding, the good in people.

3. Senses the spiritual and emotional condition of a group or individual.

Never	Seldom	Sometimes	Usually	Mostly	Always
0	1	2	3	4	5
	✗				
	POINTS				

One can almost visualize invisible feelers or antennae on the heads of those with the motivational gift of compassion. They are incredibly sensitive to the emotional status of others. They know if people are up or down, elated or blue, confident or fearful.

Jeanette told us she's always been sensitive to the spiritual needs of people. "God has gifted me with the ability to see when people are intimidated or hurt by other people in conversation. I'm automatically drawn to help them."

Compassion people are also good at reading body language. Some experts in communication have proposed that 75 to 85 percent of human communication is nonverbal. The way we stand, sit or even hold our arms can say, "I'm open to you" or, "I won't receive a thing you say" or, "I'm hanging loose today." On top of this, our facial expressions are often a dead giveaway of feelings even when we don't say a thing. Or if we do, the tone of our voice can reveal far more than the words we use.

All of us can "read" this type of communication to some degree, but compassion people are the experts. And since they function in this area constantly, they are often more or less in tune with the deepest feelings of others.

4. Is attracted to people who are hurting or in distress.

Never	Seldom	Sometimes	Usually	Mostly	Always
0	1	2	3	4	5
		✗			
	POINTS				

This is an always-present, ready-to-function characteristic of compassion people. It starts in early childhood and continues all through their lives.

They are the ones as children who brought home the lost dogs and the stray cats. They also brought home the lonely kids no one else cared for.

Our daughter Linda was that way. We remember how in her older grade school days she started to bring home some unusual new girlfriends. One was such a social misfit that we asked, "Linda, why do you want to play with *her*?"

She replied, "This girl doesn't have a single friend at school. So I'm going to be her friend!"

Not everyone understands the compassion person's attraction to the hurting, nor can everyone handle it.

Arlene tells how—when she was ten years old—she found out that a little Mexican girl in her small town had never had or even seen a Christmas tree. So she invited her over for Christmas dinner. "When Maria arrived in her ragged clothes my mother was horrified," Arlene recalled. "Mother had been raised with a lot of racial and class prejudice, and she just couldn't understand why I'd invite such a person to our home. When Mother said she'd have to leave I cried my heart out. Maria got to stay for dinner and see our tree, but Mother was far from comfortable about it."

5. Takes action to remove hurts and relieve distress in others.

Never	Seldom	Sometimes	Usually	Mostly	Always
0	1	2	3	4	5
		✗			
POINTS					

Compassion people are not only drawn to the hurting, they also do something about it.

A woman with this gift gave us a capsule definition of the difference between sympathy, empathy and compassion:

Sympathy says: "I'm sorry you hurt!"

Empathy says: "I'm sorry you hurt, and I hurt with you!"

Compassion says: "I'm sorry you hurt, and I hurt with you, and I'm going to stay right here with you until the hurt is gone."

Mollie, a nurse who loves ministering to others, told us, "Working with the Native Americans in the field of public health and midwifery has given me the opportunity to share my gift and help others in a very practical way."

Bonnie, who today works with Parents in Crisis, a support organization for those dealing with child abuse and drug addiction, tells how she wanted to help the hurting from the time she was a child.

"When I was six years old," she relates, "I used to rush home from school and go over to a neighbor's to share what I had learned that day with their little girl who was five years old and still confined to a baby buggy. She had an enormous head, the body of a baby, and a large growth on her back. I felt so bad for her and wanted to help, and this was the only way I knew how."

6. Is more concerned for mental and emotional distress than physical distress.

Never	Seldom	Sometimes	Usually	Mostly	Always
0	1	2	3	4	5
			✗		
POINTS					

Suppose you have to go to the hospital. Guess who's going to be the first to come and visit you? The compassion person will inquire about your comfort and the medical prognosis. But he or she will then move on to find out how you are *feeling* about being in the hospital. Are you worried about things getting taken care of at home? Are you battling fear? Do you sense the Lord's presence in this time of need? Do you need prayer?

He or she may just sit by your bed and hold your hand, or will literally weep with those who weep.

Sharon was so concerned about people in distress that she started a group in her church called Caring & Sharing, where people can come together and talk about their hurts and find others in similar situations.

Jacquie, who heads up the prayer chain at her church, has found herself drawn to informal counseling. "I always seem to have someone in my life who needs my emotional support. As soon as I'm able to help one work through her problems, the Lord sends me another."

7. Is motivated to help people have right relationships with one another.

Never	Seldom	Sometimes	Usually	Mostly	Always
0	1	2	3	4	5
POINTS					

Compassion people grieve over broken relationships. They are builders of bridges and menders of breaches. They are the peacemakers. They want to see the Body of Christ united and functioning in love. They love Jesus' prayer in John 17, and work to that end.

Alma, now a missionary in Japan, has exemplified this characteristic constantly in her life. While she was still living in the United States, we watched her arrange gatherings in her home, bringing together people from different churches and different backgrounds so that they could get to know and love one another.

When we visited her in Japan we saw that she was continuing to do the same thing. She would invite Japanese people she had met in different settings to come to her residence for dinner. "It gives them a chance to get to know Christians outside their own church," she said. "The Japanese tend to limit their Christian fellowship to their own small groups. They need to know there are many more who love the Lord, too. I love to see friendships spark and develop from these encounters. I'm delighted if I can expand anyone's vision of the Body of Christ."

We've seen Barbara Ann Chase try to bring whole Christian organizations together to work for common causes.

And David DuPlessis, with his outstanding compassion gift, used to visit the heads of almost every denomination to foster understanding, love and fellowship among churches.

8. Loves opportunities to give preference or place to others.

Never	Seldom	Sometimes	Usually	Mostly	Always
0	1	2	3	4	5
POINTS					

These are the people who will open the door for you, let you step in line in front of them, give you the best chair.

Lynn Koontz had a 10:00 A.M. doctor's appointment for back pain. The doctor was running late when about 10:30 an elderly woman came into the waiting room, obviously very ill. The receptionist said that they were already overbooked but that they would try to work her in as soon as possible.

Lynn couldn't stand it. She got up and went over to the receptionist. "Please, let that woman have my appointment. I'll wait to be worked in."

Lynn had to wait until noon to see the doctor, but sat there with a hurting back and a rejoicing heart. "I was so grateful," she said, "that God had placed me there at the right time to be able to give that dear woman my appointment."

9. Is careful with words and actions to avoid hurting others.

Never	Seldom	Sometimes	Usually	Mostly	Always
0	1	2	3	4	5
		POINTS			

The last thing a compassion person wants is to be the cause of hurt to another person. Therefore they are careful of their own actions and speech. We've seen them stop in the middle of a sentence in order to choose just the right word, lest they say something that might offend.

Dixie shared with us, "When I was just five years old I refused to choose between my parents when my father would ask, 'Which of us do you love the most?' Though I loved Mother more, I'd always answer, 'I love you both the same.'

"Then at age nine, when I had to be sent into isolation with a contagious disease, my father asked, 'Who do you want to go with you, Mother or me?' I knew I was again being asked which I loved more. So I said, 'I can go by myself. I don't want either of you to catch it.'"

Henry tells how this characteristic affected his job. "I was working in the complaint department of a department store and when customers would come in 'hoppin' mad,' instead of arguing I immediately empathized with them, and spoke to them with such genuine concern that they sometimes forgot what they were mad about. Often they would drop their complaint altogether. My boss was so pleased I got a nice raise in pay!"

10. Easily detects insincerity or wrong motives.

Never	Seldom	Sometimes	Usually	Mostly	Always
0	1	2	3	4	5
		POINTS			

The compassion people's "built-in radar system" helps them to detect ulterior motives or insincerity of any kind. They will back off from a person or a group when they sense this.

Virginia had gone to a prayer group upon the recommendation of a friend. At first she was impressed. The leader seemed to be committed to praying for the world and the nation as well as individual needs. "But something bothered me about her," Virginia said. "At first I couldn't put my finger on it—it was just a little 'warning signal' going off inside me."

Virginia returned to the group the next week. "About halfway through the morning I suddenly realized what had been bothering me," she declared. "The leader had mixed motives. I think she really believed in the power of prayer, but she was also controlling the women in the group.

It was not just firm leadership; she was dominating the direction of the meeting and relishing her power. I never went back again."

Jill, a woman with a compassion gift who as a child spent most of her time with animals "because they loved me so much," explained to us: "Insincerity in people bothered me as a little girl. It still does."

Shelly, who has a prayer counseling ministry in her church, shared with us, "I sense insincerity quickly and have learned to trust my impressions. Even when people come for prayer I can tell if their motives are right. I've learned to minister as the Lord directs, not necessarily as people request."

11. Is drawn to others with the gift of compassion.

Never	Seldom	Sometimes	Usually	Mostly	Always
0	1	2	3	4	5
POINTS					

Those with the motivational gift of compassion are naturally drawn to each other. They enjoy sharing with each other, praying together and just being together. It isn't so much that they think alike, but that they *feel* alike. They have the same emotional reactions to people and situations. They share the same concerns.

It's amazing how many compassion people have confided in us that their best friend is another compassion person. This is especially true while growing up. They often cannot relate well to those with the speaking gifts—the perceiver, the teacher, the exhorter and the administrator—feeling rather overwhelmed by them. But they can relate well to the server, the giver and especially to fellow compassion people.

While fewer than 5 percent of people marry someone with the same gift, about half of those who do are compassion people. Our friend's compassion daughter is married to a compassion man. He is exceptionally gentle, loving and caring. "That's why I was drawn to him," she tells us. "He's so good to me!"

When a person marries someone with the same gift and the couple is immature, the negative characteristics tend to be amplified in the relationship. But we've run across several mature "compassion couples" who have what they describe as a marriage made in heaven. They are so loving and caring for each other that it's a beautiful thing to behold. Even some of these admit, though, that it was not always so and they had to work through a variety of problems in the early years of their marriage.

12. Loves to do thoughtful things for others.

Never	Seldom	Sometimes	Usually	Mostly	Always
0	1	2	3	4	5
POINTS					

These are the people who remember birthdays, anniversaries, Mother's and Father's Day and Valentine's Day—and find a host of other occasions on which to send cards or notes just to say they care.

If you're married to one of these people, you're fortunate. A compassion husband will whisk his wife off to a dinner rendezvous more often than a man with any other type of gift. A compassion wife will serve an intimate candlelight meal more often than those with other gift types would ever think to do.

The thoughtfulness extends to every relationship. Compassion daughters and sons will be more affectionate to their parents, and vice versa. Compassion friends tend to put a lot more of themselves into friendships.

Gail was a single woman who was in our home group for many years. Her compassion gift prompted her to bless many of us with her kindnesses. Sometimes she would single out people just to tell them how special they were to her. How often the rest of us forget to do things like that!

We would get beautiful cards from her on Father's Day and Mother's Day, saying that she loved us just like another dad and mom. Sometimes we'd get unbirthday cards, or just a note for "no reason at all except to tell you how much you mean to me."

Never	Seldom	Sometimes	Usually	Mostly	Always
0	1	2	3	4	5
		✗			
	POINTS				

13. Is trusting and tries to be trustworthy.

It's because they are trustworthy that compassion people expect others to be so, too. They assume that everyone is honest and reliable until absolutely proven otherwise. They can be so trusting, in fact, that they can be in danger of becoming gullible.

They are greatly disappointed when someone proves not to be reliable. But you know what? They will continue to expect the best from that person anyway. They believe in people's capacity to change for the better. Often this very expectation brings out the best in those around them. But it can also work to the compassion person's harm.

From compassion people who have taken our seminar, we've heard these comments:

Doug: "I am trusting sometimes to the point of being stupid. I always expect people to treat me in the same way I would treat them. And even if I'm burnt, I will continue to trust."

Donna: "My attitude has always been that every person I meet is a good person. I still experience a feeling of shock when occasionally I find out that's not true. I'm crushed when someone is dishonest."

Cathy: "When someone I have trusted has taken advantage of me I get angry—mostly at myself for being so easily fooled."

Never	Seldom	Sometimes	Usually	Mostly	Always
0	1	2	3	4	5
		✗			
	POINTS				

14. Avoids conflicts and confrontations.

Even small children with the compassion gift find it very difficult to cope with conflict. They long for peace and harmony in the home, and when parents quarrel or split up, the compassionate youngster assumes it is his fault: "If I had just been a better child my mom and dad would still be together." Here's how two of them expressed it:

Ben: "When my parents fought, I found myself crying and begging them to make up. I kept telling them how much I loved them and asking them to love each other."

Ruth: "I always disliked conflict, but I seemed to be the 'middle man' in strained relationships, including my parents'. I was always trying to repair relationships and at the same time keep people from being hurt."

Compassion people are not confronters. They may hint that they are unhappy about something, but will seldom—unlike the perceiver or exhorter—address a problem straight on.

The effect of this characteristic on young boys can be a problem since they usually avoid fighting and may be labeled sissies by their classmates.

Michael recalls, "I never fought back when bullies picked on me because I never believed fighting was worthwhile. Most of my friends were the quiet type, like me. We were the ones who played on the fringes of the playground to stay clear of the more aggressive kids."

In the business world, this characteristic can be either positive or negative. Compassion people get along well with their peers but sometimes do not stand up for themselves when they should.

15. Doesn't like to be rushed in a job or activity.

Never	Seldom	Sometimes	Usually	Mostly	Always
0	1	2	3	4	5
POINTS					

Compassion people have one speed, and it's *slow* forward. As children, these were the kids who had to be pushed out the door so they'd get to school on time. They just didn't pay much attention to clocks.

How often we used to say to Linda, "Hurry up or you'll miss the school bus!" I wish I had the proverbial nickel for every time I had to drive her to school.

Punctuality remains a problem as they grow older. Given a job to do, they will finish it, but not necessarily on schedule. Somehow time just isn't that important to them. They are *now* people. They live for the moment. They figure the future will take care of itself, as long as they are doing all they can in the present.

One compassion woman we worked with was always late to meetings. She'd show up fifteen minutes after we'd started, always with a "good excuse." She'd say something like, "I ran into a friend who needed prayer." Or, "My watch stopped and the time slipped by before I realized how late it was."

We really needed her to be with us from the beginning of the meeting but we couldn't afford to waste everyone else's time. So, we decided to schedule the actual starting time fifteen minutes later, without informing her. Unsuspectingly, she made the start of every meeting!

Never	Seldom	Sometimes	Usually	Mostly	Always
0	1	2	3	4	5
POINTS					

16. Is typically cheerful and joyful.

Compassion people are positive people. The Amplified Bible says they are to show mercy and compassion "with genuine cheerfulness and joyful eagerness" (Romans 12:8). They love showing love. It gives them joy to do so.

One person said, "I love being around compassion people. Their cheerfulness buoys me up."

Since they yearn to relieve hurts and encourage relationships, they are constantly working to bring the level of happiness in others up to their own and beyond. How often we all need that kind of help!

One compassionate man had the responsibility of caring for his elderly parents. Both were somewhat senile and their care demanded much of Bart's time. As a result there were many events he and his wife were unable to participate in. Yet each time we did see him he would assure us that things were going "just great" for him. No complaints. He considered it a joy to help his parents.

Robert, a popular physical therapist, has the reputation of being especially loving to his wife, both in public and at home. Other women say they wish their husbands treated them as well. But we notice that Robert treats everyone lovingly. His voice and manner are so gentle, and his face glows with an inner joy. It's hard to feel "down" around Robert.

Never	Seldom	Sometimes	Usually	Mostly	Always
0	1	2	3	4	5
POINTS					

17. Is ruled by the heart rather than the head.

The heart plays the major role in the compassion person's life. The heart is the channel through which he or she shares God's wonderful love with others.

Compassion people are not normally tagged thinkers, intellectuals or analyzers. Rather, they are the *feelers*. They rely on emotions rather than mental processes to guide their lives. They're the ones who could say, "Don't confuse me with the facts; my feelings are already made up." This is not to say that they do not use their minds. They do—but always in relationship to what they feel.

We'd shared our testimony at an Anglican church in Timaru, on the South Island of New Zealand, when a man came to talk with us. "What you said touched me deeply," he said, "but I wish I didn't cry so easily when I feel that way. It seems unmanly. I try to hold back the tears but they come anyway."

We asked him several questions about himself and determined quickly that he had a compassion gift. "Don't hold back the tears," we advised. "God has given you a sensitive and caring heart and He expects you to respond with deep feelings. The world needs more men who are free to care and to cry."

"You mean it's okay to be this way?" he asked.

"Of course," we replied, briefly describing the gift of compassion.

"What a relief," he said, looking as though a weight had been taken off his shoulders. "All my life I've condemned myself for being this way."

It is obviously more difficult for a man to have this gift than for a woman. Society allows a woman to be led by her heart and easily moved to tears. Not so a man. The social expectations of most cultures tend to pressure a man into a macho mold, but the compassion gift is just not going to fit. Our hope is that wider understanding of the motivational gifts will allow compassion people of both sexes to be the beautiful, tenderhearted people they were created to be.

18. Rejoices to see others blessed and grieves to see others hurt.

Never	Seldom	Sometimes	Usually	Mostly	Always
0	1	2	3	4	5
POINTS					

The person with the compassion gift has an immense capacity to identify with what others are going through. He or she will literally rejoice with those who rejoice and weep with those who weep. There are times in all of our lives when we need someone to do just that with us.

Have you ever shared some great happiness with someone only to have him or her reply indifferently, "Oh, that's happened to me many times; it's no big deal." It bursts your bubble. You wish you'd never brought it up.

But share the good news with a compassion person and he or she is apt to jump for joy, saying, "I'm so happy for you," or, "Praise God! I'm so glad you told me." And you are, too.

Earl admits his gift just spills out. "I can just put my arms around a hurting person and feel his pain. And if someone's joyous, I share that joy as if it were my own."

There are times in our lives when we need someone to empathize with our sorrow or hurt. We don't need advice, exhortation or evaluation, but just someone who can sit and feel for and with us. We need someone who cares.

When Jane was in the hospital after a serious automobile accident and knew that if she did survive she would never look the same, the visitor who meant the most to her was a compassionate friend who would just sit by her bedside, hold her hand and weep. "Very few words were said," Jane told us, "but my friend's tears spoke volumes."

19. Is a crusader for good causes.

Never	Seldom	Sometimes	Usually	Mostly	Always
0	1	2	3	4	5
POINTS					

In the eyes of the compassion person, right needs to prevail. If there is evil at work in society he or she strives to overcome it, usually in "silent witness" fashion such as sit-ins, picketing, peace marches, emails or mail-outs. Those who have more extroverted personalities or a strong secondary "speaking gift" may also address political rallies or appear on TV. But all work to bring about change.

They tend to be altruistic, not wanting any special benefit for themselves, but for others.

Shannon shared how her gift went into action when her first husband's mother died leaving his brother, age eighteen, and sister, age thirteen, orphaned. "My husband, who has a secondary gift of compassion, and I went to court to fight an uncle who wanted the kids separated. We brought them to live with us. The boy finished high school and eventually got a good job and went out on his own. The girl stayed with me, even after my husband died, until she married. I still like to champion a good cause."

Stan tells how he lost his job one time (in 1974) because he went on strike—not for more wages for himself, but for equal benefits for the women in his office.

We suspect that a high percentage of the "flower children" of the sixties were compassion people who could not cope with an "unjust war." The subculture they formed enabled them to venture out to champion causes in society as a whole, while withdrawing from time to time into the security of their group.

Never	Seldom	Sometimes	Usually	Mostly	Always
0	1	2	3	4	5
POINTS					

20. Intercedes for the hurts and problems of others.

This is the third of the seven motivational gifts that is called to and anointed for intercessory prayer. They intercede primarily for the hurts and problems they have become aware of in other people's lives.

Theirs are deep, heartfelt prayers. If you've heard a compassion gift in action at a prayer meeting you may have thought, *Oh, how beautiful. I wish I could pray like that.*

They are so expressive because they feel what they are praying so deeply. It is not unusual for them to be moved to tears as they intercede. They pray with abandonment, almost forgetting there are others present, unashamed of their tears or other expressions of emotion.

Those who are drawn to become regular members of an intercessory prayer group are the perceiver, the giver and the compassion person. Each will bring his or her own special approach to the gathering.

The *perceiver* will pray for the will of God to be done in nations, in churches, in other groups and in individual lives.

The *giver* will pray for the salvation of lost souls, specifically and generally.

The *compassion person* will pray for the problems and hurts of people and for unity in the Body of Christ.

It is a beautiful thing to behold such a group in action. We believe it is the actualization of Jesus' declaration:

Again I tell you, if two of you on earth agree (harmonize together, make a symphony together) about whatever [anything and everything] they may ask, it will come to pass and be done for them by My Father in heaven.

For wherever two or three are gathered (drawn together as My followers) in (into) My name, there I AM in the midst of them.

Matthew 18:19–20

Notice that "agree" (the Greek word is *sumphoneo*) means to "harmonize together, or make a symphony," a beautiful picture of what happens when these three gifts pray together. Just as a chord is richer and lovelier than a single note, so when each gifted person prays wholeheartedly from his unique perspective, the resulting harmony is exquisite. It touches the heart of God and produces results.

We encourage churches not to pressure *everyone* to come to intercessory prayer meetings, but to let the Holy Spirit draw those who are called. Three or four people from the three gift groups mentioned above will accomplish more in intercession than dozens of people from the other four.

This does not mean that we are not all to pray. We are *all* called to pray. But not all are called to intercession.

THE GIFT OF COMPASSION

Characteristics

Characteristics		Never	Seldom	Sometimes	Usually	Mostly	Always	POINTS
		0	1	2	3	4	5	
1. Has tremendous capacity to show love.	1.			X				
2. Always looks for good in people.	2.		X					
3. Senses the spiritual and emotional condition of a group or individual.	3.		X					
4. Is attracted to people who are hurting or in distress.	4.			X				
5. Takes action to remove hurts and relieve distress in others.	5.			X				
6. Is more concerned for mental and emotional distress than physical distress.	6.				X			
7. Is motivated to help people have right relationships with one another.	7.		X					
8. Loves opportunities to give preference or place to others.	8.		X					
9. Is careful with words and actions to avoid hurting others.	9.			X				
10. Easily detects insincerity or wrong motives.	10.			X				
11. Is drawn to others with the gift of compassion.	11.		X					
12. Loves to do thoughtful things for others.	12.	X						
13. Is trusting and tries to be trustworthy.	13.			X				
14. Avoids conflicts and confrontations.	14.			X				
15. Doesn't like to be rushed in a job or activity.	15.		X					
16. Is typically cheerful and joyful.	16.			X				
17. Is ruled by the heart rather than the head.	17.		X					
18. Rejoices to see others blessed and grieves to see others hurt.	18.			X				
19. Is a crusader for good causes.	19.			X				
20. Intercedes for the hurts and problems of others.	20.			X				
							TOTAL	31

Problems of the Compassion Person

The motivational gift of compassion is potentially both the most beautiful gift of all and the most emotionally destructive. It all depends upon the degree to which the compassion person has overcome his or her own emotional wounds.

Compassionate people are the most vulnerable to hurts because their hearts are most open to others. When they are hurt or betrayed there is virtually no protection, no shell, no tough hide or callousness to deflect the attack.

Of all the recipients of gifts, the compassion child needs the most love, tenderness and adult protection. Those who receive this nurturing emerge into adulthood reasonably whole emotionally and are able to cope with life's challenges. Those who don't often require much encouragement, counseling, deliverance and healing in order to come into their rightful inheritance of a life free of encumbrances.

We've found that the compassion person is more apt to become an alcoholic or a drug abuser or to need psychiatric care than any other. Compassion people are also idealists who are prone to live in a fantasy world if the real world becomes intolerable.

Unfortunately many compassion people grow up in homes where strife and unkindness—even abuse and molestation—prevail. But the good news is that Jesus can heal all those hurts. Our experience with ministering to the emotionally hurt has verified this.

So, if you find you are hurting, let Jesus heal you and set you free. Often that happens even as you ask. Or, let someone else assist you—

your pastor or a mature Christian who ministers inner healing. Then you will be able to function in all the beauty and fullness of your gift.

Never	Seldom	Sometimes	Usually	Mostly	Always
0	1	2	3	4	5
		✗			
POINTS					

1. Tends to be indecisive.

It is difficult for the compassion person to make decisions. He or she will ponder the possible consequences, delay as long as possible or transfer the responsibility to others if possible.

One young man with the gift of compassion fell in love with a young woman from our church with the same gift. The first year of their marriage was a real challenge.

"Let's go out to dinner tonight," he would say.

"Okay," she'd reply.

"Where would you like to go?"

"Oh, I don't care, you decide."

"No, you pick the place."

"I'd feel better if you did."

"I had to make the choice last time. It's your turn."

"Well, any place is okay with me."

"Just pick one, then."

"I don't want to!"

"Well, I don't either."

By this time they'd be too angry to go out together. The problem was they went at every decision this way, until finally they went to their pastor for counseling in decision making.

This characteristic is especially detrimental in childrearing. Often compassion parents are not willing to confront their children with their improper behavior. They hope the other parent will take care of it. Actually, in their indecisiveness and permissiveness, they *are* training their children—to be disobedient and disrespectful.

Never	Seldom	Sometimes	Usually	Mostly	Always
0	1	2	3	4	5
✗					
POINTS					

2. Is often prone to take up another person's offense.

Because a compassion person cannot stand to see another person hurt or offended, he or she is quick to take up the offended person's cause.

Here's how it goes. Person A says something hurtful to person B. The compassion person observes this and joins person B in being upset with person A. Meanwhile A and B make up and restore their relationship. But the compassion person is still holding a grudge against person A.

They need to learn, first, that these matters are none of their business—except as they pray for those involved. We are not accountable for the actions of others unless we are in a position of authority with them, like a parent, pastor, teacher or group leader.

And second, they need to learn that prayer *will* move mountains. Just as prayer can defuse the perceiver's critical attitude, so prayer can defuse the compassion person's tendency to take up offenses. He or she needs to give the offense to the Lord, let Him deal with the situation and then let go of it.

Sometimes taking up an offense gets in the way of God's dealing with the other person. The compassion person also has a tendency to be easily offended. He or she reads meaning into other people's words or actions that are not there at all.

A good prayer for the compassion person is, "Lord, help me to be slow to be offended, on my own behalf or another's."

3. Is easily hurt by others.

Never	Seldom	Sometimes	Usually	Mostly	Always
0	1	2	3	4	5
POINTS					

This is the big one! No one gets hurt as easily as the compassion person. They are the most vulnerable.

It usually starts in childhood, even in infancy. One woman we counseled was an unwanted child. She was an inconvenience and her parents never let her forget it. As an adult she continued to feel she was in people's way. She would often break down and sob, "Please, somebody love me." Jesus did—in a very personal encounter—and she was healed.

Brian shared that he had a difficult home life. "My mom and dad would get in fierce yelling arguments. My heart would bleed, but I was afraid so I'd pretend I didn't hear anything. To this day it hurts to hear people fight."

Unfortunately compassion children often assume the blame for strife between parents. They tend to take everything so personally.

Gary was only seven when his parents divorced. "I was sure it was my fault," he recalls. "Along the way I kept thinking, if only I could be a better child, maybe all this would not happen. The guilt was almost unbearable at times. It's taken years of counseling to enable me to see that I was not the cause of my parents' problems."

It's ironic, but the very people who are the best at relieving the hurts of others are the ones who are most easily hurt themselves. Or . . . is it that God doesn't waste anything that we go through—if we let Him use it?

4. Can empathize too much with the suffering of others.

Never	Seldom	Sometimes	Usually	Mostly	Always
0	1	2	3	4	5
POINTS					

This is another danger area for those with the gift of compassion. If they empathize too completely with the suffering of others, it can weigh them down and render them ineffective in ministry.

Dinah wrote to us about this problem in her life. "I always want to help someone who is hurting because I hurt for them. But I have a tendency to take their worries on myself and go through it all with them. Then I'm not objective enough to really be of help."

Dinah's answer was to remember that Jesus has already borne our sorrow and grief. He's the only One with a heart large enough to carry them. We need to commit the suffering of the world to Him, rather than trying to take it upon ourselves.

In some cases we've even seen compassion people take on the illnesses of others. We're not to do that either. Jesus bore our sicknesses on the cross at the same time that He bore our sins.

One woman in California (we'll call her Amanda) was hurting for a friend who had cancer. Amanda had begun to exhibit similar cancer symptoms in her own body, although her doctor could find no physical base for them.

We cautioned Amanda that she must not try to take a sickness into her own body, no matter how deeply she cared about her friend. She kept insisting that she wanted to suffer with her friend. Even Amanda's husband could not get her to stop. She became almost completely debilitated, and did not recover until after her friend died.

5. Has an affectionate nature that is often misinterpreted by the opposite sex.

Never	Seldom	Sometimes	Usually	Mostly	Always
0	1	2	3	4	5
			POINTS		

Because compassion people have such ability to show love, and because so many people need to feel loved, it is easy for their affection to be misconstrued by a member of the opposite sex.

One time we were responsible for a tour group to the Holy Land that included two single women with the compassion gift. They wanted so much to share the love of Jesus with the tour guide and the bus driver that they took every opportunity to make conversation. Soon Don and I could see that the men were taking the women's *agape* love as personal interest. When we found out that they'd been invited to the guide's apartment, Don had to put the brakes on the situation.

At first the women resented his interference, for they saw the invitation as an opportunity to talk to the two men about Jesus. He convinced them at last that he was acting for their own protection; if the men were really ready to hear the Gospel, they could do so within the safety of the group.

Sheila, a college student with a score of 98 on compassion, shared this: "I have to be very careful ministering to the opposite sex even within our church's young adult group. More than once a 'brother' has fallen in love with me just because I showed some loving concern for him, and boy—what a problem. It's so difficult to straighten out their perspective and not hurt their feelings in the process."

We recommend that a compassion person *never*, and we mean *never* counsel someone of the opposite sex *alone*. (In fact, this is a good rule for everyone.)

If you know some compassion people, take time to let them know you love them and minister positive input into their lives.

Typical problem areas of the gift of compassion	Never	Seldom	Sometimes	Usually	Mostly	Always	POINTS
	0	1	2	3	4	5	
1. Tends to be indecisive.			✗				
2. Is often prone to take up another person's offense.	✗						
3. Is easily hurt by others.		✗					
4. Can empathize too much with the suffering of others.		✗					
5. Has an affectionate nature that is often misinterpreted by the opposite sex.	✗						
						TOTAL	4

Biblical Compassion People

Those with the gift of compassion are the easiest of all to spot in action. These are feeling people and their deeds of caring and mercy give identifiable evidence.

Jesus' story of the Good Samaritan is a classic portrait of a compassion person. The setting underscores the tremendous importance of this gift. Jesus has just pinpointed to a devious lawyer that life in the Kingdom of God has to do with loving God and loving one's neighbor.

Scripture: Luke 10:30–35	Your Comments:
30 A certain man was going from Jerusalem down to Jericho, and he fell among robbers, who stripped him of his clothes and belongings and beat him and went their way, [unconcernedly] leaving him half dead, as it happened.	
31 Now by coincidence a certain priest was going down along that road, and when he saw him, he passed by on the other side.	
32 A Levite likewise came down to the place and saw him, and passed by on the other side [of the road].	
33 But a certain Samaritan, as he traveled along, came down to where he was; and when he saw him, he was moved with pity and sympathy [for him],	
34 And went to him and dressed his wounds, pouring on [them] oil and wine. Then he set him on his own beast and brought him to an inn and took care of him.	

Scripture: Luke 10:30–35	Your Comments:
35 And the next day he took out two denarii [two day's wages] and gave [them] to the innkeeper, saying, Take care of him; and whatever more you spend, I [myself] will repay you when I return.	

Neither the priest nor the Levite, the religious leaders of their time, showed any compassion for the man who had been robbed and beaten. Religiosity without the Spirit can insulate us from "feeling with" the people around us.

The Samaritan, on the other hand, was so full of the gift of compassion that his caring broke through the social barriers that separated Samaritans and Jews. Though ostracized by Jews, the compassionate traveler reached out to a fellow human being in need. Here are our observations:

Scripture: Luke 10:30–35	Our Comments:
30 A certain man was going from Jerusalem down to Jericho, and he fell among robbers, who stripped him of his clothes and belongings and beat him and went their way, [unconcernedly] leaving him half dead, as it happened.	
31 Now by coincidence a certain priest was going down along that road, and when he saw him, he passed by on the other side.	Note: the priest had no compassion.
32 A Levite likewise came down to the place and saw him, and passed by on the other side [of the road].	Note: the Levite had no compassion.
33 But a certain Samaritan, as he traveled along, came down to where he was; and when he saw him, he was moved with pity and sympathy [for him],	**#1** has great capacity for love **#4** is drawn to the hurting **#17** responds with the heart **#18** empathizes
34 And went to him and dressed his wounds, pouring on [them] oil and wine. Then he set him on his own beast and brought him to an inn and took care of him.	**#5** takes action to remove hurt **#6** removes physical distress **#17** is ruled by the heart
35 And the next day he took out two denarii [two day's wages], and gave [them] to the innkeeper, saying, Take care of him; and whatever more you spend, I [myself] will repay you when I return.	**#6** removes potential emotional distress **#12** takes thoughtful action **#13** trusts innkeeper

We see the Good Samaritan not only taking care of the victim's physical hurt, but also anticipating his emotional distress: coming out of his coma in an inn and realizing that he had no money to pay for his care. Truly the Samaritan covered all the bases of compassion as only those with this gift can do.

Another obvious example of the motivational gift of compassion is John, "the disciple whom Jesus loved" (John 21:7). Certainly compassionate people are exceptionally lovable. In addition, we see John's loving, sensitive nature coming through in his writing. See how much the gift is evidenced in his Gospel!

Other compassion people to look at are:

Ruth: Ruth

Joseph, the legal father of Jesus: Matthew 1:16–24; 2:13; Luke 1:27; 2:4–51; 3:23; 4:22; John 1:45; 6:42

Jeremiah (but with the *call* of a prophet; note that he's often called the "weeping prophet"): Jeremiah

Rachel: Genesis 29–31; 35; 46; 48:7; Ruth 4:11; 1 Samuel 10:2; Jeremiah 31:15

Rebekah: Genesis 22:23; 24; 35:8; 49:31

Evaluating Your Profile Sheet

28

Now you have your profile sheet completed. Your scores have all been tallied and transferred and you see something like the following sample profile sheet. What does this all mean? How can you evaluate it? What if you have a tie for first and second place? What if there's not much difference between any of your seven scores? What if your scores seem too high? Or too low? We'll try to answer these questions.

We'll use our own profile sheets as examples:

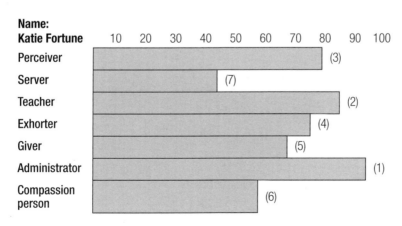

Name:
Katie Fortune

	10	20	30	40	50	60	70	80	90	100
Perceiver								(3)		
Server				(7)						
Teacher							(2)			
Exhorter						(4)				
Giver					(5)					
Administrator								(1)		
Compassion person			(6)							

Here's what we see from my profile sheet:

1. My primary gift is administration. It is a high score (94) indicating that I function in it nearly all the time. It means that I am capable of and comfortable in leadership and that I lead easily.

2. My secondary gift of teaching (82) is also high. This indicates that I am also operating in that gift a lot of the time. It shows that my teaching gift is constantly modifying my primary gift of administration. It also indicates that I can operate specifically in my secondary gift, although the way in which it functions will still be colored by my primary gift. For instance, when I prepare to teach I will do lots of research, but always with the overall picture in mind and a view to systematically organize the material.

3. My third gift of perceiving (74) is medium high. Therefore this third gift will have some influence in my life, but not nearly so much as the first two. It is not high enough to make me a regular intercessor, especially since my first two gifs are not intercessory gifts. However, it is strong enough to provide me with a keen sense of right and wrong and a desire to see God's will done through the use of my primary gifts.

4. Close to my third gift is exhorter (72), which is, like the first three, a speaking gift. Therefore my communication skills are strong and fluent.

5. My three lowest gifts are in the category of serving gifts: giving (63), compassion (56) and serving (42), which means that I am not adapted well to serving in general.

6. My lowest score is server, indicating that I am least capable in that area. My viewpoint, of course, is that I "serve" when I give myself to leadership and teaching for the benefit of others.

7. The fact that Don and I both scored low on server indicates that our home and yard will sometimes be neglected in favor of our involvement with people in areas where we can both use our speaking type gifts. Now that we are in our retirement years, we can afford to hire people to do some housecleaning and landscaping for us. Our gifting makes us grateful for that.

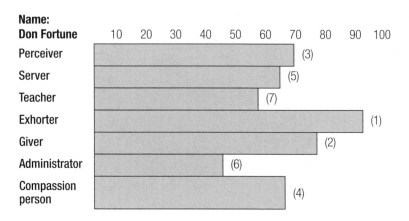

Name: Don Fortune

Gift	Rank
Perceiver	(3)
Server	(5)
Teacher	(7)
Exhorter	(1)
Giver	(2)
Administrator	(6)
Compassion person	(4)

Now about Don's profile sheet:

1. Don's primary gift is exhortation. The high score of 89 reveals that he functions in it most of the time. Don just naturally encourages people in every situation in which he finds himself. This is also a speaking and leadership gift, and he does a lot of both.
2. His secondary gift of giving (73) is also strong. This has given him a keen interest in missions and evangelism and it's why he especially likes ministering on the mission field. This gift also motivates him to support missionaries and outreach projects financially.
3. Perceiver (69), his third gift, is close to his giver gift; from this combination comes his call to a ministry of prayer and intercession. For many years he participated in the early morning prayer meeting from 6:00 to 7:00 A.M. each day at church, finding it both essential and fruitful.
4. Compassion (62) and serving (61) are almost a tie for fourth and fifth place, while Don's two lowest scores, administration (55) and teaching (54), are also only a point apart. Don's teaching ability stems from his exhortation gift, not his teaching gift.
5. Notice that his last two gifts are my first two. This means we are complementary to each other in our approach to things. This makes for some interesting challenges from time to time in our marriage—but one thing is for sure, we are never bored.

Don has exercised his primary gifts as a home fellowship leader, as a church elder, in teaching seminars in many countries, in heading up missions outreach at our church, in overseeing caring ministries like the food bank and in counseling.

This is the kind of evaluation you can make from your profile sheet. Remember, there's only one of you in all the world, and God has designed you to be a vital part of the Body of Christ.

Reasons for Close Scores

In some cases a person will have such close scores that he or she has difficulty determining the primary gift. There can be a number of reasons for this:

1. First of all, it may be that your motivational gifts have been squelched in childhood or are being hindered by some present circumstance. Therefore, another gift may at this point be taking precedence over the primary one.
2. A second reason could be a self-image so poor that you are unable to get in touch with your underlying personality and your actual giftedness.

3. A third reason may be that you are currently involved in activities or employment that make use of some secondary gift; your scoring may be influenced more by your present involvement than by your innate giftedness.
4. A fourth reason could be that you're trying to be something you're not (or trying not to be something you are).
5. Finally, you may indeed have two motivational gifts that are equally strong because God gifted you in just that way. It has been our experience that when this happens the two gifts modify each other in order to bring the balance that is needed for the type of ministry that person is to have. See the end of the chapter for more information on this.

The Breakers

If you find that you have nearly identical scores on your first two gifts, how do you determine whether they are in fact equally strong, or whether one belongs ahead of the other? Here's a test to show which gift is stronger. The questions are based on a matter of preference—yours. It is a subjective way to determine which gift primarily motivates you.

Answer every question, even if you feel "I really like to do both." *Make yourself make a choice*, even if the margin of preference is very small.

If two or three of your answers are (a), yours is probably the first of the two gifts named. If the majority of your answers are (b), then yours is the second gift.

This procedure can also be used as a tiebreaker in determining the relative strength of your second and third gifts, or your third and fourth gifts, and so on.

Perceiver/Server

1. *Would you rather spend time*
___ a. interceding for others (or)
___ b. entertaining houseguests?

2. *Would you consider it more loving and caring to*
_✳_ a. help a person to change for the better (or)
___ b. do something to meet a special need he or she has?

3. *Would you rather help a person get rid of*
_✳_ a. sin in his life (or)
___ b. clutter in his house?

Perceiver/Teacher

1. *When you share Scriptures with people, would you most likely*
___ a. tell them if their interpretation is right or wrong (or)
_✳_ b. instruct them to study and find the truth themselves?

2. *Would you rather*
___ a. spend time in intercessory prayer (or)
_✗_ b. teach a Bible study class for believers?

3. *To form an opinion about something, would you probably*
___ a. go by what you feel and/or believe already (or)
_✗_ b. research it until you are confident enough?

Perceiver/Exhorter

1. *To be of genuine help to people, would you rather*
___ a. tell them to repent and change their ways (or)
_✗_ b. encourage them to get their relationships right?

2. *In counseling people, do you*
___ a. tell them where they are wrong and what to do (or)
_✗_ b. accept them where they are, then suggest change?

3. *In giving advice, do you*
___ a. quote Scripture as an absolute basis for action (or)
___ b. give practical steps of action to follow?

Perceiver/Giver

1. *To be helpful to others, would you tend to*
___ a. give scriptural advice (or)
___ b. do something for them?

2. *Would you rather*
___ a. pray for someone (or)
___ b. provide for him or her?

3. *When dealing with unbelievers, would you be more likely to*
___ a. tell them they are sinners and need to repent (or)
___ b. simply show them the way of salvation?

Perceiver/Administrator

1. *When helping someone spiritually, would you more likely*
___ a. tell him or her, "This is what Scripture says" (or)
_✗_ b. help him or her to see the overall view of Scripture?

2. *In giving advice to people, would you*
___ a. tell them where they're right or wrong (or)
_✗_ b. try first to find out all you can about their problems?

3. *Would you rather spend time*
_✗_ a. in prayer and fasting (or)
___ b. organizing a Christian project?

Perceiver/Compassion Person

1. *In helping people, do you tend to meet*
___ a. their spiritual needs first (or)
___ b. their emotional needs first?

2. *When someone is hurting, do you*
___ a. show from Scripture how to overcome the hurt (or)
___ b. identify with the hurt, staying with him or her until it's gone?

3. *Would you rather participate in*
___ a. an intercessory prayer group (or)
___ b. a program to help the poor?

Server/Teacher

1. *Do you teach primarily by*
___ a. demonstrating the caring nature of God (or)
___ b. expounding on the Word of God?

2. *If someone needs something would you rather*
___ a. provide it for her (or)
___ b. show him how to provide for himself?

3. *Would you rather*
___ a. help set up for or serve a church dinner (or)
___ b. speak to the group after dinner?

Server/Exhorter

1. *Would you rather*
___ a. work with your hands (or)
___ b. speak with your mouth?

2. *If a person didn't follow your instructions properly, would you*
___ a. just go ahead and do it yourself (or)
___ b. explain more thoroughly so he or she could do it?

3. *After a meeting, do you feel it is more important to*
___ a. make sure the room is left in order (or)
___ b. spend time socializing?

Server/Giver

1. *Do you view hospitality mainly as an opportunity to*
___ a. serve (or)
___ b. give?

2. *Would you rather*
___ a. help people with their practical needs (or)
___ b. spend time witnessing?

3. *Would you rather help someone in need by*
___ a. doing something for him or her (or)
___ b. anonymously giving money?

Server/Administrator

1. *Would you rather*
___ a. help someone accomplish something (or)
___ b. tell him or her how to accomplish it on his or her own?

2. *If a room needed to be cleaned, would you*
___ a. get a broom and sweep it (or)
___ b. figure out who could do the job best?

3. *Do you*
___ a. take things as they come (or)
___ b. plan ahead?

Server/Compassion Person

1. *Do you care more about*
___ a. people's practical needs (or)
___ b. how people feel?

2. *Would you rather*
___ a. help with a church work party (or)
___ b. visit the shut-ins?

3. *Do you*
___ a. work at a project until it's completed (or)
___ b. get sidetracked by the emotional needs of others?

Teacher/Exhorter

1. *Would you rather help people by*
___ a. teaching a Bible study class (or)
___ b. counseling them with their problems?

2. *Would you prefer to*
___ a. read a good book (or)
___ b. be with people?

3. *Do you like to have*
___ a. a few select friends with similar interests (or)
___ b. lots of friends—the more the better?

Teacher/Giver

1. *Would you like to see God increase your ability*
___ a. to teach effectively (or)
___ b. to give generously?

2. *Would you rather*

___ a. research and study (or)

___ b. witness and evangelize?

3. *Are you most likely to be successful in a*

___ a. teaching career (or)

___ b. business venture?

Teacher/Administrator

1. *Would you rather*

___ a. train others to do a job (or)

___ b. delegate work to others?

2. *Do you find that more often you are*

___ a. reading a good book (or)

___ b. making lists of things to do?

3. *Would you rather*

___ a. do thorough research on a subject (or)

___ b. organize and lead a group project?

Teacher/Compassion Person

1. *Is your decision making*

___ a. based on research (or)

___ b. difficult for you?

2. *Do you*

___ a. keep your emotions in control (or)

___ b. cry easily?

3. *Do you find that you*

___ a. are drawn to intellectual pursuits (or)

___ b. daydream or fantasize a lot?

Exhorter/Giver

1. *Do you encourage people*

___ a. by sharing your own experiences (or)

___ b. by giving them practical help?

2. *Would you rather*

___ a. let your life be an example to an unbeliever (or)

___ b. lead someone to the Lord through verbal witnessing?

3. *Would you prefer to*

___ a. speak in front of a group (or)

___ b. function supportively in the background?

Exhorter/Administrator

1. *Would you prefer to*
___ a. do individual counseling (or)
___ b. take on group leadership?

2. *When working on a project, do you tend to*
___ a. stay with it until it is finished (or)
___ b. delegate as much as you can to others?

3. *Do you find that you*
___ a. adapt easily in almost any situation (or)
___ b. get frustrated with delays and red tape?

Exhorter/Compassion Person

1. *Would you rather*
___ a. do personal counseling (or)
___ b. help with caring type ministries?

2. *Are you*
___ a. likely to see a problem as a challenge (or)
___ b. sometimes overwhelmed by a problem?

3. *Are decisions*
___ a. easy for you (or)
___ b. hard to make?

Giver/Administrator

1. *Would you rather*
___ a. assist an ongoing project (or)
___ b. organize a project?

2. *Would you rather be*
___ a. a supporter (or)
___ b. a leader?

3. *Would you prefer to spend your time*
___ a. doing door-to-door witnessing (or)
___ b. pioneering a new project?

Giver/Compassion Person

1. *Is your prime interest in*
___ a. people's needs (or)
___ b. people's feelings?

2. *If you're working on a project when someone expresses a need, would you*
___ a. finish the project and then meet the need (or)
___ b. meet the need and then finish the project?

3. *Would you rather encourage people to*
___ a. give generously to further the Gospel (or)
___ b. minister to those who are hurting?

Administrator/Compassion Person

1. *When you look at situations, do you focus on*
___ a. the long-range view (or)
___ b. what's happening now?

2. *Would you prefer to spend your time*
___ a. organizing people and projects (or)
___ b. ministering to someone in distress?

3. *Would you rather work with*
___ a. a group (or)
___ b. one person at a time?

Clarifying Close Scores

Here are some other suggestions that can help you make sure of your primary motivational gift:

1. Set your test aside for a few days, a few weeks—even a few months. Become more observant of your behavior, your interests and what seems to be motivating you. Now that you're familiar with the seven gifts, you'll be more aware of them operating in your life. Then take the test again; this time it may be more decisive.
2. If you tended to avoid giving yourself fives and zeros, do the test again with a willingness to record the extremes where appropriate. Remember, it is not prideful to score a five. If you always do something, this is just a fact.
3. Look for patterns. Go over the scoring sheets for consistency within a major gift. For instance, you may have had a similar score on two gifts but on one the scores range from twos to fives, while on the other, most of the scores are fours. The latter is most likely your primary gift.
4. Look at the problem characteristics. Some people have told us, "The problem areas shouted the loudest, 'That's you!'" This will be especially true if you are a fairly new Christian or one who still has a lot of problems to resolve.
5. Examine the children's characteristics in chapter 33, beginning on page 262. Many have said that as they thought back into their growing-up years they saw their giftedness clearly. (This will not help, however, if your personality was squelched or controlled in your growing-up years.)

Some have found it helpful to personalize that chapter by circling all the traits that were characteristic of them as children. Then look to see which gift predominates.

Another device is to score yourself on the youth scoring sheets, or even the children's scoring sheets (also found in chapter 33). Be sure to score *as you were at that age.*

6. Ask your spouse or a close friend or relative to help you score or even to score the test for you. He may be able to see things about you that you don't see. However, use this only as confirmation, for the person who knows you best is you!

7. Ask the Lord. This may well be the most important thing you can do. After all, He created you and He knows you best of all. If He knows (and He does) how many hairs are on your head at this moment (and you certainly don't), He surely knows the gifts that He has built into you. Remember, He wants you to be a well-functioning member of His Body. He wants you to use your gifts to help others. He wants you to have the joy that comes from using your motivational gift(s) to the fullest.

Combination Gifts

Suppose that you've done all of the above and two (or more) gifts are still tied for first place in your makeup. Accept this: *about two-thirds of all people have combination gifts.* Only about one-third have just one strong gift, making them a classic example of that gift.

Please understand that neither a classic gift nor a combination of gifts is better. God has endowed people the way they are for His own purposes. A person with two gifts of equal or similar strength can be assured both will be needed to fulfill God's plans for his or her life and/or ministry. A person with one strong gift will need that focus of characteristics that will enable him or her to fulfill God's plans.

In some circumstances a person with a combination gifting will draw on one of the gifts, but in another situation he or she will draw on the other gift—while in a third case the interaction of both gifts is needed.

Each combination produces an interesting modification. For instance, a man gifted in both perceiving and compassion will find that his perceiver gift is softened by the compassion gift. Sensitive to the hurts of others, he will not be so blunt and judgmental.

His compassion gift is also modified in such a way that he is able to be reasonably decisive and to counsel with a reliable amount of objectivity. His tendency to compromise is balanced by his perceiver's refusal to compromise—which means he will compromise only when there is valid reason.

The teacher/exhorter combination produces an individual especially suited to teaching, with the ability not only to present well-researched facts but to get them across with colorful, interesting and life-related anecdotes.

The giver/perceiver combination equips a person to become a powerful evangelist or missionary, with outstanding success at calling people to repentance and salvation.

The server/giver combination creates a well-rounded Christian who both serves in person and provides financial support for others' ministries.

The list goes on and on. If you are a combination gift, praise God for your unique blend of equipping.

Here are some charts that will help you to see how your gifts affect or modify each other. We have prepared comparison scales, one or more for each of thirty categories we have designated, plotting the seven gifts in relationship to each other.

We have used abbreviations for the gifts: *P* for perceiver, *S* for server, *T* for teacher, *E* for exhorter, *G* for giver, *A* for administrator and *C* for compassion.

Circle the two letters representing your two gifts and place an "X" at the midpoint between them. This will show you where you would be in the scale when the two gifts are modifying each other. We have included only a few of the thirty categories here, but you can receive a free PDF file of the rest by emailing us at fortune@heart2heart.org to request the rest of the Combination Gifts Charts, and add the code word "chosen."

EMOTIONS

T	-	A	-	E	G	S	P	-	C

Unemotional — Balanced — Emotional

E	A	-	T	G	-	P	C	S	-

Outgoing — Balanced — Shy

T	S	A	E	G	-	C	-	-	P

Not easily angered — Average — Easily angered

C	-	E	G	A	-	P	T	S	-

Very loving — Average — Hard to express love

C	-	-	S	G	E	A	T	P	-

Easily wounded — Average — Not easily wounded

C	S	G	E	A	T	-	P	-	-

Forgiving — Average — Slow to forgive

VERBAL EXPRESSION

E	A	T	P	-	G	C	-	S	-

Easy   Average   Difficult

E	-	A	T	P	G	-	C	-	S

Interrupter   Average   Non-interrupter

A	E	T	P	G	-	-	C	-	S

Comfortable speaking in public   Average   Not comfortable

INTELLECT

T	A	E	P	G	-	S	C	-	-

Very intellectual   Average   Nonintellectual

T	P	A	-	E	G	-	S	-	C

Questioning   Average   Accepting

P	T	A	E	-	G	S	-	C	-

Highly opinionated   Balanced   Unopinionated

T	A	P	E	-	G	-	S	-	C

Very analytical   Balanced   Nonanalytical

T	-	A	P	E	-	G	S	-	C

Likes to correct   Average   Does not correct

T	A	P	E	G	-	S	-	C	-

Very studious   Balanced   Seldom studious

CONFLICT RESOLUTION

E	A	T	P	G	-	S	-	-	C

Resolves conflicts well   Average   Avoids conflict

T	A	E	-	G	S	-	C	-	P

Manages anger well   Average   Difficulty handling anger

P	-	A	T	E	-	G	S	-	C

Argumentative   Average   Nonargumentative

CONFLICT RESOLUTION

A	E	T	G	-	S	C	-	-	P
Accepts reponsibility for actions				Average					Tends to blame

C	S	G	E	A	T	-	-	-	P
Apologetic				Average					Stubborn

E	A	P	T	-	G	-	S	-	C
Addresses issues				Average					Clams up

Suppose you are an administrator with a close secondary gift of serving. In many ways these are opposite gifts, but the resulting modification will enable you to do both the overall organization and the meticulous detail work.

Look at the first scale under "Emotion" and circle the *A* and the *S*. The *A* is three sections to the right of "Unemotional," and the *S* is four sections to the left of "Emotional." You would tend to be neither extremely emotional nor unemotional. This near-central position would make you an easygoing person.

If a person is an administrator/teacher, we see the scores falling only on the extreme left. The characteristics have been enhanced further by the "doubling-up" process. Expect this person to be cool, calm and collected, quite social and exceptionally skilled in speech.

Should you have three strong gifts, circle all three on each comparison scale and observe how they modify each other.

If you are a combination gift, proceed through all the comparison scales and you will gain a more comprehensive picture of your personality. Remember, these scores are general; individuals may vary from the norm.

Biblical Exhortations

No matter what gift or combination of gifts you have been given, the most important thing to remember is that it should operate in love—always!

Following the list of motivational gifts in Romans 12, the remainder of this chapter is devoted to various exhortations, setting forth the way in which we are to put love into action as we use our gifts. While some verses may seem to relate specifically to certain motivational gifts, we think they relate to *all* the gifts; we are *all* to practice the principles laid out here. Such things as hospitality, harmony, forgiveness and kindness are both the privilege and the responsibility of every believer. It seems as if Paul has pinpointed the most important exhortations from his own writings and other biblical sources and condensed them into a precise presentation of positive Christian conduct.

One could say that if a person—no matter what his or her motivational gift—were to live by these exhortations, life would be good and relationships would be healthy. The converse is also true, to the degree that if we do not abide by them, we fall short of fulfilling the law of love. Here is an encapsulated prescription for following Paul's exhortations.

1. Love others (Romans 12:9).
2. Hate evil (Romans 12:9).
3. Focus on good (Romans 12:9).
4. Practice brotherly love (Romans 12:10).
5. Honor others (Romans 12:10).
6. Be zealous in the Spirit (Romans 12:11).
7. Serve the Lord (Romans 12:11).
8. Be joyful in hope (Romans 12:12).
9. Endure affliction (Romans 12:12).
10. Pray faithfully (Romans 12:12).
11. Share with others (Romans 12:13).
12. Practice hospitality (Romans 12:13).
13. Bless when persecuted (Romans 12:14).
14. Don't curse (Romans 12:14).
15. Rejoice with rejoicers (Romans 12:15).
16. Mourn with mourners (Romans 12:15).
17. Live in harmony (Romans 12:16).
18. Avoid pride (Romans 12:16).
19. Don't be conceited (Romans 12:16).
20. Don't return evil (Romans 12:17).
21. Do what is right (Romans 12:17).
22. Live at peace (Romans 12:18).
23. Don't take revenge (Romans 12:19).
24. Let God settle accounts (Romans 12:19).
25. Show kindness to enemies (Romans 12:20).
26. Overcome evil with good (Romans 12:21).

Jesus' Characteristics

Only Jesus has demonstrated the complete and perfect operation of all seven of the motivational gifts in His life.

As a Perceiver

1. He spoke only what He heard the Father speak.
   "For I did not speak of my own accord, but the Father who sent me commanded me what to say and how to say it" (John 12:49, NIV).

2. He was the Truth.
   "Jesus answered, 'I am the way and the truth and the life'" (John 14:6, NIV).

3. He saw into people's hearts.
   "The fact is, you have had five husbands, and the man you now have is not your husband" (John 4:18, NIV).

   "You brood of vipers, how can you who are evil say anything good? For out of the overflow of the heart the mouth speaks" (Matthew 12:34, NIV).

4. He prayed and interceded.
   "Very early in the morning, while it was still dark, Jesus got up, left the house and went off to a solitary place, where he prayed" (Mark 1:35, NIV).

5. He hated evil.
   "'It is written,' he said to them, '"My house will be called a house

of prayer," but you are making it a "den of robbers"'" (Matthew 21:13, NIV).

6. He was frank and outspoken.
"Woe to you, teachers of the law and Pharisees, you hypocrites! You are like whitewashed tombs, which look beautiful on the outside but on the inside are full of dead men's bones and everything unclean" (Matthew 23:27, NIV).

As a Server

1. He worked with His hands, a carpenter with His father, Joseph.
"Then he went down to Nazareth with them and was obedient to them" (Luke 2:51, NIV).

2. He demonstrated service.
"After that, he poured water into a basin and began to wash his disciples' feet" (John 13:5, NIV).

3. He exalted serving.
"Whoever wants to become great among you must be your servant" (Mark 10:43, NIV).

4. He had a high energy level and kept pace with the demands of His ministry.
"Again crowds of people came to him, and as was his custom, he taught them" (Mark 10:1, NIV).

As a Teacher

1. He taught God's truth.
"He told them another parable: 'The kingdom of heaven is like a mustard seed, which a man took and planted in his field'" (Matthew 13:31, NIV).

2. He fulfilled the Law.
"Do not think that I have come to abolish the Law or the Prophets; I have not come to abolish them but to fulfill them" (Matthew 5:17, NIV).

3. He quoted Scripture.
"Jesus answered, 'It is written: "Man does not live on bread alone, but on every word that comes from the mouth of God"'" (Matthew 4:4, NIV; quoting Deuteronomy 8:3).

4. He built on scriptural truth.
   "You have heard that it was said to the people long ago, 'Do not murder, and anyone who murders will be subject to judgment.' But I tell you that anyone who is angry with his brother will be subject to judgment" (Matthew 5:21–22, NIV).

5. He was intelligent and curious.
   "After three days they found him in the temple courts, sitting among the teachers, listening to them and asking them questions" (Luke 2:46, NIV).

6. He was self-controlled.
   "He plied him with many questions, but Jesus gave him no answer. . . . Then Herod and his soldiers ridiculed and mocked him" (Luke 23:9–11, NIV).

As an Exhorter

1. He taught people to live victoriously.
   See the Sermon on the Mount, Matthew 5–7.

2. He gave positive exhortations.
   "Love your enemies . . . bless . . . give . . . lend . . . be merciful . . . do not judge. . . forgive" (Luke 6:27–37, NIV).

3. He prescribed precise steps of action.
   "Go now and leave your life of sin" (John 8:11, NIV).

   "Jesus answered, 'If you want to be perfect, go, sell your possessions and give to the poor. . . . Then come, follow me'" (Matthew 19:21, NIV).

4. He accepted people as they were.
   The woman at the well (see John 4:4–30); the tax collector (see Mark 2:13–16).

5. His own life was a witness to the truth.
   "Jesus answered, . . . 'In fact, for this reason I was born, and for this I came into the world, to testify to the truth'" (John 18:37, NIV).

As a Giver

1. He fed the five thousand.
   "Taking the five loaves and the two fish . . . he gave them to his disciples to set before the people" (Mark 6:41, NIV).

2. He gave His time, energy, abilities and love to others.
   He trained His disciples, taught the multitudes, healed the sick, cast out evil spirits and raised the dead.

3. He taught on giving.
   "But a poor widow came and put in two very small copper coins, worth only a fraction of a penny. Calling his disciples to him, Jesus said, 'I tell you the truth, this poor widow has put more into the treasury than all the others'" (Mark 12:42–43, NIV).

4. He had a strong focus on the Gospel.
   "But he said, 'I must preach the good news of the kingdom of God to the other towns also, because that is why I was sent'" (Luke 4:43, NIV).

5. He gave His life for us.
   "Greater love has no one than this, that he lay down his life for his friends" (John 15:13, NIV).

As an Administrator

1. He organized His followers.
   He had an inner circle of three. "After six days Jesus took Peter, James and John with him and led them up a high mountain, where they were all alone" (Mark 9:2, NIV).

   He trained twelve disciples. "Jesus went up on a mountainside and called to him those he wanted, and they came to him. He appointed twelve—designating them apostles" (Mark 3:13–14, NIV).

   He sent out the seventy two by two. "After this the Lord appointed seventy-two others and sent them two by two ahead of him to every town and place where he was about to go" (Luke 10:1, NIV).

2. He was highly motivated to fulfill His mission.
   "Jesus . . . who for the joy set before him endured the cross, scorning its shame, and sat down at the right hand of the throne of God" (Hebrews 12:2, NIV).

3. He was a man under authority and taught about authority.
   "Then Jesus . . . said, 'All authority in heaven and on earth has been given to me'" (Matthew 28:18, NIV).

4. He was an effective leader.
   "These twelve Jesus sent out with the following instructions: . . . 'Heal the sick, raise the dead, . . . freely give'" (Matthew 10:8, NIV).

5. He endured criticism for the long-range goal of the cross.
"The Son of Man . . . [came] . . . to give his life as a ransom for many" (Matthew 20:28, NIV).

As a Compassion Person

1. He had a tremendous capacity to show love.
"When Jesus . . . saw a large crowd, he had compassion on them and healed their sick" (Matthew 14:14, NIV).

2. He was aware of people's physical needs.
"Jesus . . . said, 'I have compassion for these people; they have already been with me three days and have nothing to eat. I do not want to send them away hungry, or they may collapse on the way'" (Matthew 15:32, NIV).

3. He was alert to emotional and psychological needs.
"When he saw the crowds, he had compassion on them, because they were harassed and helpless, like sheep without a shepherd" (Matthew 9:36, NIV).

4. He cared for children.
"Jesus said, 'Let the little children come to me, and do not hinder them'" (Matthew 19:14, NIV).

5. He had empathy for others.
"When the Lord saw [the widow whose son had died], his heart went out to her and he said, 'Don't cry'" (Luke 7:13, NIV).

6. He expressed emotion.
"Jesus wept" (John 11:35, NIV).

7. He mourned over Jerusalem.
"O Jerusalem, Jerusalem . . . how often I have longed to gather your children together, as a hen gathers her chicks under her wings, but you were not willing" (Matthew 23:37, NIV).

Each of us, as part of the corporate Body of Christ on this earth, has received one or more of the motivational gifts to enable us to continue the work He began here. Working together, we can (in a sense) accomplish as much and even more than Jesus did in His three years' earthly ministry. "I tell you the truth, anyone who has faith in me will do what I have been doing. He will do even greater things than these, because I am going to the Father" (John 14:12, NIV).

Even the Communion service has taken on greater meaning for Don and me since we've come to understand how the motivational gifts tie in with it. We can almost see Jesus at that Last Supper as He broke the bread, representing the body through which He had ministered to people, saying something like:

"Here, Peter. You are obviously part of My gift of exhortation. I want you to increase in your capacity to speak boldly for this group.

"Here, Thomas. I want you to continue as the part of My gift of teaching that I have made you. Always check out purported truth by what I have taught you.

"And here, John. I want you to continue to grow as part of My gift of compassion. Let My Father's love increasingly flow through your life to others."

Jesus exhibited perfectly *all* of the motivational gifts. As His Body today we can work with Him to minister to and bless others. When Don and I take Communion now we look around at the people with whom we are joined and say with deep appreciation, "Thank You, Jesus, for our pastor, who gives so endlessly of himself to this flock. His gifts of exhortation and administration are such a marvelous combination. And thank You, Lord, for Gigi and the candid but loving honesty that comes through her perceiver gift. How we praise You for Barbara's gift of serving. What would we do without her faithfulness to handle all the detailed tasks behind the scenes? And Lord, we so appreciate Bob's ability to exhort and encourage people as he teaches. Thanks for Brian's giving gift: It's so good to see him bringing people to You. We are grateful for Brent's strong gift of administration and Ted's meticulous research into Your Word. And thank You, Lord, for Ardy's beautiful, gentle and abundant gift of compassion."

Each time we take Communion we celebrate with joy the fact that each person in the Body of Christ is gifted uniquely and generously by God!

Part III

Practical
Applications

Living Your Gift

Now that you know your giftedness you can follow the commands found in 1 Peter 4:10 and Romans 12:6–8 to use it. You will discover what a joy it is to function in your gifts. Even if you've realized that you have been doing so naturally and spontaneously in the past, you will be more delighted as you consciously observe your gift in action in the future.

You will be able to make wise choices and decisions. You will be able to live life to the fullest, to deliberately be a blessing to others and to accept and appreciate others as they operate in their giftedness. Truly, you will be able to know experientially the fulfillment of Jesus' prayer in the seventeenth chapter of John.

In any given situation, you will be able to recognize the motivational gifts in action—in conversations, in groups, in preachers, in leaders and in those who work quietly behind the scenes. You'll spot a person's gift as he speaks or teaches, or even as she appears on television or radio. Biographies will make more sense. Even newspaper reports, if enough details are given, will reveal a person's giftedness.

We'd like to share the following example that shows how naturally the motivational gifts go into action.

Suppose that you have seven people over for dinner and each just happens to have a different motivational gift. You are bringing three salad plates to the table when one slips from your grip and crashes to the floor, scattering bits of glass and salad in one big mess. How will each person react?

Perceiver: "That's what happens when you try to carry too many plates."

Server: "I'll clean it up."

Teacher: "The reason you dropped that plate was that it was not balanced properly."

Exhorter: "Next time, let someone help you carry the plates."

Giver: "I'll be glad to help you make another salad."

Administrator: "John, get the broom and dustpan. Sally, bring the mop. Marie, help me fix another salad."

Compassion person: "Don't feel embarrassed, it could have happened to anyone."

Marriage Challenges

We have found that opposites usually attract in marriage. Usually one spouse will have a speaking type gift and the other will have a serving type gift. A perceiver may be attracted to a compassion person, or a teacher to an exhorter, or a server to an administrator—seemingly contrary gifts.

We could write a whole book on this subject (and we did! See *Discover Your Spouse's Gifts*) but we'd like to say here that many marriage conflicts and stresses can be eliminated simply by coming to know and accepting each other's motivational gifts.

Take Tim and Darlene, for instance. Tim is the quiet type who likes to work with his hands, a boat builder by trade. He is easily moved to tears, easily swayed in the stands he takes. Darlene is more outgoing, highly opinionated, unmovable in her standards and drawn to a ministry of prayer.

There were many conflicts at first for them. Darlene would get irritated at Tim's "wishy-washiness" and changeability. He was upset with her dogmatic and unbending ways and easily hurt by her outspokenness.

Then the motivational gift test revealed that she was a perceiver and he was a compassion person. Almost immediately their relationship improved. Darlene realized that she needed to pray more and comment less. She began to appreciate her husband's sensitivity and gentleness as a beautiful gift from the Lord, and understood that he could hear from God, too.

Tim realized that Darlene's giftedness was from the Lord and that he could value, rather than be threatened by, her strong standards. He saw that it was okay for her to be the more verbal of the two.

They began to encourage each other's giftedness instead of resisting it. Differences were seen as an asset, and they have since become one of the most loving and spiritually mature couples we know. Darlene said, "I realized if both of us were just alike, one of us wouldn't be needed."

Then there's Gill and Gloria. He's a dynamic speaker type who for years tried to push his quiet, reserved wife into public ministry with him, accusing her of stubbornness and rebellion for not complying. Her attempts to talk in front of groups left her drained, embarrassed and devastated. She, on the other hand, accused Gill of being dominating, controlling and prideful for wanting such a visible public ministry.

After taking the motivational gift test they both repented for their judgments of each other. They discovered he was an administrator/perceiver combination and she was a server with a secondary gift of compassion. Gill released Gloria to be a behind-the-scenes support person and she accepted the fact that Gill's giftedness, not pride, was the reason he enjoyed a high-profile ministry. They are getting along just fine now.

We recommend that every married couple, and every couple considering marriage, get to know their motivational gifts. (See the back of the book for ordering additional books and materials.)

All types of relationships, not just husband/wife, can benefit from a heightened awareness of giftedness. Use the following chart to gain insight into the people with whom you tend to have problems or conflicts. Write the names and the relationship to you in the first column. Then in the second column briefly define the problems in that relationship. In the third column list what you think their gifts might be (you may even want to give them the test if they'd be open to that) and how these relate to the friction between you. The fourth column is for possible solutions. Indicate what you can do to help reduce the stressors. It may be that just seeing how different your gifts are (or in some cases, how similar) will relieve much of the pressure.

THE PERSON & THE RELATIONSHIP	CONFLICTS & PROBLEMS	MOTIVATIONAL GIFT	POSSIBLE SOLUTIONS
husband/wife:			
mother/father:			
brother/sister:			
other:			

Others you might list include your employer, fellow worker, pastor, leader, teacher, in-law, child, friend, roommate or neighbor.

Ask the Lord to guide you as you seek solutions. Remember, *you cannot change anyone else, but you can change yourself—both your attitudes and your actions.*

Counseling Clues

We find that knowing a person's motivational gift is invaluable in the counseling we do. A polluted gift may well be responsible for the difficulty he is having. Or she may simply be in conflict with someone who has an opposite gift or in competition with someone who has the same gift. The counsel we give to one type of gift is different from that which we give another type of gift. Sometimes the very nature of the problem is an indicator of the gift. A wife who feels constantly crushed by her husband may be a compassion person. A father who expects too high a level of academic performance from his son may be a teacher parent with a server child.

Often we can discern a person's gift by interviewing him or asking a few pointed questions. We asked a man who expected unquestioning obedience from his wife if he believed he was always right about everything. His "yes" answer was a clue to his perceiver gift.

Other times we give the motivational gift test to the counselee to score at home and bring back to the next counseling session.

Here are some problems we encounter repeatedly:

Perceiver: judgmental, intolerant, critical, prideful, domineering, controlling, unforgiving or poor self-image.

Server: perfectionist, critical, interfering, overdependent on appreciation or won't cut apron strings.

Teacher: prideful, intolerant, legalistic, dogmatic, opinionated, aloof, unromantic or know-it-all attitude.

Exhorter: opinionated, interruptive, compromising, overtalkative, pushy or stretches the truth.

Giver: stingy, manipulative, too focused on money, workaholic, too frugal, spoils children or steals.

Administrator: bossy, domineering, insensitive, callous, overzealous, procrastinates or neglects routine work.

Compassion person: easily wounded, overemotional, compromising, indecisive, undependable, tardy, illogical or overly empathetic.

We can't imagine being able to counsel constructively without such clues and an understanding of the counselees' motivational gifts. It has cut our counseling time down to one-half to one-third of the time it used to take, and our counselees wind up with information that will be useful for the rest of their lives.

Witnessing Styles

Most classes and seminars on witnessing assume there is a basic formula that works for everyone. We have not found this to be so. Rather, the most effective witnessing approach will be different with each of the seven motivational gifts. Therefore we see great value in knowing something about the person's giftedness before sharing our faith. The buckshot method may win some to Christ, but how much better it is to target our witnessing.

I can remember at age fifteen being accosted by a group of well-meaning but overzealous Christian young people who confronted me in a public place with, "Are you saved?" They succeeded only in making me mad.

First of all, they were brash and abrupt. They made no effort to strike up a conversation first or give any opportunity for me to relate to them.

Secondly, the statement was threatening and judgmental. It implied that if I didn't answer yes I was by implication "lost." They were using "Christianese," which does not communicate with unbelievers—or even some believers from more traditional backgrounds.

Thirdly, they knew nothing of my individual approach to new ideas, and so I automatically rejected what they said. I answered, "Of course I am!" even though I had no real idea of what they were asking. I only knew it got them off my back and I walked away thinking, *I'm glad I'm not like them!*

That encounter, far from being an effective witness, prompted me to ignore future witnessing attempts for the next eleven years. It had done more harm than good.

Here are some observations on witnessing within the framework of a person's gift that will at least earn you the right to be heard. In all cases, strive to build a bridge first. Let people know you are genuinely interested in them, their needs and their opinions.

Perceivers will respond best to questions about right and wrong, good versus evil, God's justice or other ultimate things: "Why do you think there is so much evil in the world?" or "How can God be both loving and just?" or "Do you know what happens to people when they die?" Depending on their answers you can lead into what you believe about these things and why.

Servers will respond to a Gospel that is practical and useful. Questions like "What is a man's greatest need?" "Do you think 'good works' will help a person get into heaven?" or "Have you ever considered how much Jesus focused on the importance of having a servant's heart?" will arouse interest and response.

Teachers will want to know facts and the reliable basis or proof for what you share. Ask something like "Why do you think God sent Jesus to live on this earth?" or "Look at this verse. Isn't that compelling proof that Jesus really was the unique Son of God?" or "Have you ever considered the claims of Christ? Do you think they are valid?"

Exhorters are concerned with people and their problems and what they can do to help. Questions like "What's the best way to help people overcome their problems?" or "What do you consider to be of greatest importance for having a fulfilled life?" or "Would you like to hear how I dealt with the same problem you are facing now?" will bring responses.

Givers have an inborn eager responsiveness to the Gospel. Your approach can be more direct: "Do you know what it means to be born again?" or "What do you think the word *salvation* means in the Bible?" or "What is the greatest gift you can give to God?"

Administrators are interested in the overall view of life and the universe. Catch their interest with "Why do you think God created people?" or "What is the most important thing that the Bible teaches?" or "What do you think will happen to the human race?"

Compassion people will relate best on a feeling level; logic leaves them cold. Try "How do you feel God wants us to treat each other?" or "If Jesus were here today, what do you feel He'd want to spend His time doing?" or "Do you feel there is any hope for the suffering people in the world?"

You'll develop your own questions, of course. Just remember that the focal point for each gift is different. After you've attracted the interest of a person, you will find that each comes to Jesus with a different emphasis:

> The *perceiver* will likely feel the need to repent and make salvation a deliberate choice of the will.
>
> The *server* will be attracted by the good works of Jesus and receive Him because he or she wants to do good works, too.
>
> The *teacher* may want to read through the New Testament to gain the facts needed to make an intellectual decision.
>
> The *exhorter* will be glad to learn about Jesus' methods of helping people and want to be joined together with Him.
>
> The *giver* will be excited when the Gospel suddenly makes sense and will want to witness to others right away.
>
> The *administrator* will examine the whole story from creation to the Millennium before deciding Jesus is the Son of God.
>
> The *compassion person* will be moved to tears of joy over the greatness of God's love for him or her personally.

31
Every Christian a "Minister"

Growing up in a traditional church, I thought that the only person who was a minister was the pastor. I never had a clue that every Christian was a minister.

In Ephesians 4:12 Paul tells us that all of us are to be equipped for the work of the ministry, which will help build up and mature the Body of Christ. But we will minister in various ways, depending upon our motivational gift(s), our possible ministry gift (verse 11) and how we flow in the manifestation gifts.

Not everyone is called, as most of those with ministry gifts are, to the full-time Christian service of equipping the "saints," but *all of us are called to minister in the name of the Lord Jesus Christ*. Most of us will have a full-time job outside the organizational church or a full-time responsibility in the home. We will find, however, that there are plenty of opportunities to minister our gifts to others: the neighbor with a problem, our son's best friend, the elderly shut-in down the street, the wrong number who turned out to be in crisis, the guy at work, the discouraged woman in the prayer group.

Here are some specific instances.

Ministry to Neighbors

Suppose an illness keeps a woman bedridden for a month. If each of her seven immediate neighbors has a different motivational gift, how will each one express love to her?

The *perceiver* will pray both privately and at her bedside for healing, strength and endurance.

The *server* will take over meals, offer to do housework, run errands and mow the lawn.

The *teacher* will find it hard to relate to her, but will finally take her some good books and tapes.

The *exhorter* will go right over to encourage her and share uplifting Scripture.

The *giver* will bring food and other gifts, spend time talking and listening.

The *administrator* will find out what she needs and organize the neighborhood to meet those needs.

The *compassion person* will ask how she feels, empathize, hug, weep and stay by her bedside.

Ministry in Sunday School

There's a place for everyone to minister in a Sunday school program. Not everyone will want to teach, but there are plenty of other jobs.

The *perceiver* will want to teach, especially the older youth or the adult classes.

The *server* will prefer to assist a teacher, help in the nursery, handle the custodial work or be the Sunday school secretary.

The *teacher* will aim at teaching the adult or college-age classes or preparing and providing enrichment material.

The *exhorter* will be happy to teach any age and will be especially good with older children and teenagers.

The *giver* will do well teaching any age, and may also want to handle finances or promote missionary support and offerings.

The *administrator* will be delighted to be in charge, be a department superintendent or teach an adult class.

The *compassion person* will migrate to teaching or helping in the primary age, preschool or nursery departments.

Ministry in Bible Studies

Everyone can minister by teaching a Bible study group. But the subject and approach will differ with each gift.

The *perceiver* will:
1. Spend much time in prayerful preparation.
2. Use the Bible as the basic text.

3. Focus on subjects like prayer, prophecy and God's will.

The *server* will:
1. Prefer to use prepared materials.
2. Do a detailed preparation of the lesson.
3. Focus on practical subjects that demonstrate faith.

The *teacher* will:
1. Want to prepare his or her own lesson plans.
2. Spend much time in biblical research.
3. Prefer teaching an entire book of the Bible or a thematic topic.

The *exhorter* will:
1. Use prepared materials.
2. Draw from life experience for illustrations.
3. Choose subjects that help people live victoriously.

The *giver* will:
1. Enjoy doing his or her own preparation.
2. Tend to gear each lesson to win someone to Christ.
3. Focus on subjects like evangelism and missions.

The *administrator* will:
1. Organize materials into his or her own special lesson plan.
2. Bring in resource people for added interest.
3. Cover broad subjects from a variety of aspects.

The *compassion person* will:
1. Use prepared materials.
2. Be spontaneous in teaching methods.
3. Focus on God's love and right relationships.

Ministry to the Body of Christ and Others

Paul tells us in Ephesians 4:16 that the Body of Christ actually grows and builds itself up in love and maturity as *each part* does its work properly. Every person is needed. Every person ministers to others, knowingly or unknowingly.

Perhaps you've never thought of some of the spontaneous things you do to help others as being ministry, but they are. We are naturally drawn to those types of ministries that enable us to use our motivational gifts. If you don't function in your giftedness in ministry to others, there is a lack in the Body of Christ. You are needed!

To demonstrate the wide variety of service areas available, we've compiled the following list, grouped under general headings, although many overlap. We have indicated which motivational gift usually ministers in these areas, but that does not mean that other gifts do not minister in those areas, too. Two or three other possibilities are listed in parentheses. Also, your secondary gift may lead you into areas of ministry that your primary gift might not otherwise be drawn to.

As you study this list ask the Holy Spirit to trigger ideas for ways in which you could minister.

Possible Areas of Ministry

Prayer and Healing Ministries: Perceivers (givers and compassion people)

__ intercessory prayer
__ anointing with oil
__ prayer breakfasts
__ prayer groups
__ hospital calls
__ praying by phone
__ prayer chain
__ fasting
__ prayer counseling

Practical Ministries: Servers (givers and compassion people)

__ office help
__ church secretary
__ doing mail-outs
__ writing letters
__ preparing Communion
__ childcare
__ financial support
__ rolling bandages
__ bazaar crafts
__ tape ministry
__ baby showers
__ church kitchen help
__ nursery work
__ organizing files
__ phone calling
__ handling registration
__ advertising
__ making gifts
__ missionary barrels
__ sports programs
__ ushering
__ wedding showers
__ custodial work
__ repairing
__ bake sales
__ wedding hostess
__ making choir robes
__ hospitality
__ church treasurer
__ work parties
__ recreation programs
__ helping people move
__ news releases

Educational Ministries: Teachers (exhorters, administrators and perceivers)

__ Bible teacher
__ workshop leader
__ youth ministry
__ retreat speaker
__ researching
__ church library
__ seminar leader
__ adult classes
__ children's ministry
__ discipling
__ word studies
__ book reviewing
__ Sunday school teacher
__ women's Bible study
__ editing
__ Bible school instructor
__ tutoring
__ teaching new believers

Counseling Ministries: Exhorters (perceivers, compassion people and administrators)

__ prayer counseling
__ marriage counseling
__ teen counseling
__ pregnancy counseling
__ encouraging others
__ home visitation
__ hospital visitation
__ problem solving
__ follow-up calls
__ crisis center
__ inner healing
__ hotline help

Outreach Ministries: Givers (perceivers and exhorters)

__ child evangelism
__ mime teams
__ bus ministry
__ drama
__ in high schools
__ political causes
__ missions
__ crusades

__ TV/radio programs
__ college students
__ street witnessing
__ outreach center
__ coffeehouse outreach
__ men's breakfasts
__ women's luncheons
__ door-to-door witness
__ Vacation Bible School
__ placing Bibles

Leadership Ministries: Administrators (exhorters, teachers and perceivers)

__ organizer
__ emcee
__ Sunday school superintendent
__ department head
__ planner
__ troubleshooter
__ home group leader
__ missions coordinator
__ leader
__ committee chairperson
__ Christian education director
__ church administrator

Caring Ministries: Compassion person (servers and givers)

__ hospitality
__ food bank
__ hospital visitation
__ food for shut-ins
__ driving service
__ babysitting
__ AA/Al-Anon
__ dial-a-prayer
__ missions
__ street ministry
__ overnight guests
__ clothing bank
__ nursing homes
__ deliver Communion
__ crisis center
__ hospice care
__ assisting mentally impaired

__ prayer helpline	**Creative Ministries:** All the	__ mime presentations
__ abuse aid	gifts (depends on talents and	__ puppetry
__ women's shelter	interests)	__ interpreting
__ entertaining	__ music	__ bulletin boards
__ prison visitation	__ choirs	__ writing
__ helping elderly	__ playing piano	__ songwriting
__ food for new moms	__ dramatic readings	__ church orchestra
__ helping handicapped	__ trio/quartet	__ church band
__ helping needy	__ translation work	__ church decorating
__ rides to church	__ designing posters	__ making banners
__ feeding hungry	__ drama	__ arts and crafts
__ halfway house	__ leading worship	
__ help unwed mothers	__ playing organ	

In addition to all of these personal and church-related ministries there are hundreds of civic, environmental and parachurch organizations in which you may be led to be involved. Just remember to keep your priorities straight: God, family, job—and then outside ministry.

Ministry Success Possibilities

On the following pages we list some of the eight hundred occupational and volunteer Job/Ministry Position Profiles typical to working or serving in most churches or Christian organizations. We have indicated to what degree we feel each of the motivational gifts will cause a person to be fulfilled and successful in these areas of work or volunteer service.

We offer the chart simply as our opinion, based on more than thirty years of research and experience working with motivational gifts. We have also received input from a dozen of our most experienced Certified Gifts Teachers. We hope it will be helpful as you seek God's will for your life's work and/or service to Him and others.

Remember that many other factors besides giftedness contribute to success in any field: passions, talents, special abilities, training, education, background, experience, dependability, commitment, adaptability and so forth. People with little gifting in an area can succeed because of an eagerness to learn and apply themselves, whereas people with great gifting in the same area can fail because of poor attitude, laziness, indifference or unwillingness to make a serious commitment.

Some fields of service are so broad that everyone can find a place where their gifts are well utilized. To identify these something-for-everyone ministries we have placed a plus sign (+) immediately following them.

The entire list of about eight hundred ministries is too large for this book, so we are presenting only about two hundred selected ministries. To recieve an email of the free additional Ministry Success Possibilities List in PDF format, you can contact Katie Fortune at (360) 297-8878 from noon to five p.m. (PST) Monday through Friday. The code word is "chosen."

How to Score

Here is how we've coded the following Job/Ministry Positions:

If success in a position is highly unlikely for a person with a particular motivational gift (because it would not use the person's natural motivations or because the demands of the position go beyond the capabilities of that gift), then we've given the position a minus sign (–) in the column under the gift.

If success is not likely, but there could be other factors enabling an individual to enjoy this position (like a strong secondary gift), then we have coded the position by leaving the space blank.

If success is possible, especially with other positive factors entering in, then we have coded it with an asterisk (*).

If success is very possible—if that person's motivational gift would be an asset in the position—then we have coded it with two asterisks (**).

If success is highly probable—if that person's motivational gift is especially suited to the position and he or she would excel and be fulfilled—then we have coded it with three asterisks (***).

To score your probability for success in a Job/Ministry Position, circle all the three-star (***) and two-star (**) codes under your primary motivational gift. If you have a strong secondary gift, do the same in that column. Then put a check mark in front of all the positions thus identified. Now look to see which positions have the highest number of stars. Record the positions (except the ones that you already know you would not be interested in) on the chart provided at the end of the chapter. It will be from among these that you could confidently choose areas to work in or volunteer in, knowing that you are well gifted for top performance in any of them. Your ministry may change from time to time, or in various places or situations, or time of life.

Here's the scoring at a glance:

Scoring	
–	highly unlikely
(blank)	not likely
*	possible
**	very possible
***	highly possible

Gifts Letter Key			
P	Perceiver	G	Giver
S	Server	A	Administrator
T	Teacher	C	Compassion
E	Exhorter		

	P	S	T	E	G	A	C
Pastoral							
Pastoral Staff							
Administrative Pastor	**		**	**	*	***	–
Administrative Assistant	**	**	**	***	***	***	–

	P	S	T	E	G	A	C
Assistant Pastor	***	**	**	***	**	**	*
Associate Pastor	***	*	**	***	***	**	*
Benevolence Minister	***	*		**	***	**	***
Chaplain	**	*	**	***	***	***	**
Children's Pastor		**		***	**	*	***
Church Planting Pastor	***	—	**	**	***	***	
Congregational Care Pastor	*	**		***	**	***	**
Director of Christian Education	**		***	***	*	***	
Executive Secretary	*	***		**	***	*	*
Evangelist	***			***	***	**	*
Family Life Pastor	**		**	***	**	***	*
Missionary	***	**	**	***	***	**	**
Missions Pastor	***	*	**	***	***	***	*
Senior Pastor	***		***	***	*	***	
Spiritual Life Pastor	***		**	***	**	**	*
Theologian	***		***	**	*	***	
Visitation Pastor	*	**	*	***	**	*	***
Worship/Fine Arts Director	***		**	***	*	**	*
Youth Pastor	**			***	**	**	
Media							
Media Director	*	—	*	*	*	***	—
Audio Technician	*	***	**		***	*	—
Duplication Director		***	*		***	*	—
Lighting Technician		***	*		**		—
Microphone Supervisor		***			**		—
Multimedia Operator	*	***	*	*	***	**	
Photographer	**	***	**	**	**	***	***
Power Point Programmer	*	***	*	*	***	**	*
Power Point Projectionist		***			**	*	—
Technology Designer	**	***	***		**	**	
Videographer	*	***	**	*	***	*	*
Video Technician	*	***	*		***	*	—
Ministerial Assistance							
Baptism							
Baby/Child Dedication Facilitator	—	**	—	*	**	*	***
Baptismal Assistant		***		*	**		***
Training Class Teacher	**		***	**	*	***	
Communion							
Communion Preparer		***	—		***	—	**
Greeters							
Greeters Coordinator	**			**	**	***	
Greeter	*	***	—	***	**	*	***
Ministry Team							
Altar Ministry Leader/Trainer	***		***	**	*	**	

	P	S	T	E	G	A	C
Altar Ministry Provider	***	*	*	**	***	*	***
Armor Bearer	***	***		–	***	*	–
Prayer Room Attendant	***	*	*	**	***	*	***
Ushers							
Head Usher/Coordinator	*		–	**	**	***	–
Usher	*	***		**	***		**
Prayer & Healing Ministry							
Prayer Ministry Coordinator	***			*	***	**	**
Anointer	***	*	*	**	***	**	***
Email Prayer Coordinator	***	*		*	***		**
Healing Service Leader	***		*	**	***	**	*
Healing Service Worker	***	*	*	*	***	*	***
Home Communion Giver	***	*		*	***		***
Hospital Visitor	*	**	–	**	***	*	***
Intercessor Leader	***			*	**		**
Intercessor	***	*		*	***		***
Nursing Home/Hospice Visitor	**	*	–	**	***		***
Phone Prayer Coordinator	***			**	***	*	**
Prayer Breakfast Program Director	***			**	***	**	*
Prayer Breakfast Cook	*	***	–		***		*
Prayer Breakfast Host/Hostess	***	**		**	***	*	***
Prayer Breakfast Leader	***			*	**		*
Prayer Counselor	***		*	**	***	**	***
Prayer Group Leader	***			*	***		**
Prayer Group Member	***	*		*	***	–	***
Prayer Ministry Coordinator	***			*	**	*	**
Practical							
Bookstore							
Bookstore Director/Manager	**		***	*	**	***	
Bookkeeper	*	***	*		***		–
Sales Clerk	*	***	*	**	***		
Childcare							
Childcare Director	*		–	***	***	**	**
Nursery Worker		***	–	*	**	–	***
Preschool Worker		***	–	*	**	–	***
Supply Coordinator	–	***	–		***	*	*
Construction							
Carpenter	*	***		*	***	*	*
Contractor	**	**	**	*	***	***	–
Electrician	*	***	*		**	*	
Handyman		***	–	*	**		*
Painter	*	***		*	**	–	*
Plumber	*	***			**		*

	P	S	T	E	G	A	C
Repairer		***		—	**		—
Telephone System Specialist	*	***	*	*	**	*	—
Work Party Coordinator		*	—	**	***	**	—
Work Party Worker		***	—		**		*
Crafts							
Bazaar Leader	*		—	***	***	***	
Bazaar Worker	*	***	—	*	***		**
Craft Designer	**	**	*		***	*	**
Craft Worker	*	***		*	***		***
Facilities							
Facilities Director	*	*	—	—	***	**	—
Gardener		***	—	—	**		**
Gardening Assistant		***	—	—	**		**
Interior Decorator	*	**		**	**	**	***
Janitor/Custodian	—	***	—	—	**	—	*
Seasonal Decorator	*	***		**	**	*	***
Security Director	***	**	—		***	**	—
Security Assistant	***	***	—		**	—	
Special Events Facility Worker		***	—	*	**	—	*
Sprinkler System Operator	*	***	—		**	—	
Tree Trimmer	*	***	—		**		—
Window Washer		***	—		**	—	*
Women's Lounge Attendant		***	—	*	**	—	*
Food							
Baker		***	—		**	—	*
Bake Sale Organizer	*	**	—	**	***	*	*
Barista	—	***	—	**	**	—	**
Cashier	**	**	—	*	***	—	*
Cook		***	—	*	***	—	**
Food Service Director	*		—	*	***	**	—
Food Service Assistant Director	—	**	—		**	—	*
Host/Hostess	*	**	*	***	**	*	***
Kitchen Director		**	—	*	***	*	
Kitchen Helper		***	—		***	—	**
Linen Tablecloth Caretaker		***	—		**	—	**
Meal Coordinator	*	**		*	***	**	*
Meal Provider	*	***	*	**	***	*	***
Pantry Organizer		**	—		***		*
Server		***	—	*	***		**
Shut-In Server	*	***	—	*	***		***
Snacks and Treats Coordinator		**	—		***	*	*
Snacks and Treats Server		***	—		***		***
Table Decoration Director		***		*	**	*	***

	P	S	T	E	G	A	C
Home Service							
Babysitter		***	—	*	**	—	***
Car Care Specialist	*	***			**	—	—
Carpet Cleaner		***	—		***	—	*
Home Care Giver		***	—	*	**	—	**
House Cleaner		***	—	*	***	—	*
Repair Team Member		***	—	—	***		*
Library							
AV Specialist	*	***			***	*	
Book Reviewer	**		***	**	*	**	
Desk Clerk		***	*	**	**	—	*
Historian	*	*	***		**	**	
Librarian	**		***	*	*	**	
Assistant Librarian	**	**	*	*	**	*	
Library Worker	*	***	*		**		*
Medical Ministry							
Alzheimer's Caregiver	*	***	—	*	**	—	***
Chiropractic Doctor	**	*	***	**	***	**	*
Chronic Illness Caregiver	**	***	—	*	**		***
Dentist	**	*	***	**	**	***	*
Doctor	***	*	***	**	**	***	*
Emergency Medical Responder	***	*	**	***	**	**	—
First Aid Worker	***	**	—	**	***		***
House Visitor	*	***		*	**		—
Medical Ministry Director	***		**	*	**	***	
Medical Missionary	***	**	*	**	***	*	***
Naturopathic Doctor	**	*	***	**	**	***	*
Nurse	*	**	**	***	**	**	***
Certified Nursing Assistant	*	***		**	***	*	***
Nutritionist	***	*	***	**	*	**	*
Paramedic	***	**	**	***	**	*	—
Physician's Assistant	**	*	**	***	**	*	
Respite Caregiver		***	—	**	***		***
Missionary Assistance							
Clothes Drive Leader		**		**	***	*	**
Educational Supply Director	**	*	***	*	*	**	
Medical Supply Organizer	**	*	**	*	***	**	
Missionary Assistance Director	**		*	**	***	**	*
Missionary Closet Organizer		**		**	**	**	*
Missionary Correspondent	*	***	**	***	***	*	***
Missionary Fundraiser	**		*	**	***	***	
Moving Help							
Church Relocation Advisor	*		**	***	*	***	

	P	S	T	E	G	A	C
Moving Help Coordinator	*		—	**	***	**	*
Moving Help Worker		***	—	**	***		**
Welcome Basket Chairman		**		**	***	**	**
Welcome Basket Creator		***		*	**		***
New Baby Ministry							
Baby Clothes Exchange Leader		**		*	***		**
Baby Shower Coordinator		**		**	**	*	***
New Baby Instructor	**		***	**	*	**	
New Baby Ministry Director				***	***	*	**
Parenting Instructor	**		***	***	*	***	
Pregnancy Instructor	***		***	**	*	***	*
Office Help							
Bulletin Board Designer	*	***	*	*	**		***
Bulletin Stuffer	—	***	—	*	**	—	**
Church Directory Designer	*	*		***	**	***	*
Church Directory Photographer	**	***	**	**	**	***	***
Computer Network Specialist	*	***	**		***	*	—
Computer Operator	**	***	***	*	***	**	*
Computer Servicer	**	***	**		***	*	—
Data Entry Operator/Administrator	*	***	*		**	*	
Errand Runner	—	***	—	—	**	—	*
File Organizer	*	***	*		***	*	
Filer	*	***	—		***	—	
Graphics Designer	**	***	**		**	*	**
Letter Writer	*	***	*	**	*	**	*
Mail-Out Worker		***	—	—	**	—	**
Mail Processor	—	***	—		**		
Ministry Appreciation Coordinator	*		*	***	*	***	
News Release Writer	**		***	*	*	***	
Newsletter Editor	**		***	**	*	***	
Newsletter Reporter	**	*	***	**	**	**	*
Newspaper Article Clipper		***		*	**	—	*
Phone Worker	*	***		***	**		**
Photocopier	—	***	—	*	**	—	**
Printed Materials Assembler	*	***	—	*	**	—	**
Promoter/Advertiser	*		*	***	***	**	
Proofreader	*	**	***	*	**	**	
Public Relations Director	**		**	***	*	***	
Media Contactor	*	*	**	***	**	***	
Public Relations Writer	**		***	***		***	
Receptionist	*	***		***	**		*
Records Administrator	*	***		*	***	*	
Registrar	*	***		**	***	*	

	P	S	T	E	G	A	C
Researcher	**	*	***		*	***	
Secretary	*	***		***	***		*
Secretarial Assistant		***	—	*	***	—	**
Special Events Worker	*	***		**	***		**
Ticket Sales Director	**	*		**	***	*	
Ticket Salesperson	*	***		**	***	—	*
Typist	*	***		*	***	—	*
Volunteer Recruiter	**			***	**	***	
Webmaster/Designer	*	***	***	*	***	**	*

JOB/MINISTRY SUCCESS POSSIBILITIES SUMMARY

Job/Ministry Position	Number of Stars	My Preferences

Careers and Occupations

One of the questions most frequently asked us is, "How do I relate my motivational gift scores to my career or occupation?" In this chapter we have related the gifts to 305 of the most common careers and occupations. If you do not find yours in the list, you can probably find similar ones and draw appropriate conclusions from the comparison.

But first, we want you to consider a specific way of relating your motivational gift(s) to any occupation or career choice you might consider, including your present situation. Here are some general guidelines for determining how likely you are to be successful and fulfilled in a career or occupation.

Your Core Motivations

As part of your motivational gift you have received certain built-in core motivations or modes of operating. The utilization of your core motivations is what gives you satisfaction and a feeling of accomplishment. Whenever you are considering particular employment, you should ask yourself the following question: *To what degree will this enable me to do what I am motivated to do?*

To assist you in answering that question we have prepared the following lists that are indicative of what each motivational gift enjoys doing. Go over the items listed under your primary gift—and your secondary gift if it's a strong one—and check off all the things that you would be able to do in a given occupation. If many of the items are checked, it is likely that you will be happy and successful in that position. If very few items are checked, it is probable that you are not suited to it. It is much better to be able to recognize ahead of time if a career or occupation is one you will enjoy, rather than to become committed to it and struggle with ongoing frustration.

Statistics indicate that two out of every three people are dissatisfied with their present positions. How sad! Many people spend all their working years doing something that fails to use their motivational gifts.

We do not believe that is God's intention. He wants us to feel fulfilled in what we do.

Here's what a person with each motivational gift tends to do. It is what comes naturally, as a result of his or her inner core motivation. These tendencies are generic enough to apply to anyone's situation.

Motivational gift of perception

__ admonish	__ defend	__ moralize
__ advise	__ discipline	__ negotiate
__ advocate	__ dramatize	__ overcome
__ analyze	__ enforce	__ persevere
__ assess	__ evaluate	__ persuade
__ caution	__ evoke	__ preach
__ challenge	__ expose	__ prevail
__ change	__ forewarn	__ proclaim
__ combat	__ identify	__ reveal
__ convict	__ impact	__ solve
__ convince	__ inspire	__ strengthen
__ correct	__ intercede	__ urge
__ decide	__ judge	__ warn

Motivational gift of serving

__ assemble	__ fix	__ meet needs
__ assist	__ follow	__ minister
__ be useful	__ follow up	__ obey
__ build	__ fulfill expectations	__ operate
__ carry out plans	__ handle	__ perfect
__ carry through	__ help	__ persist
__ complete	__ host	__ produce
__ construct	__ implement	__ repair
__ detail	__ maintain	__ run effectively
__ develop	__ make	__ serve
__ do	__ make effective	__ tend
__ entertain guests	__ make work	__ wait on
__ finish	__ master	__ work for

Motivational gift of teaching

__ analyze	__ establish truth	__ inspire
__ communicate	__ evaluate	__ instruct
__ comprehend	__ examine	__ interpret
__ discipline	__ experiment	__ interview
__ discover	__ expound	__ investigate
__ edit	__ figure out	__ learn
__ educate	__ formulate	__ lecture
__ enlighten	__ improve	__ observe

__ present truth
__ publish
__ recommend
__ research
__ search

__ solve
__ study
__ systematize
__ teach
__ theorize

__ train
__ tutor
__ use logic
__ validate
__ write

Motivational gift of exhortation

__ achieve potential
__ admonish
__ advise
__ advocate
__ assure
__ build up
__ coach
__ communicate
__ convince
__ counsel
__ cultivate
__ demonstrate
__ develop

__ direct
__ edify
__ encourage
__ endure
__ entreat
__ exhort
__ explain
__ expound
__ foster
__ gain response
__ give response
__ guide
__ improve

__ influence
__ inspire
__ instruct
__ modify
__ motivate
__ persuade
__ prescribe
__ relate
__ stimulate
__ strengthen
__ talk
__ teach (practical)
__ urge

Motivational gift of giving

__ accommodate
__ acquire
__ advocate
__ aid
__ assist
__ back up
__ bargain
__ benefit
__ bless
__ bolster
__ budget
__ contribute
__ corroborate
__ develop
__ donate
__ encourage

__ endow
__ entertain
__ espouse
__ evangelize
__ expedite
__ furnish
__ gain
__ give
__ grant
__ help
__ host
__ improve
__ improvise
__ invent
__ invest
__ make better

__ modify
__ multiply assets
__ patronize
__ perform
__ proclaim
__ procure
__ prompt
__ rescue
__ share
__ shore up
__ succeed
__ supply
__ support
__ sustain
__ testify
__ witness

Motivational gift of administration

__ accomplish
__ achieve
__ administrate
__ attain
__ authorize
__ be challenged
__ be in charge
__ be responsible
__ build
__ command
__ communicate
__ conduct
__ control
__ coordinate
__ create
__ delegate

__ design
__ develop
__ envision
__ establish
__ excel
__ explore
__ facilitate
__ govern
__ guide
__ handle projects
__ influence
__ initiate
__ instigate
__ lead
__ operate
__ organize

__ oversee
__ motivate
__ pioneer
__ plan
__ preside
__ proceduralize
__ promote
__ put together
__ rule
__ schedule
__ set goals
__ shape
__ shoulder
__ strategize
__ supervise
__ visualize

Motivational gift of compassion

__ accept	__ condole	__ promote unity
__ accommodate	__ console	__ relieve distress
__ affirm	__ crusade	__ relieve hurts
__ assist	__ defer to	__ renew
__ assure	__ empathize	__ repair hearts
__ avoid hurting	__ feel	__ rescue
__ befriend	__ forgive	__ respond
__ be gentle	__ give preference	__ restore
__ be thoughtful	__ harmonize	__ serve
__ bring together	__ heal	__ show compassion
__ build relationships	__ help	__ show kindness
__ build up	__ intercede	__ show mercy
__ care for	__ look after	__ support
__ cheer up	__ love	__ sustain
__ cherish	__ nurse	__ sympathize
__ comfort	__ nurture	__ trust

These lists can also be applied when you are asked to help with a project, program or task in your church or organization, as well as the selection of an appropriate ministry or volunteer work—or even a temporary job, or just helping out a friend or relative.

Occupational Success Probabilities

We list 305 specific career and occupational possibilities, indicating to what degree we feel each of the motivational gifts will enable a person to be fulfilled and successful in these fields. We offer the chart simply as our *opinion*, based on more than thirty years of research and working with people in the area of the motivational gifts. We hope it will be helpful as you seek God's will for your life's work.

Remember that many other factors besides giftedness contribute to success in any field: talents, special abilities, training, education, background, emotional stability, dependability, commitment, adaptability and so forth. People with little gifting in an area can succeed because of their eagerness to learn and apply themselves, whereas people with great gifting in the same area can fail because of poor attitude, laziness, indifference or unwillingness to make a nine-to-five commitment.

Some fields are so broad that everyone can find a place where his or her motivational gifts are well utilized—a writing career, for example. Anyone can enter this field. However, the gifts can determine what types of writing jobs each person will be drawn to and excel in. Let's look at this field more closely to show you what I mean.

When I taught at a Billy Graham Writers' Conference, my goal was not only to help writers discover their motivational gifts but also to identify the various kinds of writing in which they might be successful.

For instance, *perceivers* will do well in high-pressure jobs such as news reporting and editorial positions. Their field of interest will be strictly nonfiction. They will be good at writing articles and books that deal with good and evil, spiritual principles, politics, prophecy, prayer, character development and spiritual growth. They make good drama critics, probing interviewers and challenging editorialists. Their writing is persuasive, highly opinionated and often blunt.

Servers will not be happy in high-stress jobs or in leadership positions. They do well as editorial assistants, copyeditors or rewriters. They are good at proofreading, detailed writing and being supportive staff persons. Servers like fiction, poetry and writing for the children's market. They write excellent articles dealing with the practical application of Christian principles, how-to subjects and self-help ideas.

Teachers will excel in almost every area of writing and will make the finest editors and nonfiction book authors. They work well under stress and within schedules. They are top-notch curriculum and Bible study writers and do well on any biblical subject. They love research and often include generous amounts of information. They are good at writing about education, religion, science, medicine, history and law. They write probing editorials and excellent descriptive pieces. They make good reporters and also do well with textbooks or research books. They could also be good playwrights and poets.

Exhorters will excel in writing anything with a self-help or how-to approach. Their writing is practical and encouraging and often drawn from their own experiences. They are good at biographies and nonfiction and they make dialogue come alive. Their focus will be people, not facts or places. They are among the most prolific writers and their material is exceptionally readable. They write true-life stories, inspirational pieces, how-to articles and books, testimonies, advice columns, articles on psychology, ministry, interpersonal relationships and also humor and poetry—anything life-related.

Givers are so well-rounded that they are able to write on a wide range of subjects and handle a variety of jobs. They make especially good editors and publishers. Ghostwriting is acceptable. They write both fiction and nonfiction with a focus on business, success, evangelism and missionary endeavors.

The *administrator* will also make an excellent editor or publisher, and will do well in other management positions. Bored with copyediting or routine writing assignments, they'd rather pioneer. Their area is definitely nonfiction with comprehensive coverage of broad subjects. They will organize their material well. Freelancers will find it a challenge to discipline themselves to "office hours" at the computer keyboard because of their desire to interact with people. They will delegate routine writing tasks to others, if possible.

Compassion people are the most creative of all writers—with a focus on fiction, from true confessions to science fiction. They are exceptionally good with children's stories, devotionals and poetry. Their articles and books deal with feelings, human interest episodes, interpersonal relationships, animals, inspiration and overcoming handicaps. They are not into research, and are not suited to newspaper or magazine reporting unless it is strictly human interest writing.

Thus, there is a place for each gift in the field of writing, and this applies to many other careers as well. To identify these something-for-everyone occupations in our list we have placed a plus sign (+) immediately following them.

How to Score

We've coded the following 305 occupations in the same way we coded the Job/Ministry Positions in the previous chapter.

If success in a job is highly unlikely for a person with a particular motivational gift (because it would not use the person's natural motivations or because the demands of the job go beyond the capabilities of that motivational gift), then we've given the job a minus sign (−) in the column under the gift.

If success is not likely, but there could be other factors enabling an individual to enjoy this work (like a strong secondary gift), then we have coded the job by leaving the space blank.

If success is possible, especially with other positive factors entering in, then we have coded it with an asterisk (*).

If success is very possible—if that person's motivational gift would be an asset in the job—then we have coded it with two asterisks (**).

If success is highly probable—if that person's motivational gift is especially suited to the job and he or she would excel and be fulfilled—then we have coded it with three asterisks (***).

To score your probability for success, circle all the three-star (***) and two-star (**) codes under your primary motivational gift. If you have a strong secondary gift, do the same in that column. Then put a check mark in front of all the occupations thus identified. Now look to see which jobs have the highest number of stars. Write those occupations (except for ones that you already know you would not be interested in) in the spaces provided at the end of the chapter. It will be from among these that you could confidently choose a career, knowing that you are well-gifted for top performance in any of them. For instance, if you circle three-star codes for a certain occupation beneath both your primary and your secondary gift, such a career would be one of the very best that you could follow.

Here's the scoring at a glance:

Scoring	
−	highly unlikely
(blank)	not likely
*	possible
**	very possible
***	highly possible

Gifts Letter Key			
P	Perceiver	G	Giver
S	Server	A	Administrator
T	Teacher	C	Compassion
E	Exhorter		

Now proceed to circle the two-star and three-star codes under your motivational gift(s):

	P	S	T	E	G	A	C
General Occupations							
Auctioneer	*	*		***	**	*	—
Automobile Dealer		*		**	***	**	
Firefighter	**	***		*	**		*
Funeral Director	*	**		*	***		*
Philosopher	***		***	**	*	**	***
Postman		***		**	***		*
Printer	*	***	*	*	**	**	*
Realtor	**	*	*	***	***	***	*
Recreation Director	*	*		***	**	***	*
Technician	*	***	**	*	***	*	*
Animal Care							
Animal Care (Training, Kenneling)		***		*	***	*	***
Pet Groomer		***		*	***		***
Taxidermist		***			**		*
Veterinarian	*	**		*	***	*	***
Zookeeper		***		*	**	*	***
Zoologist	*	***	**	*	**	**	***
Architecture & Engineering							
Aerospace Engineer	***		***	*	***	**	
Agricultural Engineer	**	*	***	—	**	***	—
Architect	**	***	**	*	**	***	
Cartographer & Photogrammetrist	*	***	**	—	***	*	*
City Planner	**	—	**	**	**	***	—
Civil Engineer (Land)	**	*	**		***	***	—
Engineer	**	*	***	**	**	**	
Environmental Technologist (GeoTech)	**	*	***	**	**	**	
Forester	**	**	***		**	***	*
Land Developer	**		**	*	***	***	
Machinist	**	***	*		***	*	
Marine Architect	**	*	***		**	***	
Marine Engineer	***	*	***	*	**	**	—
Mechanical Drawing	*	***	*	*	**		**
Mechanical Engineer (Equipment)	**	***	**		**	*	—
Product Safety Engineer	***	**	***		**	**	
Railroad Engineer	*	***		*	***		
Technical Writer	***	**	***	—	**	**	—

	P	S	T	E	G	A	C
Business Management							
Accountant	**	***	*		***	−	
Advertising Executive	*	−	**	***	**	***	−
Auditor	**	***	**	*	***	*	
Bookkeeper	*	***	*		***		−
Business Consultant	**	*	**	*	***	**	−
Business Owner	**	*	**	**	***	***	
Economist	**	*	**	*	***	**	
Human Resource – Compensation, Benefits & Job Analysis	*	**	***	**	***	***	
Human Resource – Employee Trainer/Leadership Development	**		***	***	**	***	
Human Resource – Labor Relations (Contract Negotiation, Etc)	***		**	**	***	***	−
Human Resource Assistant		***	*	**	***	*	**
Management Analyst (Business Consultant)	**		**	*	***	***	−
Market Researcher/Analyst	***	*	***	**	*	***	
Marketing Executive	**		*	**	***	***	
Office Worker	*	***		*	***		***
Personnel Manager	*		*	***		***	*
Public Relations Director	**		**	***	*	***	
Receptionist		***		***	**		**
Secretary	*	***		**	**		**
Speech Writer	**		***	**	*	***	
Statistician	*	**	***	−	***		−
Construction/Labor							
Agricultural Worker	*	***			**	−	*
Aircraft Mechanic	**	***	**	*	**	*	
Assembler/Fabricator	**	***	*		***	−	*
Builder	*	***	*	*	***	**	*
Carpenter	*	***		*	***	*	*
Carpet/Floor/Tile Installer	*	***	−	*	**	−	*
Construction Laborer	*	***		*	***	−	*
Construction Contractor	**	**	**	*	***	***	−
Dock Worker		***	−		***	−	
Electrician	*	***	*		**	*	
Heating, Air Conditioning, Refrigeration	*	***	*		***	*	
Heavy Equipment Operator		***			**		
Industrial Designer	*	***	**	*	**	*	
Inspector	***	*	**	*	**	**	

	P	S	T	E	G	A	C
Janitor	—	***	—	—	***	—	*
Landscaper/Gardener		***	—	—	***		**
Line Installer & Repairer (Fiber/Cable/Power/DSL)	*	***			**		—
Mason		***		*	***		*
Mechanic	*	***		*	***		*
Metalworker		***		*	***		*
Miner	*	***			***		
Painter & Paper Hanger	**	***	—	*	**	—	*
Pest Control Worker	**	***		*	**	—	
Plumber		***		*	***		*
Semiconductor Processor	*	***	***		**		—
Sheet Metal Worker	*	***	—		**	—	
Shipbuilder	*	***	*	*	***	*	
Surveyor	**	***	*	*	***	**	*
Toolmaker	*	***			***		*
Welder	*	***			***		*
Woodworker	*	***	*	*	***		**
Education							
College Professor	***		***	***	*	***	
Guidance Counselor	***	*	**	***	*	***	**
Librarian	**		***	*	**	*	
School Administrator	**		***	**	*	***	
Teacher (Art)	**	**	***	*	*	*	***
Teacher (Business Education)	*	***	*	**	***	**	*
Teacher (Drama)	***		**	**	***	*	
Teacher (Elementary)	*	*	**	***	**	*	***
Teacher (English)	*	*	***	**	*	**	**
Teacher (Foreign Language)	**	*	***	*	**	*	*
Teacher (History)	**	*	***	**	*	***	
Teacher (Home Economics)	*	***	*	**	*	*	***
Teacher (Mathematics)	*	**	***	*	***	*	
Teacher (Music)	***	*	**	**	*	**	***
Teacher (Physical Education)	*	**		***	**	***	
Teacher (Science)	***	*	***	*	**	***	
Teacher (Social Studies)	**	*	**	***	**	***	**
Teacher (Special Ed.)	**	*	***	***	**	**	***
Entertainment: Arts							
Art Director	***		***	**	**	**	***
Artist	***	**	**	**	**	*	***

	P	S	T	E	G	A	C
Choreographer	***	*	**	**	**	***	***
Commercial Artist	***	**	**	*	*	**	***
Composer	***	*	***	**	**	***	***
Conductor (Music)	*		**	*		***	*
Curator	*	*	***		*	**	
Dancer	***	***	*	*	**	*	***
Fashion Designer	*	**		*	**	*	***
Model	*	**		***	*		***
Music Director	***		***	**	*	***	**
Musician	***	**	**	**	**	*	***
Photographer	**	***	**	**	**	***	***
Product Demonstrator		***		**	*		***
Singer	***	**	**	***	**	**	***
Entertainment: Sports							
Athletic Scout	***		**	***	*	**	—
Sports Announcer	**		*	***	*	**	
Sports Coach	**	*	**	***	**	***	
Umpire/Referee	***	*	**	***		**	—
Entertainment: TV							
Actor/Actress	***	*	**	***	***	*	***
Audio & Visual Equipment Technician	*	***	*		***	*	—
Videographer (TV/Video & Motion Picture)	*	***	**	*	***	*	*
Director (Stage/Motion Picture/TV/Radio)	***	—	**	***	**	***	—
Performing Artist	***	*	**	***	**	*	***
Producer (TV/Video/Motion Picture)	***	—	**	**	*	***	
Radio/TV Announcer	**		**	***	*	**	
Radio Producer	***	—	**	***	*	***	
Reporter	***	*	***	**	*	***	*
Set Designer	**	**	*	*	***	*	**
Talent Director (Film/TV/Radio)	***	—	**	***	*	***	*
TV Anchor	***	—	***	***	*	***	—
Entertainment: Writing							
Copywriter	*	***	**	***	**	**	
Cartoonist	***	**		***	**		***
Editor	**		***	**	**	***	—
Journalist	**	*	***	**	*	***	*
Proofreader	*	*	***	**	*	**	
Researcher	**	*	***		*	***	
Writer (Fiction)		*		***	**	*	***
Writer (Nonfiction)	***	*	***	**	*	***	

	P	S	T	E	G	A	C
Finance & Insurance							
Assessor (Property)	***	*	**	*	**	**	
Bank Teller	**	***	*	**	***	*	*
Banker	**	*	**	*	***	**	
Budget Analyst	**	*	***		***	*	—
Claims Adjustor/Appraiser/Examiner	***		**	*	***	**	
Financial Analyst	***		**	*	***	**	—
Financial Manager	***	*	***	**	***	***	—
Insurance Agent	***	*	**	**	***	**	
Investment Fund Manager	**		**	*	***	**	
Life Insurance Agent	***	*	**	**	*	**	*
Loan Officer	**		**	*	***	***	—
Meeting & Convention Planner	*	—	**	**	***	***	—
Tax Preparer	**	***	*	*	***	*	—
Food Preparation/Delivery							
Cook		***	—	*	***	—	**
Restaurant Manager	**			*	***	**	
Waiter/ Waitress		***		**	***		**
Law Enforcement/ Judicial System/Gov't							
Ambassador	***	*	**	***	*	***	
Civil Servant	*	***	*	**	**	*	**
Corrections Officer (Facility)	***	**		*	**		—
Court Reporter	*	**	**	*	*		
Criminologist	***	*	**	**	*	**	—
Judge	***		**	*	*	***	—
Lawyer	***		**	*	*	***	—
Military Officer	***		**	**	*	***	
Paralegal	***	**	***	**	*	**	
Policeperson	***			***	**	**	—
Politician	***	*	**	***	*	***	
Private Investigator/Detective	***	*	***	*	*	**	—
Probation Officer/Corrections Specialist	***	*	*	**	**		—
Public Administrator	***		**	**	*	***	
Security Guard	**	***		***	**		
Medical							
Anesthesiologist	*	*	***	*	**	*	
Biomedical Engineer	**	**	***	*	***	**	
Chiropractor	**	*	***	**	***	**	*
Clinical Lab Technician	**	**	***	*	**		—

	P	S	T	E	G	A	C
Coroner	***	**	***		**	**	—
Dental Hygienist	*	***		*	**		*
Dentist	**	*	***	**	**	***	*
Doctor	***	*	***	**	**	***	*
Home Health Aide	*	***		**	***	*	**
Hospital Administrator	***		**	**	**	***	
Licensed Practical Nurse	*	***	*	**	***	*	***
Medical Records & Health Info Technician	*	***	*		**		*
Medical Technologist	**	**	***	**	**	*	*
Medical Transcriptionist		***	*		**	—	**
Naturopathic Doctor	**	*	***	**	**	***	*
Nurse (RN)	*	**	**	***	**	**	***
Nurse's Aid	*	***		**	***	—	***
Nutritionist	***	*	***	**	**	**	*
Occupational Therapist	*	**	*	***	***	*	***
Optometrist	**	*	***	***	*	**	*
Paramedic	***	**	**	**	***	*	—
Pharmacist	***	**	***	*	**	**	*
Physical Therapist	*	**	*	**	***		***
Physician	***	*	***	**	**	***	*
Speech Therapist	*	**	***	***	**	*	***
Surgeon	**	**	***	*	*	**	
X-ray Technician	*	***		*	***		**
Ministry/Church							
Associate Pastor	**	*	**	***	***	**	*
Building Program Director	**		**	*	***	***	—
Chaplain	**	*	**	***	***	***	**
Children's Pastor		**		***	**	*	***
Christian Education Director	**		***	*	***	***	
Church Planting Pastor	***	—	**	**	***	***	
Church Secretary/Receptionist	*	***		***	**		*
Evangelist	***			***	***	**	*
Missionary	***	**	**	***	***	**	**
Missions Pastor	***	*	**	***	***	***	*
Prayer Ministry Leader	***		*	**	***	**	***
Senior Pastor	***		***	***	*	***	
Theologian	***		***	**	*	***	
Visitation Pastor	*	**	*	***	**	*	***
Worship/Fine Arts Director	***		**	***	*	**	*
Youth (Teens) & Campus (College) Pastor	*		**	***	**	**	

	P	S	T	E	G	A	C
Outdoor/ Environmental							
Archaeologist	**	*	***		*	***	*
Astronomer	***	*	***		*	***	*
Botanist	**	**	***		**	*	**
Conservationist	**	**	**	*	*	**	***
Farmer	*	***			***	*	**
Fisherman		***	—	*	**	—	*
Florist		**		*	**		***
Forest ranger	*	***		*	**		*
Geographer	**	***	***		**	*	
Geologist	**	**	***		**	*	
Meteorologist	**	**	***	—	**	**	
Oceanographer	**	**	***	—	**	*	
Personal Services							
Barber/Beautician		***		*	***	—	**
Certified Personal Trainer	**	**		***	***	*	**
Childcare Provider	*	***	—	**	**	—	***
Dietitian	***	**	*	***	*	*	**
Fitness Worker	*	***		***	***		**
Home Economist	*	***	*	**	**	*	***
Interior Decorator	*	***	*	**	**	**	***
Massage Therapist		***	—	*	**		***
Professional Housecleaner		***		*	**		**
Psychiatrist	***		***	***	*	**	*
Psychologist	***		***	***	*	**	**
Rehabilitation Counselor (Substance Abuse)	***		**	***	**	*	***
Seamstress/Tailor	*	***		*	**		***
Social Worker	**	*	*	***	**	*	***
Sociologist	**		***	***	**	**	**
Spa/Salon Manager	*	***		***	***	*	***
Retail/Manufacturing							
Assembly Line Worker		***	—		**	—	*
Bill & Account Collector (Past Due)	***	**		**	*		—
Billing Clerk (Processes Company Billing)	*	***			***		—
Buyer	**	*	**	*	***	**	
Cashier/Checker		***		*	**		**
Clerk	*	***	—	**	***	—	**
Courier/Messenger	*	***	—		**	—	*
Customer Service Representative		***	*	***	***		*
Department Store Manager	**		**	**	***	***	

	P	S	T	E	G	A	C
Manufacturer	**	*	*	*	***	***	
Merchandise Displayer		***	—		**	*	***
Payroll & Timekeeping Clerk		***		**	***	—	*
Purchasing Agent	*	**	*	*	***	**	
Retailer	**	*	*	**	***	**	
Sales Person	*	***	*	**	***		
Shipping & Receiving Clerk		***	—		***	—	**
Store Clerk (Order Filler)	*	***		***	**	—	***
Telemarketer	**	**	—	***	**	—	—
Wholesaler	*			*	***	***	
Science							
Anthropologist	**	*	***	**	*	**	
Biologist	**	*	***	*	*	**	*
Chemist	**	*	***	*	**	**	
Mathematician	**	***	***	*	**	**	
Physicist	**		***	*		**	
Research Scientist	**	*	***		*	**	
Scientist	***	*	***	*	**	**	*
Technology/Telecommunications							
Computer & Information Systems Manager	***		**	**	***	***	—
Computer Animator		***	*		**	*	***
Computer Hardware Engineer	*	***	***		***	*	—
Computer Operator	**	***	**	*	***	**	*
Computer Programmer	**	***	***	*	**	**	
Computer Support Specialist	*	***		***	**		—
Database Operator/Administrator	*	***	*		**	*	
Desktop Publisher	*	**	***	*	***	***	*
Graphic Designer	**	***	**		**	*	**
Software Programmer	**	**	***	*	**	**	*
Systems Administrator	*	*	***	*	***	***	—
Systems Analyst	***	**	**	*	***	**	
Telephone Operator		***		*	**	*	***
Website Designer	**	***	***	*	***	**	*
Travel/Transportation							
Air Traffic Controller	***	**	**	*	**	***	—
Airplane Pilot	***	*	**	**	*	***	
Bus Driver	*	***	—	*	***		*
Concierge, Porter, Bellhop		***	—	**	***		***
Dispatcher (of Drivers)	*	***	—	*	**	*	
Dispatcher (of Emergency Units)	***	*	**	*	*	***	—

	P	S	T	E	G	A	C
Flight Attendant	*	***		**	**	*	**
Hotel Manager	**		**	**	***	***	—
Hotel, Motel, Resort Clerk	*	***		***	**	*	**
Interpreter/Translator	**	*	***	***	**	**	*
Taxi Driver/Chauffeur		***	—	**	***	—	**
Travel Agent	*	*	**	***	***	***	*
Truck Driver	*	***		*	***		**

Now, record the occupations in which you have the highest number of stars. You could be successful in any of these. Remember, these "success probabilities" are just *guidelines and suggestions*. Individual circumstances, opportunities, talents, education, training, experience, available finances, timing, interest and passions will help you determine your actual choice. The most important thing is to pray about it and seek the Lord's guidance.

Commit the choice (or change) of your vocation to the Lord. He is the one who has gifted you, and He has a specific plan for your life. Ask Him to lead you in this decision.

MY LIST OF OCCUPATIONAL POSSIBILITIES

Best Occupations	Number of Stars	My Preferences

33
Your Children's Gifts

Over twenty years ago we distributed a two-page questionnaire to seminar participants in order to learn more about their motivational gifts as they were growing up. With over one thousand responses, we've assembled a composite portrait that enables parents not only to discover the motivational gifts of their children, but also to know better how to train their children up in their giftedness as Proverbs 22:6 indicates we should do: "Train up a child in the way he should go [and in keeping with his individual bent or gift], and when he is old he will not depart from it."

The feedback questionnaires were collected from a broad cross section of people from both the United States and Canada, representing all walks of life, all ages and most denominations. Allowing for the variables discussed earlier, we've found normative characteristics that consistently show up in the lives of even young children, depending on their motivational gifts.

We have written a whole book on this subject, *Discover Your Children's Gifts*, but here we will present only a general picture, stressing that the recognition of the motivational gifts in children makes us aware of the need to treat and train children differently. There is no such thing as an ideal, model child any more than there is any one type of ideal, model adult. Rather, we could say there are seven.

Children's Learning Styles

Just as the different learning styles of children have been recognized in secular education circles, so it is evident from the study of motivational gifts that children learn in various ways.

While we cannot cover the subject in detail here, we've observed that children with the "serving" gifts (serving, giving and compassion) perform better when separated from the more aggressive "speaking" gift children (perceiver, teacher, exhorter and administrator). The former are not competitive and are easily overwhelmed by those who thrive on competition.

When the teachers we work with divide these two groups of children for some activities, they've seen the "server" children function much better both academically and socially.

Parenting Styles and Children's Gifts

Children with different motivational gifts require different types of care, discipline and training in the family setting. We found that our perceiver son required about four times the amount of discipline as our administrator son or our compassion daughter. Compassion children are the most easily wounded and the most in need of protection. Yet they also need to be taught how to express appropriately the negative feelings they often hold in; otherwise they could suffer deep emotional damage.

Teacher children will exasperate you with their questions and challenges while exhorter children will talk your ear off. Server children will delight you with their helpfulness but be hurt if you don't show appreciation. Giver children will amaze you with their frugality yet often prove to be stingy. And administrator children may try to take over the organizing of family activities, yet thrill you with their accomplishments at school.

We hope the following brief overview will give you some clues to enhance your parenting skills.

An Overview of the Tallied Data

We have tallied more than a thousand responses to this questionnaire. Respondents were asked to answer all the following questions about their childhood experiences and feelings as descriptively as possible.

1. Emotions: Describe your emotional makeup as a child.
2. Expression: How easy was it for you to communicate verbally?
3. Self-image: How did you feel about yourself as a person?
4. Approach to life: Describe how you generally approached life (i.e., realistically, idealistically or systematically).
5. Reality/imagination: To what degree were you imaginative or realistic?
6. Behavior: Describe your usual behavior patterns.
7. Personal habits: What were your good and bad habits?

8. Friends: How many friends did you usually have? How did you feel about it?
9. Relationships: How did you relate to peers, older children, parents and teachers?
10. Intellect: Describe your mental capacity as a child.
11. Leadership: To what degree were you a leader or follower?
12. School: How well did you do in school?
13. Best subjects: What were your best subjects in school?
14. Reading: What did you like to read for enjoyment?
15. Sports: In what sports did you participate regularly?
16. Games/toys: What were your favorite games and toys?
17. Pets: Did you have pets? How did you feel about them?
18. Qualities: List three positive qualities that were evident in you as a child.
19. Interests: What were your general interests?
20. Joy: What brought you the most joy as a child?
21. Other comments on your childhood:

We have summarized the various responses in the chart on pages 265–67 based on the gifts evident in the adults who filled out the questionnaire. The age span covers earliest memories through high school age. While the data is typical for each gift, please remember that the child's secondary gift, the variables of life and the amount of freedom from polluting factors can all affect the degree to which each child may match the data.

To use this tool we suggest that you select a different colored pencil for each child. Then read the description across from each of the 21 categories, and circle the qualities that match one child. The column with the most circles will most likely indicate his or her primary gift; the one with the next most frequently circled items could likely be his or her secondary gift. Then do the same for the next child, and so on.

Record the information below.

Name of Child	Color Code	Primary Gift	Secondary Gift

Category	Perceiver	Server	Teacher	Exhorter	Giver	Administrator	Compassion
1. Emotions	1. Sensitive 2. Intense 3. Extremes of secure and insecure	1. Shy 2. Sensitive 3. Emotional 4. Easily embarrassed	1. Stable disposition 2. Unemotional 3. Reserved	1. Happy 2. Sensitive 3. Balanced	1. Happy 2. Expressive of feelings 3. Sometimes shy	1. Stable 2. Confident 3. Sensitive 4. Happy 5. Enthusiastic	1. Sensitive 2. Shy 3. Hard to express negative feelings
2. Expression	1.Verbalizes easily	1. Verbalizes with difficulty 2. Quiet 3. Shy in class	1. Verbalizes easily 2. Articulate 3. Dislikes small talk	1. Very verbal! 2. Likes public speaking	1. Some verbalize easily 2. Some verbalize with difficulty	1. Very verbal 2. Expresses self easily	1. Verbalization hard to easy, depending on feelings 2. Soft-spoken
3. Self-image	1. Self-image problems 2. Negative 3. Introspective	1. Low self-image 2. Needs to be appreciated 3. Security in doing	1. Good self-image 2. Objective	1. Most have good self-image 2. Positive personality	1. Average self-image	1. Good to very good self-image 2. Basically secure	1. Poor to good self-image 2. Insecure 3. Takes guilt for conflict
4. Approach to Life	1. Idealistic 2. Practical 3. Creative 4. Can get depressed	1. Practical 2. Idealistic and realistic 3. Oriented toward doing	1. Realistic 2. Idealistic 3. Practical 4. Searcher for truth	1. Idealistic 2. Creative 3. Realistic 4. Practical 5. Adaptable	1. Balanced between realistic and idealistic 2. Wholehearted	1. Practical 2. Systematic 3. Creative 4. Wide areas of interest	1. Idealistic 2. Creative 3. Subjective 4. Loving 5. Peacemaker
5. Reality/Imagination	1. Can be both but mostly imaginative	1. Excellent imagination 2. Good at pretending 3. Realistic	1. Very realistic 2. Poor imagination	1. Imaginative and also practical	1. Very imaginative	1. Both realistic and imaginative 2. A visionary	1. Very imaginative 2. Daydreamer
6. Behavior	1. Obedient 2. Extremes of good/bad 3. Very strong-willed	1. Obedient 2. Quiet 3. Likes to do things on own terms	1. Obedient 2. Independent 3. Entertains self easily	1. Obedient 2. Outgoing 3. Adaptable	1. Obedient 2. Industrious	1. Obedient 2. Gregarious 3. Competitive 4. Pleasing	1. Obedient 2. Loving 3. Indecisive 4. Crusader for good causes
7. Personal Habits	1. Dependable 2. Wants to be right! 3. Tattletale	1. Neat, tidy 2. Helpful 3. Completes projects	1. Neat 2. Good study habits 3. Punctual 4. Intolerant	1. Neat, clean 2. Helpful 3. Accepting 4. Not saver 5. Interrupts	1. Neat 2. Helpful 3. Friendly 4. Makes money 5. Saves money	1. Studious 2. Plans ahead 3. Saves things 4. Procrastinates	1. Neat, clean 2. Helpful 3. Unorganized 4. Not punctual
8. Friends	1. Few or no friends 2. Loner	1. Only a few friends	1. Just a few friends with similar interests	1. Many friends 2. Gregarious 3. Joiner 4. Well-liked	1. Just a few friends 2. Supportive	1. Usually many friends 2. Likes large groups 3. Joiner	1. A few close friends 2. Drawn to friendless
9. Relationships	1. Relates best to adults and teachers 2. Relates poorly to peers	1. Relates best to parents 2. Good to teachers 3. Shy toward peers	1. Relates best to parents and teachers 2. Some difficulty with peers	1. Relates well to everyone	1. Relates well to everyone	1. Relates very well to all 2. Tends toward broad relationships	1. Relates best to adults and teachers 2. Average to peers

Category	Perceiver	Server	Teacher	Exhorter	Giver	Administrator	Compassion
10. Intellect	1. Above average	1. Average to good 2. Good at details	1. Very intelligent 2. Highest IQs 3. Investigative	1. Above average to excellent	1. Average to good	1. Good to excellent 2. Investigative	1. Average to above average 2. Concern for feelings
11. Leadership	1. Can be either leader or follower	1. Follower 2. Prefers smaller groups	1. Some are leaders	1. Mostly leaders	1. Primarily follower 2. Sometimes will lead	1. Excellent leader 2. Organizer 3. Delegator	1. Follower 2. Supporter
12. School	1. Above average 2. Focuses on facts and truth	1. Average to good 2. Meticulous	1. Excellent student! 2. Self-motivated 3. Over-prepares	1. Above average	1. Average to good	1. Excellent student 2. Excels 3. Enjoys a challenge	1. Average to above average
13. Best Subjects	1. English 2. Math 3. History 4. Art 5. Drama	1. Math 2. English 3. History 4. Science 5. Home Ec./ shop	1. History 2. English 3. Good in all subjects	1. English 2. Math 3. History 4. Likes most subjects	1. English 2. Math 3. Business 4. History	1. English 2. Math 3. History 4. Good in all subjects	1. English 2. Math 3. Art/music 4. History
14. Reading	1. Biography 2. Romance 3. Adventure 4. Mystery	1. Adventure 2. Mystery 3. Romance 4. Historical novel	1. Prolific reader 2. Historical novel 3. Mystery	1. Biography 2. Fiction 3. Nonfiction	1. Loves to read 2. Fiction 3. Adventure 4. Animal	1. Wide range of interests 2. Mystery 3. Biography	1. Romance 2. Mystery 3. Fairy tale and fantasy 4. Animal
15. Sports	1. Prefers individual sports: swim, ski, bicycle	1. Group sports 2. Noncompetitive sports: swim, skate 3. Some: none	1. Not much interest 2. Prefers watching or books	1. Loves active sports 2. Group sports 3. Swimming	1. Most like group sports 2. Some don't like any sports	1. Group sports 2. Competitive sports	1. No sports or non-competitive sports
16. Games & Toys	1. Makes up own games 2. Plays alone 3. Toys are real things	1. Card games 2. Table games 3. Manual skill and crafts 4. Puzzles	1. Table games 2. Active games 3. Prefers books	1. Active games 2. Group games 3. Toys with a purpose: ball, skates	1. Outdoor games 2. Construction toys 3. Creative play	1. Table games 2. Group games 3. Creative play	1. Table games 2. Card games 3. Quiet, imaginative play
17. Pets	1. Loves pets 2. Needs their companion-ship	1. Loves pets 2. Feels they are special friends	1. Indifferent about pets 2. Would rather read a book	1. Likes them but prefers people	1. Enjoys pets but people even more	1. Loves pets but not the routine care	1. Adores pets 2. They are their friends 3. Brings homes strays
18. Qualities	1. Sensitive 2. Honest 3. Loyal 4. Responsible	1. Helpful 2. Reliable 3. Sensitive 4. Obedient	1. Diligent 2. Dependable 3. Considerate 4. Perfectionist	1. Friendly 2. Loving 3. Obedient 4. Happy	1. Helpful 2. Kind 3. Honest 4. Thrifty	1. Capable 2. Responsible 3. Honest 4. Gregarious	1. Loving 2. Caring 3. Helpful 4. Obedient

Category	Perceiver	Server	Teacher	Exhorter	Giver	Administrator	Compassion
19. Interests	1. Reading 2. Sports 3. Music	1. Handwork 2. Animals 3. Homemaking skills/building/fixing	1. Reading 2. Studying 3. The arts	1. People 2. Outdoor activities 3. Reading	1. Reading 2. Friends 3. Domestic 4. Make money	1. Wide areas of interest 2. Doing things with others 3. Reading	1. Music/art 2. Reading 3. People
20. Joy	1. Family activities 2. Nature 3. "Being"	1. Family activities 2. Appreciation 3. Serving	1. Family activities 2. Learning 3. Being accepted	1. Family activities 2. Making others happy 3. People	1. Family activities 2. Helping others 3. Travel	1. Family activities 2. Accomplishments 3. People	1. Family activities 2. Friendships 3. Being appreciated
21. Other	1. Strong conscience 2. Opinionated 3. Blunt	1. Good dexterity 2. Not college-oriented	1. Bookworm 2. Teacher's pet	1. Encourager 2. Gives lots of advice 3. Talkative	1. All-around personality 2. Gives generously	1. Makes to-do lists 2. Writes notes 3. Loves to plan	1. Easily hurt 2. Easily moved to tears

Questionnaires Designed for Children

Through teaching about motivational gifts in Christian schools—from primary grades through high school—we have gained much insight in actually testing students at various levels. This, along with the information gleaned over the years from the survey feedback sheets, is the basis for our children's and youth questionnaires.

The Junior Questionnaire

The Junior Questionnaire is designed for young people from ages nine to twelve years old, or grades four through six. The testing should be done with the help of a parent or teacher. Some concepts are somewhat difficult to put into simple language and will need some explanation on the part of the assisting adult. The Junior Questionnaire can be used by schoolteachers, home school parents, Sunday School leaders, young people's groups and, of course, by parents of junior age children. (See the back of the book to order.)

The Primary Questionnaire

The Primary Questionnaire is designed for children from ages six to eight, or grades one through three. The testing would be done by the parent(s) or by teachers who know their students well—and then confirmed by the parent(s). This can also be used by teachers or leaders of young children's groups or programs. (See the back of the book to order.)

Parents or teachers may want to retest children every year or so. The older the child, the more reliable and indicative the test scores usually are.

Questionnaires Designed for Youth

Youth Questionnaires

We have especially enjoyed working with teenagers in school settings and church groups, as well as individually. We find they are very eager to know about themselves. And, since they are at an age where they are making lifelong career decisions, it is especially helpful for them to discover their motivational gifts.

It also helps them to build an acceptable self-image and to understand and cope with some of the teenage problems and stresses they are going through. It helps with interpersonal relationships, peers and parents—and to be able to make more responsible decisions in the future, including the choice of a mate. So often adults say to us, "Oh, how I wish I had known about the gifts when I was a teenager." We would personally love to see all teenagers discover their motivational gifts. (College-age youth can use this test, found on pages 269–83, or the adult one.)

The scoring procedure is the same as the adult questionnaire described in chapter 6. Remember that the negative characteristics do *not* go on the profile sheet. They're to be scored just for the young person's own information and to provide an indicator of areas that need prayer and maturing. (See the back of the book to order.)

Student Questionnaires

For teenagers who are not Christians or have little knowledge of Christian terms, or for a group of teens where some are not Christians, we recommend our Student Questionnaire. It is a secular version of the Youth Questionnaire, suitable for use in public schools or other secular situations. (See the back of the book to order.)

Youth Questionnaire

YOUTH MOTIVATIONAL GIFT PROFILE SHEET

Gift	0	10	20	30	40	50	60	70	80	90	100
Perceiver											
Server											
Teacher											
Exhorter											
Giver											
Administrator											
Compassion Person											

#1 GIFT _____

#2 GIFT _____

#3 GIFT _____

NAME _____

ADDRESS _____

CITY/ST/ZIP _____

Copyright © 1987 Don & Katie Fortune, P.O. Box 101, Kingston, WA 98346

Youth Questionnaire

THE GIFT OF PERCEPTION

Characteristics

	Never	Seldom	Sometimes	Usually	Mostly	Always	POINTS
	0	1	2	3	4	5	
1. Quickly sees what is good or evil and hates evil.							
2. Sees everything as either right or wrong.							
3. Can easily tell the character of others.							
4. Encourages others to be sorry for doing wrong.							
5. Believes problems and difficulties can produce spiritual growth.							
6. Has only a few or no close friendships.							
7. Views the Bible as the basis for truth, belief and action.							
8. Boldly lives by spiritual principles.							
9. Is frank, outspoken and doesn't have much tact.							
10. Is very convincing with words.							
11. Feels bad when others sin.							
12. Is eager to see their own blind spots and help others see theirs, too.							
13. Desires above all else to see God's will done in everything.							
14. Loves to encourage the spiritual growth of others.							
15. Prays a lot for others and for God's will to be done.							
16. Has a tendency to be dramatic.							
17. Looks inside self a lot.							
18. Has strong opinions and beliefs.							
19. Has strict personal standards.							
20. Feels strong desire to be obedient to God.							
						TOTAL	

Typical problem areas
of the gift of perception

	Never	Seldom	Sometimes	Usually	Mostly	Always	POINTS
	0	1	2	3	4	5	
1. Tends to be judgmental and blunt.							
2. Forgets to praise others for small improvements.							
3. Pushy in trying to get others to grow spiritually.							
4. Doesn't like opinions and views that differ from his or her own.							
5. Struggles with self-image problems.							
TOTAL							

Youth Questionnaire

THE GIFT OF SERVING

Characteristics		Never	Seldom	Sometimes	Usually	Mostly	Always	POINTS
		0	1	2	3	4	5	
1. Is quick to meet the needs of others.	1.							
2. Especially enjoys working with his or her hands.	2.							
3. Keeps everything neat and in order.	3.							
4. Remembers details easily.	4.							
5. Enjoys having people at his or her house.	5.							
6. Wants to complete what is started.	6.							
7. Has a hard time saying no to requests for help.	7.							
8. Is more interested in meeting the needs of others than own needs.	8.							
9. Enjoys working on projects that can be finished in a short time.	9.							
10. Shows love for others in deeds and actions more than words.	10.							
11. Needs to feel appreciated.	11.							
12. Tends to do more than asked to do.	12.							
13. Finds highest joy in doing something that is helpful to someone.	13.							
14. Does not want to lead others.	14.							
15. Has a high energy level.	15.							
16. Cannot stand to be around clutter.	16.							
17. Wants everything to be perfect.	17.							
18. Thinks serving is the most important thing in life.	18.							
19. Would rather do a job than ask someone else to do it.	19.							
20. Likes to help others who are in leadership get the job done.	20.							
							TOTAL	

Typical problem areas
of the gift of serving

	Never	Seldom	Sometimes	Usually	Mostly	Always	POINTS
	0	1	2	3	4	5	
1. Upset with others who do not offer to help out with needs. 1.							
2. May forget to help family by being too busy helping others. 2.							
3. May become pushy in eagerness to help. 3.							
4. Hard to accept being served by others. 4.							
5. Easily hurt when not appreciated. 5.							
						TOTAL	

Youth Questionnaire

THE GIFT OF TEACHING

Characteristics		Never	Seldom	Sometimes	Usually	Mostly	Always	POINTS
		0	1	2	3	4	5	
1. Likes to present truth in a logical way.	1.							
2. Always likes to check out the facts.	2.							
3. Enjoys studying.	3.							
4. Enjoys learning the meaning of words.	4.							
5. Likes to use biblical illustrations to make a point.	5.							
6. Does not like Scripture to be used out of context.	6.							
7. Wants truth to be established in every situation.	7.							
8. Able to analyze without personal feelings getting in the way.	8.							
9. Easily develops and uses a large vocabulary.	9.							
10. Believes facts are more important than feelings.	10.							
11. Always wants to be sure that what is learned is true.	11.							
12. Prefers helping believers grow as opposed to witnessing.	12.							
13. Feels this gift is the best one for a strong Christian life.	13.							
14. Solves problems by using principles found in the Bible.	14.							
15. Is an excellent student.	15.							
16. Is self-disciplined.	16.							
17. Emotionally self-controlled.	17.							
18. Has only a few close friends.	18.							
19. Has strong beliefs and opinions.	19.							
20. Believes truth has the power to produce change in people.	20.							
							TOTAL	

Typical problem areas of the gift of teaching

	Never	Seldom	Sometimes	Usually	Mostly	Always	POINTS
	0	1	2	3	4	5	
1. Tends to forget to apply truth in practical ways.							
2. Slow to accept viewpoints of others.							
3. Tends to feel smarter than most others the same age.							
4. Tends to be a "know-it-all."							
5. Easily sidetracked by new interests.							
TOTAL							

Youth Questionnaire

THE GIFT OF EXHORTATION

Characteristics		Never	Seldom	Sometimes	Usually	Mostly	Always	POINTS
		0	1	2	3	4	5	
1. Loves to encourage others to live fully and happily.	1.							
2. Wants others to pay attention when speaking.	2.							
3. Would rather apply truth than research it.	3.							
4. Prefers learning things that can be used in practical ways.	4.							
5. Loves to tell others what to do in order to improve.	5.							
6. Loves to work with people.	6.							
7. Encourages others to develop in their ability to help others.	7.							
8. Finds truth most often in experience.	8.							
9. Loves to help others with their problems.	9.							
10. Will stop helping others with their problems if they don't change.	10.							
11. Prefers teaching that can be applied to life.	11.							
12. Believes trials and problems can help people grow.	12.							
13. Accepts people as they are.	13.							
14. Is positive about everything.	14.							
15. Prefers to witness through the way he or she lives life rather than talking about it.	15.							
16. Makes decisions easily.	16.							
17. Completes what is started.	17.							
18. Wants to clear up problems with others quickly.	18.							
19. Expects a lot of self and others.	19.							
20. Needs a close friend to share ideas and thoughts with.	20.							
							TOTAL	

Typical problem areas
of the gift of exhortation

	Never	Seldom	Sometimes	Usually	Mostly	Always	POINTS
	0	1	2	3	4	5	
1. Tends to interrupt others in eagerness to give opinions.							
2. Will use Scriptures out of context in order to make a point.							
3. May tend to give the same advice again and again.							
4. Speaks out boldly on opinions and ideas.							
5. Can be too self-confident.							
TOTAL							

Youth Questionnaire

THE GIFT OF GIVING

Characteristics	Never	Seldom	Sometimes	Usually	Mostly	Always	POINTS
	0	1	2	3	4	5	
1. Gives freely of money, things, time and love.							
2. Loves to give quietly, without others knowing about it.							
3. Wants to feel a part of the ministry he or she gives to.							
4. Prays a lot for the salvation of others.							
5. Delighted when his or her gift is an answer to someone's prayer.							
6. Wants gifts to be the best he or she can give.							
7. Gives only by the leading of the Holy Spirit.							
8. Gives to support and bless others or to help a ministry.							
9. Sees having people in his or her home as an opportunity to give.							
10. Has ability to handle money wisely and well.							
11. Quick to help where a need is seen.							
12. Prays about the amount to give.							
13. Believes in tithing and in giving more besides.							
14. Loves to share the Gospel more than anything else.							
15. Believes God will take care of all his or her needs.							
16. Works hard to earn money so more can be given away.							
17. Good at making money.							
18. Careful not to waste money on self.							
19. Has a good business ability.							
20. Has both natural and God-given wisdom.							
						TOTAL	

Typical problem areas
of the gift of giving

	Never	Seldom	Sometimes	Usually	Mostly	Always	POINTS
	0	1	2	3	4	5	
1. May try to control how money given is used.							
2. Pushy in trying to get others to give.							
3. May upset others who do not understand how and why he or she gives.							
4. May spoil someone by giving too much.							
5. May become stingy in some cases.							
TOTAL							

Youth Questionnaire

THE GIFT OF ADMINISTRATION

Characteristics		Never	Seldom	Sometimes	Usually	Mostly	Always	POINTS
		0	1	2	3	4	5	
1. Loves to organize anything.	1.							
2. Can explain ideas and organization to others clearly.	2.							
3. Is glad to be under authority in order to have authority.	3.							
4. Will not try to take leadership unless given by those in authority.	4.							
5. Will take leadership when needed if there is no leadership.	5.							
6. Enjoys working on long-range goals and projects.	6.							
7. Can easily see the broad picture of what needs to be done.	7.							
8. Knows how to pick the right people to get a job done.	8.							
9. Enjoys delegating responsibility to others to get more done.	9.							
10. Doesn't mind criticism as long as things get done.	10.							
11. Has great interest and enthusiasm for whatever he or she does.	11.							
12. Finds greatest fulfillment and joy in working toward a goal.	12.							
13. Is willing to let others get the credit in order to get a job done.	13.							
14. Prefers to move on to something new once a goal is completed.	14.							
15. Constantly writes both notes to self and lists of things to do.	15.							
16. Is a natural and good leader.	16.							
17. Knows when to change ways of doing things and when not to.	17.							
18. Enjoys working with and being around people.	18.							
19. Wants to see things completed as quickly as possible.	19.							
20. Does not enjoy doing the same things over and over again.	20.							
							TOTAL	

Typical problem areas
of the gift of administration

	Never	Seldom	Sometimes	Usually	Mostly	Always	POINTS
	0	1	2	3	4	5	
1. Becomes upset when others do not work together well toward a goal. 1.							
2. Can hold in hurts due to being a target for criticism. 2.							
3. Can sometimes "use" people to accomplish own goals. 3.							
4. Can tend to drive self and neglect personal needs. 4.							
5. Can neglect home chores due to intense interest in activities. 5.							
						TOTAL	

Youth Questionnaire

THE GIFT OF COMPASSION

Characteristics		Never	Seldom	Sometimes	Usually	Mostly	Always	POINTS
		0	1	2	3	4	5	
1. Great ability to show love.	1.							
2. Always looks for the good in people.	2.							
3. Senses the spiritual and emotional condition of others.	3.							
4. Attracted to people who are hurting or in distress.	4.							
5. Takes action to remove hurts and relieve distress in others.	5.							
6. More concerned for mental and emotional hurts than physical hurts.	6.							
7. Helps others have right relationships.	7.							
8. Loves to give others the better place or opportunity.	8.							
9. Careful with words and actions to avoid hurting others.	9.							
10. Can easily tell when others are insincere or have wrong motives.	10.							
11. Drawn to others with the gift of compassion.	11.							
12. Loves to do thoughtful things for others.	12.							
13. Trusting and tries to be trustworthy.	13.							
14. Avoids conflicts with others.	14.							
15. Doesn't like to be rushed in a job or activity.	15.							
16. Usually cheerful and joyful.	16.							
17. Ruled by heart rather than head.	17.							
18. Rejoices to see others blessed and grieves to see others hurt.	18.							
19. A crusader for good causes.	19.							
20. Prays a lot for the hurts and problems of others.	20.							
							TOTAL	

Typical problem areas
of the gift of compassion

	Never	Seldom	Sometimes	Usually	Mostly	Always	POINTS
	0	1	2	3	4	5	
1. Has a hard time making decisions. 1.							
2. Can easily take up another person's offense. 2.							
3. Feelings are easily hurt. 3.							
4. Has a hard time being "on time." 4.							
5. Can be taken advantage of by others. 5.							
						TOTAL	

Closing Thoughts

You have learned about the motivational gifts, discovered your own and seen how they can function in the Body of Christ. Now the application is up to *you*!

We can honestly say that what we have learned about the motivational gifts has been and continues to be extremely useful in every aspect of our lives. It has enriched our relationships, increased our understanding and acceptance of others, equipped us to minister more effectively, enabled us to cooperate with God's plan for our lives and allowed us the freedom to be ourselves.

We trust this book has enriched your life, drawn you closer to Jesus, truly enabled you to be free to be *you* and to carry out the biblical command:

> Each one should use whatever gift he has received to serve others, faithfully administering God's grace in its various forms . . . so that in all things God may be praised through Jesus Christ.
>
> 1 Peter 4:10–11, NIV

Notes

1. Edward Ziegler, "The Mysterious Bonds of Twins," *The Reader's Digest* (January 1980), 78.

2. George Ricker Berry, *The Interlinear Literal Translation of the Greek New Testament* (Grand Rapids: Zondervan, 1973).

3. James Strong, *Strong's Exhaustive Concordance of the Bible* (New York: Abingdon Press, 1970).

4. Kenneth Wuest, *Word Studies in the Greek New Testament* (Grand Rapids: Eerdmans, 1955), Chapter 12: Romans in the New Testament.

5. Emily Binning, *Gordon Takes a Wife* (Lynnwood, Wash.: Women's Aglow Fellowship, 1977), 136–37.

6. Steve Lightle, *Exodus II* (Kingwood, Tex.: Hunter Books, 1983), 60–61.

7. Howard Pitman, *Placebo* (Bassfield, Miss.: Mississippi Christian Broadcasting, Inc., 1980), 33.

8. Used with permission.

9. Albert W. Lorimer, *God Runs My Business* (Old Tappan, N.J.: Revell, 1941), 131–32.

Epilogue

Here is a study plan designed to help teach the material in this book. While it is designed as a thirteen-week study, it may be lengthened or shortened to fit any time frame. Assign the chapters and the questions in advance of the discussion time.

1. First week: read chapters 1–2

Chapter 1: Three Categories of Gifts

a. What nine gifts are mentioned in 1 Corinthians 12:7–10? Define each one.
b. What are the functions of the five gifts that are listed in Ephesians 4:11–13? How do these gifts differ from the ones in 1 Corinthians 12?
c. How do the seven gifts found in Romans 12:6–8 shape our personalities?
d. How does Romans 12:1–5 provide a good basis for operating in our motivational gifts?
e. How does 1 Corinthians 12:28–31 relate to the lists of gifts? Is love essential?

Chapter 2: Everyone Has a Gift!

f. In what ways should others benefit from your motivational gift?
g. When do we receive our motivational gifts? What is the evidence?
h. How does a motivational gift affect a person's viewpoint?
i. In what ways are different basic needs met by the seven motivational gifts?
j. How do the seven motivational gifts relate to the three areas of the soul?

2. Second week: read chapters 3–5

Chapter 3: Placed in His Body

a. How do the seven gifts relate to different parts of the body?
b. Describe someone you know and the way his or her gift reflects his or her position in the Body.
c. What is the difference between the "speaking gifts" and the "serving gifts"?

Chapter 4: We Minister in All Areas

d. In what sense can we all function in all seven areas of the motivational gifts?
e. Why can some people minister better and more naturally in some areas?

Chapter 5: If I Have a Gift, Why Haven't I Known It?

f. Why might a person not know about his or her motivational gifts?
g. What are some of the hindrances to the flow of a person's motivational gift?
h. How is a motivational gift empowered so that it is used for God's purposes?

3. Third week: read chapters 7–9

Chapter 7: Characteristics of the Perceiver

a. What are the differences between a perceiver, a prophet and the gift of prophecy?
b. Why do perceivers hate evil but welcome difficulties?
c. Why do perceivers put so much emphasis on what the Bible teaches?
d. What are blind spots? Do you have any? How can you get rid of them?
e. Why is intercession the most important ministry of the perceiver?
f. Why are perceivers so introspective? How does it help them? Hurt them?

Chapter 8: Problems of the Perceiver

g. Why isn't it okay to be open and blunt if it is based on truth?
h. Why would perceivers tend to have self-image problems?

Chapter 9: Biblical Perceivers

   i. Who are the Old Testament people that might have been perceivers? Why?

   j. Why is John the Baptist a good New Testament example of a perceiver?

4. Fourth week: read chapters 10–12

Chapter 10: Characteristics of the Server

   a. What types of things do servers do that may not be recognized as ministry?

   b. What should a server do if he or she gets overextended?

   c. How can others adjust to the perfectionism of a server?

   d. How can a server parent rob his or her children of learning to be responsible?

   e. Why was Moses' gift of serving an asset to God's plan for the Israelites?

Chapter 11: Problems of the Server

   f. How can we help servers feel more loved and appreciated?

   g. How can you gracefully tell a server you don't want his or her help with something?

Chapter 12: Biblical Servers

   h. What do you think Jesus appreciated about Martha's serving gift?

   i. Why did Mary's and Martha's gifts clash?

5. Fifth week: read chapters 13–15

Chapter 13: Characteristics of the Teacher

   a. Why do teachers insist on such extensive researching of everything?

   b. How can a teacher's objectivity fit him or her for jobs that others could not do well?

   c. Is it possible to change a teacher's opinions? How?

   d. Why would a teacher have difficulty participating in assertive evangelism?

Chapter 14: Problems of the Teacher

e. In what ways might a teacher be less effective at teaching than an exhorter?
f. How can others cope effectively with a legalistic or dogmatic teacher gift?

Chapter 15: Biblical Teachers

g. What traits in Apollos indicate that he was a teacher?
h. What do you know about Luke that reveals his gift of teaching?

6. Sixth week: read chapters 16–18

Chapter 16: Characteristics of the Exhorter

a. Why do people usually like to be around exhorters?
b. Why do you think exhorters feel life experience is as valid as Scripture?
c. What qualities make the exhorter an exceptional counselor?
d. Can the exhorter's tendency to accept everyone be an excuse for compromising?

Chapter 17: Problems of the Exhorter

e. What justification is there for using Scripture out of context?
f. How can others cope with the overtalkativeness of an exhorter?

Chapter 18: Biblical Exhorters

g. Why would Barnabas stand by John Mark, who had deserted them once before?
h. In what ways did Peter demonstrate the characteristics of an exhorter?

7. Seventh week: read chapters 19–21

Chapter 19: Characteristics of the Giver

a. How many ways can a giver give?
b. Why is a giver most suited to be involved in evangelism?
c. Why does God enable givers to be so gifted and successful in business?
d. Why is wisdom an especially important possession for the giver to have?

Chapter 20: Problems of the Giver

 e. How can a giver be helped to "cut the strings" after he or she has given financially?

 f. In what ways can a giver's generosity have a negative effect on his or her family?

Chapter 21: Biblical Givers

 g. What clues do we have to Abraham's motivational gift of giving?

 h. Since apostles often have more than one strong gift, what were Paul's?

8. Eighth week: read chapters 22–24

Chapter 22: Characteristics of the Administrator

 a. How do you think administrators relate to authority?

 b. Why is a visionary capacity vital to the gift of administration?

 c. Why do administrators continually keep lists of things to do?

 d. How can we know if a person who desires leadership is really qualified?

Chapter 23: Problems of the Administrator

 e. How should an administrator deal with criticism?

 f. Why do administrators sometimes get their priorities out of order?

Chapter 24: Biblical Administrators

 g. How did Joseph's sharing of his dream both get him into trouble and into God's plan?

 h. Why would David and Nehemiah be considered administrators?

9. Ninth week: read chapters 25–27

Chapter 25: Characteristics of the Compassion Person

 a. In what ways is the compassion gift both a blessing and a problem to have?

 b. What draws compassion people to those who are hurting or in distress?

 c. Why do compassion people trust even those who have proven untrustworthy?

d. What conflicts could develop in a relationship between a compassion person and someone with one of the more analytical gifts?

e. Which gifts are intercessors, and how can people with these gifts work together?

Chapter 26: Problems of the Compassion Person

f. Why are compassion people the most easily hurt?

g. Why is it difficult for a compassion person to be firm or to plan ahead?

Chapter 27: Biblical Compassion People

h. To what extent did the Good Samaritan show compassion?

i. Although Jeremiah was a prophet by call, how do we know he also had the gift of compassion?

10. Tenth week: read chapter 29

Chapter 29: Jesus' Characteristics

a. Was Jesus' perception greater than ours or does the Holy Spirit enable us to have similar perception today?

b. Why do you think Jesus put such emphasis on servanthood?

c. Why did Jesus base so much of His teaching on the Old Testament?

d. How did Jesus determine whom to encourage and whom to criticize?

e. In what ways was Jesus' teaching on the good news of the Kingdom of God central?

f. Did Jesus just "let things happen" or did He have a plan for His ministry?

g. Discuss a variety of ways in which Jesus showed compassion. Which was best?

11. Eleventh week: read chapters 30–31

Chapter 30: Living Your Gift

a. How might each gift cause a person to respond if a child brought home a notice that his or her schoolwork was poor?

b. What are some marriage conflicts that may result when people with two opposite gifts marry?

c. What other interpersonal relationships might involve conflict due to their gifts? What can you do about it?

d. How can knowledge of the motivational gifts be useful in counseling?

e. Do all of the motivational gifts approach witnessing the same way? Why or why not?

Chapter 31: Every Christian a "Minister"

f. In what way is every Christian a "minister"?

g. Can people of each gifting teach effectively? How will their approaches differ?

h. What are some possible areas of ministry for those with each gift? What have you done? How were you able to use your giftedness?

i. How do talents relate to the motivational gifts?

j. What are some of the best ministries for you to pursue?

12. Twelfth week: read chapter 32

Chapter 32: Careers and Occupations

a. How do your built-in core motivations reflect your motivational gifts?

b. What did you do in childhood that was a result of your built-in motivations in action?

c. What should you do if you find your core motivations are not fulfilled in your occupation?

d. What are the occupations or careers that your testing showed you'd be successful in?

e. Are you doing anything along those lines right now? Have you in the past?

f. What does this indicate to you about your future?

13. Thirteenth week: read chapter 33 and Closing Thoughts

Chapter 33: Your Children's Gifts

a. Why would server, giver and compassion children learn better when separated from the more outgoing perceiver, teacher, exhorter and administrator children?

b. How would the parenting styles of perceivers differ from styles of compassion people? Or teacher parents versus server parents?

c. What special challenges would teacher parents have with a server child?

d. Have you discovered the gifts of your children or other children you know? How has this helped you understand them better? Work with them better?

e. Have you discovered the gifts of any teenagers? How does it help to explain any of their actions, attitudes or relationships? What can be done to help them improve those relationships?

Closing Thoughts

f. What insights have you gained from this study of motivational gifts?

g. How has it changed your life?

h. How do you view the Body of Christ now?

Additional Material Available

To assist you in testing yourself, your children or others, or in presenting the material in this or other books by Don and Katie Fortune in a teaching or sharing situation, the authors make the following items available:

Discover Your God-Given Gifts Materials

Item #100 Discover Your God-Given Gifts Study Guide (60 pages)

In a condensed, self-paced format, the Study Guide brings together in one tool the key teachings from the three separate units that are presented in our comprehensive, teacher-led seminars: *Seminar Workbook* (including Self-Assessment), *Ministry Discovery* and *Occupational Success* probabilities. For group settings, the materials can be covered in an abbreviated program (such as a half-day or full-day seminar) or can be shared over a period of weeks. An accompanying *Study Guide PowerPoint Presentation* is available.

Item #101 Discover Your God-Given Gifts (304–page book)

Here is how to discover the gifts God has built into every person according to Romans 12:6–8. This book, a comprehensive study complete with a thirteen-week study plan for teaching the Romans 12 gifts, is a continuing bestseller. It also includes a worldwide-tested assessment with profile sheets, biblical examples and life application material. The *Occupational Success* analysis is presented as well as the *Ministry Discovery* material and analysis.

Item #102 Discover Your God-Given Gifts Seminar Workbook (48 pages)

This attractive workbook is designed for use in motivational gifts seminars, or with the seminar teaching tapes or DVDs, and coordinates with the materials and subjects in *Discover Your God-Given Gifts*. Testing sheets and tiebreakers for adults are included, as well as biblical examples and practical application material.

Item #103 Adult Questionnaire (16 pages)

This includes the seven adult testing sheets from *Discover Your God-Given Gifts*, along with a profile sheet for final scoring. Tiebreakers to determine which gift is stronger when scores are close or the same are also included.

Item #104 Ministry Discovery (16 pages)

This set contains expanded material from chapter 31 of *Discover Your God-Given Gifts* and a listing of types of ministries most fulfilling for people with each gift. Selected material from chapter 30, "Living Your Gift," helps the user put gifts into practical action.

Item #105 Objective Adult Questionnaire (16 pages)

This is a blind test, designed to be used for objective (not teaching) testing situations. The adult questionnaire is arranged randomly so a person taking the test cannot tell how the characteristics relate to the seven gifts. Tiebreakers, scoring key and decoder sheet are included.

Item #106 Discover Your God-Given Gifts Seminar Audio CDs (4 CDs)

This includes eight hours of seminar teaching on motivational gifts by authors Don and Katie Fortune, based on the book *Discover Your God-Given Gifts*. *Discover Your God-Given Gifts Seminar Workbook* is also recommended for use with the tapes.

Item #107 Discover Your God-Given Gifts Home Study Course (4 DVDs plus)

This includes eight hours of seminar teaching on motivational gifts by authors Don and Katie Fortune, based on the book *Discover Your God-Given Gifts*. Great for learning at home as well as in group Bible studies. Comes with *Discover Your God-Given Gifts*, *Discover Your God-Given Gifts Seminar Workbook*, a *Ministry Discovery* unit and an *Occupational Success* unit. Additional materials can be ordered separately for group studies.

Item #107A Discover Your God-Given Gifts Seminar DVDs (4 DVDs only)

This set includes eight hours of seminar teaching on motivational gifts (as above). Great for learning at home as well as in group Bible studies. Additional materials can be ordered separately for group studies.

Item #108 Value Pack A (Items #101–6)

This packet contains one of each of the following items: *Discover Your God-Given Gifts*, *Discover Your God-Given Gifts Seminar Workbook*, *Adult Questionnaire*, *Ministry Discovery*, *Objective Questionnaire* and *Discover Your God-Given Gifts Seminar* CD Set or audio tapes.

Item #108B Variety Packet, Adult (11 items)

This packet contains one of each of the following items: *Adult Questionnaire*, *Youth Questionnaire*, *Junior Questionnaire*, *Primary Questionnaire*, *Preschool Questionnaire*, *Objective Questionnaire*, *Ministry Discovery*, *Occupational Success*, *Secular Questionnaire*, *Motivational Gifts Seminar* CD Set/audio tapes and *Discover Your God-Given Gifts Seminar Workbook*.

Item #108E Discover Your God-Given Gifts Quick Reference Guide (12 pages)

This handy reference guide has characteristics and problem areas, childhood characteristics, predominant qualities, benefits to the Body of Christ and biblical examples for each of the gifts. With special diagrams and pictures, it is possible to share about the motivational gifts quickly and graphically.

Item #109 Ministry Success Assessment (52 pages)

About eight hundred ministry and job positions found in churches and Christian organizations have been analyzed and coded to determine the degree to which people of each motivational gift would be successful in them. This is an excellent assessment tool for anyone wanting to find out how they are best suited for specific areas of service. It is also a valuable means by which church leaders can find the rightly gifted people for positions and areas of responsibility.

Item #702 Occupational Success (16 pages)

This unit contains a detailed analysis of the 305 most common careers and occupations, showing the degree to which each gift is likely to be successful in them. Also included is an evaluation of the built-in core motivations that bring joy and satisfaction to persons with each gift. Now updated to include computer, high-tech industries and more!

Discover Your Spouse's Gifts Materials

Item #201 Discover Your Spouse's Gifts (352-page book)

Learn how the discovery of the motivational gifts of Romans 12:6–8 can enhance a marriage relationship. Based on an extensive marital survey conducted by Don and Katie Fortune, the book gives valuable information on how the gifts affect marriage, how to identify problems that stem from not knowing each other's gifts and how to overcome those problems. An extensive marriage analysis is included.

Item #202 Discover Your Spouse's Gifts Seminar Workbook (48 pages)

This practical workbook is designed for use in marriage seminars or couples' groups, and covers the material in *Discover Your Spouse's Gifts*. Dual motivational gift assessments for couples are included, as well as a personal copy of the marriage survey and life application material. Ideal for couples who want to make their marriages better.

Item #203 Survey Your Marriage (16 pages)

Based on an extensive marriage survey conducted by Don and Katie Fortune, this personal copy of the survey will enable you and your spouse to pinpoint your differ-ences and problem areas in your marriage. It will give you insight and understanding that will greatly enhance your marital relationship. It is also an excellent tool for couples' groups or classes and premarital or marital counseling. The survey is based on the twenty most common categories of problems in marriage.

Item #204 The ABCs of Christian Marriage (Parchment)

This inspirational reminder, taken from *Discover Your Spouse's Gifts*, makes a thoughtful gift for engaged couples, newlyweds or any Christian couple. It is available on 8½ x 11 inch parchment-type paper suitable for framing.

Discover Your Children's Gifts Materials

Item #301 Discover Your Children's Gifts (296-page book)

Learn how to discover the gifts God has built into every child according to Proverbs 22:6. This book, a comprehensive study complete with study guide, is enlightening and practical with extensive life application material. It is a valuable tool for parents, grandparents, youth workers, teachers, daycare providers, Sunday school teachers, Christian education leaders and anyone involved with children or youth of any age.

Item #302 Discover Your Children's Gifts Seminar Workbook (48 pages)

This workbook is designed for use in seminars or with the seminar CDs/tapes, and covers the subjects discussed in *Discover Your Children's Gifts*. Many charts and practical application ideas are included.

Item #302A Forms & Charts Packet (32 pages)

This includes enough forms and charts from Part III, "Practical Insights," in *Discover Your Children's Gifts* to keep records for a family with up to five children. In 8½ x 11 inch size, it constitutes a permanent family record, but individual forms and charts can be removed. (Note: does not contain the motivational gifts testing sets.)

Item #303 Youth Questionnaire (16 pages)

Designed for teenagers (grades 7–12), this assessment is somewhat similar to the *Adult Questionnaire*, but age-appropriate for junior high and senior high youth, ages 13 to 18. It includes the seven scoring sheets for teens, a profile sheet and tiebreakers.

Item #303A Student Questionnaire (16 pages, secular)

Designed for teenagers (grades 7–12), this assessment is a secular version of the *Youth Questionnaire*. It includes the seven scoring sheets for teens, a profile sheet and tiebreakers. It is excellent for use in public schools.

Item #304 Junior Questionnaire (16 pages)

Designed for grade-schoolers (grades 4–6), this assessment should be administered by a parent, teacher or other adult. It includes the seven scoring sheets for juniors, a profile sheet and tiebreakers. It is age-appropriate for ages 9 through 12.

Item #304A Junior Student Questionnaire (16 pages, secular)

Designed for grade-schoolers (grades 4–6), this assessment is a secular version of the *Junior Questionnaire*. It should be administered by a parent, teacher or other adult. It includes the seven scoring sheets for juniors, a profile sheet and tiebreakers. It is age appropriate for ages 9 through 12. It is excellent for use in public schools.

Item #305 Primary Questionnaire (16 pages)

Designed to be completed by parents of primaries (grades 1–3), this assessment includes the seven scoring sheets about primary children, a profile sheet and twenty categories of combination gift scales. It is appropriate for ages 6 through 8.

Item #306 Preschool Questionnaire (16 pages)

This includes three sets of charted scoring sheets to help determine the gifts of children from toddler through kindergarten age. It can also help determine the gifts of older children, and help adults clarify their own scores by comparing the survey characteristics with those from their own childhood.

Item #307 The ABCs of Christian Parenting (parchment) "recorded on CD or tapes, which follow"

This inspirational reminder, taken from *Discover Your Children's Gifts*, makes a thoughtful gift for new parents or anyone with children. It is available on 9 x 12 inch parchment-type paper suitable for framing.

Item #308 Discover Your Children's Gifts Seminar CDs (6 CDs or audio tapes)

Nine hours of seminar teaching from *Discover Your Children's Gifts* by author Katie Fortune, recorded on CD or tapes, which follow the teaching outline in the back of the book. The *Children's Gifts Seminar Workbook* is recommended for use with the tapes for personal instruction or for teaching others.

Item #310 Value Pack C (Items #301–8)

This packet contains one each of the following items: *Discover Your Children's Gifts, Children's Gifts Seminar Workbook, Youth Questionnaire, Junior Questionnaire, Primary Questionnaire, Preschool Questionnaire, The ABCs of Christian Parenting* and the *Children's Gifts* CD Set/audio tapes.

Item #310B Variety Packet, Children (13 items)

This packet contains one each of the following items: *Adult Questionnaire, Youth Questionnaire, Junior Questionnaire, Primary Questionnaire, Preschool Question-*

naire, *Objective Questionnaire, Ministry Discovery, Occupational Success Questionnaire, Secular Questionnaire, Children's Gifts* CD Set/audio tapes, *Children's Gifts Seminar Workbook,* Forms & Charts Packet and *The ABCs of Christian Parenting.*

Secular Motivational Gifts Materials

Item #702 Occupational Success (16 pages)

This unit contains a detailed analysis of the 305 most common careers and occupations, showing the degree to which each gift is likely to be successful in them. Also included is an evaluation of built-in core motivations that bring joy and satisfaction to people with each gift. Now updated to include computer, high-tech industries and more!

Item #703 Adult Motivational Gifts Questionnaire (Secular) (16 pages)

This assessment is designed to be used in situations where secular adult testing is desired. Christian terms and interests have been replaced by generic ones. Tiebreakers, scoring key and decoder sheet are included.

Item #703B Adult Motivational Gifts Seminar Workbook (Secular) (32 pages)

This practical secular workbook is designed for use in motivational gifts seminars presented in secular situations, including colleges and universities. Christian terms and interests have been replaced by generic ones. Tiebreakers, scoring key and decoder sheet included.

Item #703C Adult Motivational Gifts Objective Questionnaire (Secular) (16 pages)

This unit is designed to be used for objective (blind) testing situations where secular adults are involved. This question-naire is arranged randomly so a person taking the test cannot tell how the characteristics relate to the gifts. Christian terms and interests have been replaced by generic ones. Tiebreakers, scoring key and decoder sheet are included.

Item #703D Motivational Gifts Quick Reference Guide (Secular) (12 pages)

This handy reference guide has characteristics and problem areas, childhood characteristics, predominant qualities, benefits to an organization and the greatest joy of each of the gifts. This can be used in secular or corporate environments since Christian terms and interests have been replaced by generic ones.

Foreign Language God-Given Gifts Materials

Item #101S Discover Your God-Given Gifts in Spanish (264-page book)

Now Spanish-speaking people can discover the gifts God has built into every person according to Romans 12:6–8. This book, a comprehensive study complete with study guide, has been translated into Spanish!

The Adult Questionnaire has been translated into many languages, listed below. Each is 8 pages and includes the profile sheet:

Item #103C Discover Your God-Given Gifts Questionnaire in Chinese

Item #103D Discover Your God-Given Gifts Questionnaire in Danish

Item #103F Discover Your God-Given Gifts Questionnaire in Finnish

Item #103FR Discover Your God-Given Gifts Questionnaire in French

Item #103G Discover Your God-Given Gifts Questionnaire in German

Item #103I Discover Your God-Given Gifts Questionnaire in Indonesian

Item #103J Discover Your God-Given Gifts Questionnaire in Japanese

Item #103K Discover Your God-Given Gifts Questionnaire in Korean

Item #103N Discover Your God-Given Gifts Questionnaire in Norwegian

Item #103P Discover Your God-Given Gifts Questionnaire in Polish

Item #103PO Discover Your God-Given Gifts Questionnaire in Portuguese

Item #103R Discover Your God-Given Gifts Questionnaire in Russian

Item #103RO Discover Your God-Given Gifts Questionnaire in Romanian

Item #103S Discover Your God-Given Gifts Questionnaire in Spanish

Item #103SW Discover Your God-Given Gifts Questionnaire in Swedish

Item #103U Discover Your God-Given Gifts Questionnaire in Ukrainian

Additional Materials by the Fortunes

Manifestation Gifts Materials

Item #704 Flowing in the Gifts Seminar Workbook (48 pages)
Based on 1 Corinthians 12:7–10, this practical workbook developed by Don and Katie Fortune gives a biblical perspective on each of the nine gifts of the Holy Spirit mentioned by the apostle Paul: the word of wisdom, the word of knowledge, faith, gifts of healings, working of

miracles, prophecy, discerning of spirits, various kinds of tongues and interpretation of tongues. It is designed to be used by participants being taught about these spiritual gifts. Biblical examples are given for each gift.

Ministry Gifts Materials

Item #706 Ministry Gifts Seminar Workbook (32 pages)
Based on Ephesians 4:11, this practical workbook developed by Don and Katie Fortune gives a biblical perspective on each of the five ministry gifts mentioned by the apostle Paul: apostles, prophets, evangelists, pastors and teachers. Opportunity is given to examine present-day examples of people called to be these gifts as well as biblical examples, New Testament exhortations, character qualities, probable motivational gifting, distinguishing marks and potential problem areas. The syllabus is designed to be used by participants being taught about these ministry gifts.

Other Materials by the Fortunes

Item #800 Be Free Home Study Course (Workbook and 6 CDs)
A biblical study of deliverance and spiritual warfare written by Don and Katie Fortune. Includes Part 1, "Why We Need to Be Free," Part 2, "How Jesus Set People Free," Part 3, "How to Get Free" and Part 4, "How to Keep Free." Items #801 and #802 are included.

Item #801 Be Free Seminar Workbook (32 pages)
A biblical study of deliverance and spiritual warfare written by Don and Katie Fortune. Part 1, "Why We Need to Be Free," presents the invisible war and the triune nature of man. Part 2, "How Jesus Set People Free," presents how Jesus destroyed the power of Satan and how Jesus approached deliverance. Part 3, "How to Get Free," reveals our spiritual weapons and a practical outline of

deliverance ministry. Part 4, "How to Keep Free," presents the Christian's armor and how to stay free. The syllabus is designed to be used with the *Be Free Seminar* CDs or by participants being taught the *Be Free Seminar*.

Item #802 Be Free Seminar Audio CDs (6 CDs)

This CD set by authors Don and Katie Fortune is designed to be used with the *Be Free Seminar Workbook* for personal study, or it can be used by those who plan to teach the *Be Free Seminar*.

Item #803 The Three Heavens Audio CD (1 CD or audio tape)

This study, based on the apostle Paul's declaration that he was caught up into the third heaven (2 Corinthians 12:2) and Jesus' story about the Rich Man and Lazarus, reveals why mankind is in need of a Savior. Why Jesus had to go into the place of the dead and how He rescued those who were in Abraham's bosom and took them to the third heaven is presented with biblical accuracy and exciting revelation. An excellent witnessing tool that produces amazing results. A diagram accompanies the CD.

Item #804A Dealing with Anger Diagrams (2 pages)

Item #804B Dealing with Anger Audio CDs (2 CDs or 1 audio tape)

Katie Fortune shares a life-changing teaching, based on Matthew 5:21–26, on how to get free from the negative effects of anger in the heart. With two kinds of people, expressers and stuffers (and some who become flippers), the consequences of harbored and unresolved anger produce most of the problems and dysfunctions of life. Three keys unlock the possibility of complete freedom from the effects of anger. For use by individuals and Christian counselors. A two-page diagram accompanies the CDs.

Item #809 Counseling Materials Packet (Dealing with Anger Audio CDs, 6 Diagrams and 6 Adult Questionnaires)

To assist Christian counselors, both professional and volunteer, this counseling packet contains *Dealing with Anger* Audio CDs, six *Dealing with Anger* diagrams (item #804A) and six *Adult Questionnaires* (item #103). The Fortunes have found that their counseling effectiveness has been tremendously increased by first helping the person to discover their God-given gifts through the adult questionnaire and then walking the person through the anger teaching. Extra copies of the *Dealing with Anger* diagram are available.

Item #807 Becoming the Bride of Christ (1 CD or audio tape)

The traditional Jewish betrothal and wedding customs of Jesus' day present a pattern for God's preparation of the Bride of Christ for Jesus today. In telling the story and relating it to Jesus' promises to us, His Bride, Katie Fortune unveils the depth and excitement of Jesus' promises to believers and the evidence of His work in preparing us for His return.

Item #810A Receive All God Has to Give (32-page booklet)

Over five million copies of this booklet have been produced in English, as well as thousands of copies in more than thirty languages. With graphic illustrations, it presents how to receive Jesus Christ as Savior and Lord (first section), how to receive baptism in the Holy Spirit (second section) and how to walk in the Spirit in victorious Christian life (third section). It is an excellent tool for witnessing and for helping people live a positive Christian life. Keep this handy in your purse or pocket.

Item #810B How to Avoid the Pitfalls of the Passive Mind (32-page booklet)

One of the greatest dangers Christians can fall into is to put the mind into a passive state. This booklet reveals the nature of those dangers and why a passive mind can open a Christian to demonic influence, the occult and deception. It is important to consistently choose the will of God—not try to turn one's will over to God, who cannot and will not take it, since He gave it to mankind to use.

Item #810C Guidance Guidelines (32-page booklet)

This booklet gives helpful guidelines in helping a person to receive guidance from God. It covers the promise of guidance, the purpose of guidance and the principles of guidance. It also covers God's provision of guidelines, the problems that can develop when seeking guidance and the test of inner peace.

Authors Don and Katie Fortune and Heart 2 Heart International Ministries/Discover Your Gifts provide Certified Teacher Training both by on-site/location arrangement and by correspondence/home arrangement.
Certified Gift Teachers receive:

- Certification upon completion of the study and teaching of a class
- Generous discounts on materials and supplies
- Ongoing support and training—both live and online
- Inclusion on our web list of recommended Certified Gift Teachers
- Personal contacts/relationships with Don & Katie Fortune and staff.

If you are interested in knowing more about Certified Teacher Training, contact Katie Fortune at fortune@heart2heart.org or by phone at (360) 297-8878 from noon to five p.m. (PST).

For orders or inquiries, contact:

Dan & Ileana Fortune
Discover Your Gifts
20126 Ballinger Way NE #120
Shoreline, WA 98155
phone: (206) 508-3800
toll free: (877) GIFTS-R-US or
(877) 443-8778
fax: (206) 508-3810
websites: www.heart2heart.org
www.discoveryourgifts.org

To contact the authors:

Don & Katie Fortune
Heart to Heart International
Ministries
P.O. Box 101
Kingston, WA 98346
phone: (360) 297-8878
fax: (360) 297-8865
email: fortune@heart2heart.org
websites: www.heart2heart.org
www.discoveryourgifts.org